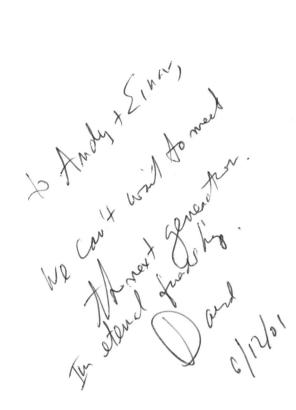

To Andy + Einar,

We can't wait to meet
the next generation.
In eternal friendship.

David
6/12/01

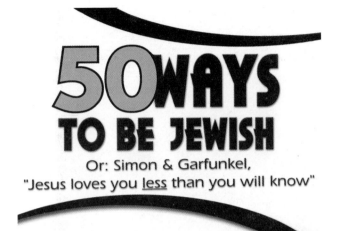

50 WAYS TO BE JEWISH

Or: Simon & Garfunkel,
"Jesus loves you <u>less</u> than you will know"

DAVID J. FORMAN

gefen
publishing house   בית הוצאה לאור
JERUSALEM ◆ NEW YORK

Typesetting: Marzel A.S. – Jerusalem
Cover Design: Studio Paz, Jerusalem
Illustrations: Bracha Trinz

1 3 5 7 9 8 6 4 2

Gefen Publishing House
POB 36004, Jerusalem 91360, Israel
972-2-538-0247 • orders@gefenpublishing.com

Gefen Books
12 New Street Hewlett, NY 11557, USA
516-295-2805 • gefenbooks@compuserve.com

www.israelbooks.com

Printed in Israel

Send for our free catalogue

ISBN 965-229-282-6 (alk, paper)

Library of Congress Cataloging-in-Publication Data:
Forman, David J., 1944-
[Fifty ways to be Jewish]
Fifty ways to be Jewish, or Simon & Garfunkel, "Jesus loves you
less than you will know" / David J. Forman
Includes bibliographical references
1. Jewish way of life. 2. Judaism—20th century. I. Title: 50 ways to be Jewish.
II. Title: Simon & Garfunkel, "Jesus loves you less than you will know". III. Title.
BM723.F47 2001 • 296.7—dc21 • CIP Number: 2001051084

For my grandchildren

"The world exists only because of the innocent breath of children…"

(*Babylonian Talmud, Shabbat* 119b)

Praise for *Jewish Schizophrenia in the Land of Israel*

David Forman offers us a painful analysis of the spirit of today's Israel, along with fresh observations on how we have gotten into our collective malaise, and how to recover. His insights are fierce, poignant and original.

Amos Oz, Israeli author

With a keen eye and a razor-sharp wit, and with an uncanny ability to cut to the heart of the matter, David Forman paints a picture of Israel that is both painful and heart-warming. Insightful and spellbinding, each page embraces a hope for a better future for the people of Israel.

Avraham Burg, Speaker of the Knesset

With wit and charm, David Forman helps readers navigate the psychological landscape of modern Israel. Whether writing about house demolitions or the sexual antics of political leaders or the existential meaning of Jerusalem to the Jewish People, he helps Israel find its true self. Forman puts Israel "on the couch," offering some healing to the patient with both spiritual insight and a hearty laugh.

Charles M. Sennott, Middle East Bureau Chief of the Boston Globe

With irreverence, humor and extraordinary insight, David Forman's *Jewish Schizophrenia in the Land of Israel* helps us to understand why Israelis think and act they way they do. What emerges from this book is a profound love for Israel, coupled with a sharp-eyed critique of Israel's failure to deal with many of its problems. This is must reading for those who want to understand Israel as it really is.

Eric Yoffie, President, Union of American Hebrew Congregations

Using the paradigm of schizophrenia, David Forman provides an informed and up-to-date analysis of the current divisiveness that characterizes Israeli society. His critique of Israel's social, political and religious insitiutions always displays a basic commitment to Judaism's principles of social justice and equality.

Dr. Alice Shalvi, Founding Chairwoman, Israel Women's Network

David Forman has given us a bold, penetrating and often hilarious look at current Israel with all its accomplishments and failures. This is a must book for all who want to understand "Jewish schizophrenia."

Dr. David Zisenwine, Chairman, Department of Jewish Education, Tel Aviv University

Praise for *Israel on Broadway, America: Off-Broadway Jews in the New Millennium*

In *Israel on Broadway*, David Forman presents a bold and controversial approach to issues of Jewish identity. He challenges Diaspora Jews to actively engage Israel. Not everyone will agree with his views, but anyone who cares about the continued vitality of Israel and the perpetuity of the Jewish People must read this book.

Alan M. Dershowitz, Professor, Harvard Law School

David Forman has presented a comprehensive, incisive and honest analysis of the relationship between Israel and Diaspora Jewry. This is obligatory reading.

A.B. Yehoshua, Author of The Lover and Mr. Mani

Bold, cutting to the quick, *Israel on Broadway* provoked me. When it was wrong, it drove me crazy, and when it was right, it made holes in my heart. I could spend the next ten years arguing with these pages. *Anne Roiphe, Author of Lovingkindness*

In this strongly and persuasively argued book, David Forman presents a powerful plea for health: the health and survival of the Jewish People.

Sir Martin Gilbert, Author of The Israelis

Forman is my kind of rabbi — smart, witty, insightful and reverently irreverent. Few know more than he does about Israel-Diaspora relations. Read this book. You'll enjoy it and learn something. *Ze'ev Chafets, Jerusalem Report*

Israel on Broadway is the book that Lenny Bruce would have written had he been in search of a healthy Jewish identity. For Forman, the challenge of the contemporary Jew is to learn the Jewish drama — to claim it, to participate in it and to write the next act. *Dr. Bernard Steinberg, Director, Harvard Hillel*

This is a passionate Zionist polemic, which juxtaposes the situation of Jews in Israel and the United States. This provocative book should stimulate debate among American Jews about the nature of their Jewish identity and commitment.

Dr. Paula Hyman, Lucy Moses Professor of Modern Jewish History, Yale University

Contents

ACKNOWLEDGMENTS

When I first conceived of the title for this book, *Fifty Ways to be Jewish*, I was not at all certain that I would find fifty ways. But when I shared my idea with others, unwittingly I invited so many suggestions for topics to write about that eventually I had to pare down the numerous paths one must follow to maintain his or her Judaism. Therefore, I am eternally grateful to family and friends for providing me with the fifty ways to be Jewish.

Special thanks must be extended to my close friend Walter (Ben) Smoke, who painstakingly read through the original manuscript, offering his always-sharp insights. I am indebted to Rabbis Lee Diamond, Shaul Feinberg, Joshua Haberman, Avi Levine, Mayer Perelmuter, Stanley Ringler and Henry Skirball. Their contributions are truly appreciated.

I also wish to express my gratitude to my copy editor, Ms. Esther Herskovics, and to my proofreader, Ms. Moriah Leilyn. I am especially grateful to Ilan and Dror Greenfield of Gefen Publishing House. Their support and enthusiasm accompanied me throughout this literary venture. Indeed, my thanks extend to the entire staff at Gefen. Their blend of the personal and professional accords a writer an environment that helps to serve his or her creative energies.

Stanley Chyet — teacher, mentor, rabbi, colleague and friend —

has been a source of encouragement throughout my career. Gently guiding me, he first taught me to write.

I must extend a special thank you to Ms. Bracha Trinz, whose illustrations so ably and creatively capture the spirit of the book.

Most importantly, I want to thank my immediate family: my wife Judith, my daughters and sons-in-law, Tamar and Michael, Liat and Eran, Shira, Orly **and** my grandchildren, Sivan and Benjamin Amichai (and those yet to be born), to whom this book is dedicated. "A child makes him- or herself known through his or her conduct" (*Proverbs* 20:11). I pray, that as my grandchildren grow older, they will find their **Jewish Way** in the world; and that their conduct will be determined by the historical traditions and practices of our people, which find their longevity and continued strength in a prophetic vision of social justice and equality, of personal commitment and collective responsibility, of familial respect and human dignity.

September 2001 — Tishrei 5762
Jerusalem

INTRODUCTION

One of Paul Simon's most famous songs is *Fifty Ways to Leave your Lover*.[1] According to the song, all one has to do is: "Slip out the back, Jack; make a new plan, Stan; no need to be coy, Roy — just listen to me. Hop on the bus, Gus; don't need to discuss much; just drop off the key, Lee — get yourself free..." If one were to examine the state of affairs of the American Jewish community, one change of Simon's song would sum up its condition: *Fifty Ways to Leave your Judaism*, because for the most part, we Jews have slipped out the back, found a new plan, don't discuss much and dropped off the key to our Jewish life. In the words of another Paul Simon song: our Jewish life is *Slip Slidin' Away*.[2]

This book will explore "Fifty Ways to be Jewish." With the exception of **Way #1 — Your Name** and **Way #50 — Your Instincts**, one should not attach any importance to the numerical order of the other forty-eight **Ways**. The reader must decide which of the fifty **Ways** speaks the most to him or her. The reason that each **Way** is designated as **"Your Way"** is to personalize each Jewish step. The book probably falls into the category of one of

---

1. From Paul Simon's album, *Still Crazy After All These Years*.
2. From Paul Simon's album, *Negotiations and Love Songs: 1971-1986*.

those "self-help" works: a guideline to better Jewish living. Or, if one is only biologically born into Judaism, but has never been interested in identifying as a Jew, then this literary adventure might help lead one back to a Jewish life.

Most of us Jews are truly uninformed when it comes to the most basic elements of Jewish life. This lack of knowledge has not been shaped by any intellectual rejection of Judaism on our part; rather, it has been colored by an indifference born out of ignorance.

Some of us Jews who think at all about the Jewish side of our existence may feel embarrassed that we know so little about Judaism, and so consciously desist from any identification with the organized Jewish community. But basically, we are lazy when it comes to our Judaism. Too many of us simply do not see any concrete advantages to being a Jew. We do not weigh the net gains against what we might perceive as the net losses of being Jewish. The vast majority of us suffers from a basic inertia when it comes to Judaism. Our belief systems and religious frameworks are reduced to a simple statement: "For lack of any proof to the contrary, I believe in God." Thus, we find ourselves subscribing to the civic religion of whatever culture we happen to be a part of.

As far as this author is concerned, if this book sells relatively well, then its entire thesis will be proven wrong, because to buy this Jewish manual means that Jews really are curious about their Judaism. Therefore, the success of this book will be ultimately determined by how many Jews fail to purchase it.

No one should expect to discover in these pages some sophisticated academic approach to Jewish life. Nor should there be any hope of finding an abundance of ideological arguments that would warrant one to jump head-first into Judaism. This slim volume is not intended to be either exhaustive or comprehensive. What is essentially emphasized in this book are some simple "why to" formulas, with an additional few "how to" and "what to" ingredients. Therefore, to help the reader out, perhaps it is best to understand the word "Jew" not as a noun, but rather as a verb, like "to Jew it" or "don't bite off more than you can Jew!"

This book is also intended to contradict the notion that "it is hard to be a Jew." What the reader will encounter here are "fifty easy steps to be Jewish." Now, one should not confuse the notion of "easy" with a concept of "demands." Let us just say that this primer is ideologically light-hearted, but practically heavy-handed.

Finally, the ultimate audience for this book is the average Jewish "John Doe" whom the author has every intention of turning into the above-average Jewish "Jonathan Doestein." It is directed to the Simon & Garfunkel generation of non-involved Jews, and to the Jewishly uninvolved children they raised. If the "words of the prophets are written on the subway walls and tenement halls," then it might help to know that the original prophets were Jewish. It is incumbent upon all us former Jewish flower children who sang the words "Jeremiah was a bullfrog" from The Three Dog Night's popular Sixties' song, *Joy to the World*,[1] that Jeremiah was one of the great Jewish social prophets; and if he were turned into a bullfrog, then that bullfrog could not have been *kosher*![2]

So Mr. Simon and Mr. Garfunkel, it is time to stop singing about "Jesus loving us more than we will know." No longer can you "find yourselves" or "search for your identity" in South Africa or in Spanish Harlem or on the 59th Street Bridge or at Graceland. You are going to have to go elsewhere — to Lithuania and Berdichev and points east; and go back further — well before the birth of your "loving Jesus." Indeed, in place of Jesus and Joe Dimaggio, you need

---

1. From the Three Dog Night Album *The Best of Three Dog Night*.
2. Adjective derived from *kashrut*, the system of dietary laws, which outlines what is and is not permissible for a Jew to eat. See **Way #33 – Your Food**.

to write a new song about Moses and Hank Greenberg.[1] Instead of "looking for America," let's look for re"Jew"venation. Let's find **fifty ways to be Jewish**.

---

1. Hank Greenberg (1911-1986) was a great Detroit Tigers baseball player who starred in the Thirties and Forties. His Jewishness prompted this poem by Edgar Guest: "Come Yom Kippur, holy fast day wide-world over to the Jew/ And Hank Greenberg to his teaching and the old tradition true/ Spent the day among his people and he didn't come to play/ Said Murphy to Mulrooney, 'We shall lose the game today/ We shall miss him in the infield and shall miss him at bat/ But he's true to his religion, and I honor him for that.'"

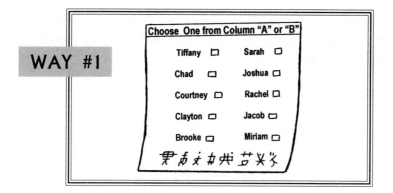

WAY #1

Choose One from Column "A" or "B"

Tiffany ☐	Sarah ☐
Chad ☐	Joshua ☐
Courtney ☐	Rachel ☐
Clayton ☐	Jacob ☐
Brooke ☐	Miriam ☐

YOUR NAME

or:

The Name Game

Let's say your Jewish parents named you Courtney or Clayton or Lindsay or Chad or Morgan or Ryan or Meagan or Shawn. With half the names — Courtney, Ryan, Meagan and Shawn — you could open an Irish law firm. With the other half — Clayton, Lindsay, Chad and Morgan — you could open a Protestant blue-blood Brahmin stock brokerage. But there are some of you who had the dubious fortune of having your parents name you after a body of water, like Brooke, or after a desert, like Sierra. I do agree that it would be inappropriate to choose the name "Dead Sea" as a Jewish alternative to "Brooke," but what would be so bad in opting for the name "Sinai" over "Sierra?"

Now, we are told that Chad was named for his dead Jewish grandfather, Haim, even as Meagan was named for her dead Jewish grandmother, Miriam. Most Jewish parents give their children two names, like Sarah Mary. After all, in the spirit of American pluralism, one needs to show respect for the Judeo-Christian tradition. Therefore, the Jewish mother Sarah must be balanced by the Christian mother Mary.

Of course, one of the challenges is that many of these names will lead one back to his or her roots in Ireland or Sweden, not Poland or the Ukraine. This phenomenon reminds one of the story of two old Jewish high school buddies, Goldstein and Cohen, who bumped into each other after a hiatus of over forty years.

Cohen: Goldstein, how are you doing?

Goldstein: I couldn't be better. I work as a doctor at Beth Israel Hospital in Boston. And what about you?

Cohen: I am also doing well. I am a partner in the law firm of Sullivan and O'Brien.

Goldstein: How nice. Sullivan and O'Brien? What a surprise!

Cohen: I've got a bigger surprise. I'm O'Brien!

Now, what about those of you who have more traditional names like Edward or James or William? While more subtle than the assimilated names of Courtney, Ryan, et. al., they certainly cannot be characterized as Jewish names. Of course, one can argue that since William is the derivative of the German name Wolf, which is the English of the Hebrew name Ze'ev (which indeed is a wolf in Hebrew), then one's name is really a Jewish name. But that would be stretching the point. I would hate to see the length of the name-tag, which the sponsors of a Jewish identity seminar would have to produce, in order that others attending the seminar would know that dear old William is indeed a Jew, and not some pretender to the British Crown!

There is a tradition of Jews changing their names. Abraham was converted from Abram. Sarah from Sarai. And Jacob became Israel. In each case, the names meant something significant; and it was incumbent upon the individual to live up to his or her name. For example, the name "David" means "beloved." The name "Michael" means an "angel of God." The name "Isaac" means "he will laugh." Imagine, a family of three rambunctious boys blessed with these names. What a magnificent challenge for them to become beloved angels of God who sit around laughing all day!

Remember this classic exchange from the popular TV show *All in the Family*:

> **Archie**: That's something the "Hebes" do. They change their last names, but keep their first names so that they'll still recognize each other.
> **Mike**: Whaddya mean Arch?
> **Archie**: Well, you take a guy like Isaac Schwartz. He changes "Schwartz" to "Smith," but he leaves "Isaac." So he's Isaac Smith. Jacob Cohen? He becomes Jacob Kane...see?
> **Mike**: Yeah, I see what you mean Arch. Like Abraham...Lincoln.
> **Edith**: I didn't know Lincoln was Jewish!

So all you Claytons out there, change your name to Rachmiel. Once you do that, you will no longer be identified as some transplanted Yankee oil tycoon who appeared on the Eighties' popular TV soap opera *Dallas*, who courted Miss Ellie shortly after her husband died. Rachmiel means "God, the Merciful One." Now isn't that a far better offering? And what a great challenge to fulfill the meaning of your new name. Also, if you can pronounce the name, you are half-way on the road to being Jewish, because it would mean that you have mastered one guttural letter of the Hebrew language (see **Way #4 — Your Language**). And for all you Courtneys, let's go for Osnat. Admittedly, there is a challenge with the pronunciation of the name — "oh, snot." But the name relates to a biblical personality, giving one a sense of longevity, as well as providing one with a feeling of historical and religious importance.

Also, some Jewish names have a certain authority to them. Take the name Samuel. It has a power to it. "Hello, this is Sam. I'll place fifty dollars on Tyson to bite his ear off in three." Or Rachel: "Listen kid, this is Rachel, like the mother Rachel, from the Bible. Now sit down and shut up!"

When Rabbi Zushya[1] was on his death-bed, his disciples gathered around him. Zushya seemed deeply troubled. His disciples asked him what was the matter. Zushya responded: "I am not afraid of dying, I only fear one question. Not that God will ask me why I was not like Moses, but why was I not like Zushya?"

A name is serious business. It labels an individual, oftentimes attaching a certain persona. It is with you from birth to death. A name gives a hint of one's identity, of one's self-definition. One of the reasons that the Jewish People has survived for so long is that Jews never gave up their names.[2] So, **the first way to be Jewish is to be immediately identified as one, by choosing a Jewish name**. Ashley and Scott won't cut it. Joshua and Deborah will. Paul and Art won't do the trick (that is, Saint Paul and King Arthur). Simon & Garfunkel might.

---

1. Rabbi Dovber of Mezeritch succeeded the Ba'al Shem Tov as the leader of the Hassidic movement. Zushya was one of his disciples.
2. According to one commentary on the story of the exodus from Egypt, the reason that the Israelites were brought out of slavery was because they held on to three things: their names, their language and their clothes.

YOUR NEIGHBORHOOD

or:

On the Street where you Live[1]

Let's say that you live in Oleana, Arkansas, or Beaumont, Texas, or Kihei, Maui, or Stockbridge, Massachusetts, or Racine, Wisconsin. How in God's name are you going to get any sort of a Jewish education? Or let's say that you study at Kansas State University, or Earlham College of Indiana, or Reed College in Oregon. How are you going to meet a prospective Jewish spouse? And what if your parents have registered you for the Lutheran High School of St. Louis, or the Ursiline High School Academy of Atlanta? The best response is: Move to another town, transfer to another college, and enroll in another high school!

Where one lives, where one goes to school, and where one

1. From the musical *My Fair Lady*, book and lyrics by Alan Jay Lerner, music by Frederick Loewe.

works all have a profound effect on the nature of one's Jewish life. If we live in a primarily non-Jewish neighborhood and go to a school where there is minority of Jews, then the chances are great that Judaism will occupy a secondary or tertiary position in our everyday life. And to be Jewish, one has to be a full-time Jew. It is ironic that even the most uninformed Jew knows at least one Jewish prayer, the *Shema*. Part of the prayer tells us: "You shall speak of them (the commandments) when you are sitting in your house, when you are walking on your way, when you lie down and when you get up" (*Deuteronomy* 6:7). Not much room for maneuverability here.

I admit that not everyone can live on Long Island or on the North Side of Chicago or in Brookline, Massachusetts (all predominantly Jewish areas), but that does not mean that a Jew should go to the extreme and opt to live Montpelier, Vermont. Besides, it is freezing there, with heavy doses of snow, and Jews don't ski! At least they never did, until they became Chad and Ryan from **Way #1 — Your Name**.

To be Jewish, one has to live in a Jewish environment. We need to have access to a Jewish library, a Jewish community center, Jewish cultural events, a synagogue, a Jewish day school, a Jewish old-age home, an Anglo-Jewish newspaper, a Jewish deli, Jewish neighbors and a good Chinese restaurant. Instead of living on Shady Grove Lane or Pine Bluff Circle, we have to live on 184th Street and Utopia Parkway in Queens. Who wouldn't want to live in Utopia?

If "knowing I'm on the street where you live" is exclusively lit up with reindeers and nativity scenes in December, then chances are that we are not hanging around in a Jewish neighborhood. In one respect, Simon & Garfunkel have it Jewishly right when they sing so lovingly about New York City. After all, more Jews live there than anywhere else in America. Thus, if we take our two "Jewish" minstrels seriously, then **the second way to be Jewish is simply to live among Jews**.

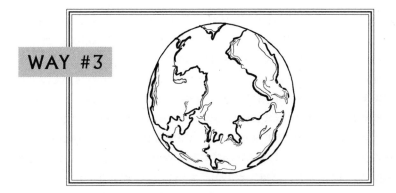

YOUR TRIPS ABROAD

or:

Around the World in Eighty Days[1]

Jews love to travel. Close to seventy-five percent have traveled abroad. Without any intention of being pejorative, we have earned the name the "wandering Jew." Even Paul Simon understood this in his song: "One and one-half wandering Jews. Free to wander wherever they choose."[2] This is a reference to his Jewish self and his then half-Jewish wife, Carrie Fisher. Her father, Eddie Fisher, was Jewish (see **Way #5 — Your Singers**), her mother, Debbie Reynolds, was not, so according to Jewish law she is technically not Jewish. Yet even though the context is quite different, his recognition of the status of Jews as wanderers is interesting,

---

1. Novel by Jules Verne.
2. Paul Simon's song "Hearts and Bones" in his *Hearts and Bones* album.

although he got it wrong when he added the words: "Free to wander wherever they choose."

So, where do American Jews go when they travel? Well, let's leave Israel aside for the moment, because that country is explored in **Way #21 — Your Israel Quotient**. Also, only about twenty percent of the American Jewish population has visited Israel. Most of them prefer European jaunts, with the Caribbean coming in a close second. We will also exclude visits to clearly defined Holocaust sites, as these are examined in **Way #36 — Your Holocaust Awareness**.

When visiting foreign countries, Jews use *Fodor's, Frommer's, The Rough Guide, The Lonely Planet* and *Michelin*. Rarely do they turn to Jewish guidebooks to Spain, Prague, Russia or Hungary. I guess this makes sense, because when one travels overseas, he or she wants to appear worldly. Signaling out Jewish points of interest might be considered too parochial. Going to an all female revue at the Crazy Horse or the Lido on the Champs-Elyses is far more of a universal eye opener than eating a French pastrami sandwich at Goldberg's Deli in the Jewish Quarter of Paris. The former gives you heartache while the latter gives you a stomach ache.

Since the destruction of the Second Temple in 70 CE,[1] the Jews have been touring the globe — unfortunately not of their own free will. They reached virtually every spot on earth. Most significantly, their influence was always felt: in the arts, philosophy and the economy, and to some extent in politics. Their religious and cultural uniqueness left their mark. By visiting Jewish sites, a Jew can learn much about his or her history, about the driving forces behind Jewish survival despite the attempts, some all too painfully real, by the European Christian community to undermine the perpetuation of the Jewish People. American Jews, who make up

---

1. Jews refer to the recording of history before the birth of Christ as BCE (Before the Common Era), and after the birth of Christ as CE (Common Era).

such an insignificant numerical minority in the United States, can learn much from the European Jewish experience.

Sunning oneself on the Spanish Costa Brava must be balanced by a visit to Jewish Cordova. Sailing on the Danube must be followed by a tour of the Jewish Museum in Budapest and the adjacent Dahony Synagogue. And of course the traditional Jewish highlights that all tourists see in Amsterdam (the Anne Frank House), in Venice (the Jewish Ghetto) and in Prague (the Jewish Quarter) are absolute musts. But what about a side trip to Kiev to see where Golda Meir grew up, or to Peryaslav where Shalom Aleichem[1] was born? If one wants to get a sense of the power of European anti-Semitism, then all one has to do is buy a coke in any city in the Ukraine with a five grivna note, which proudly displays a full frontal shot of that great Cossack butcher, Bogdan Chmielnicki.

Many American Jews have made a pilgrimage to Concord and Lexington in Massachusetts where the American Revolution began, or visited the National Civil Rights Museum at the Lorraine Hotel in Memphis, Tennessee, where Martin Luther King Jr. was assassinated, or toured the colonial village of Williamsburg, Virginia. I believe that **Jewish Americans** visit these sites, while **American Jews** visit the Rhineland cities of Worms and Mainz and the Northern French enclaves of Sens and Troyes where Rashi (Rabbi Shlomo Yitzhaki, 1040-1105), the great French biblical and talmudic commentator, established an academy of Jewish studies; or Cordova where Maimonides (Rabbi Moses Ben Maimon, also known as the Rambam, 1135-1204), the premier medieval Jewish philosopher, composed his Jewish *Guide to the Perplexed* and other philosophical works; or Prague where Franz Kafka (1883-1924), the

---

1. Born Shalom Rabinowitz (1859-1916), Shalom Aleichem ("peace unto you" in Hebrew) was the great natural genius of Yiddish literature, and one of the few modern writers who could speak for an entire people. Born in Russia, he moved to America in 1914. His literary legacy is enormous. His most famous book was *Tevye, the Dairyman* on which the popular musical *Fiddler on the Roof* was based.

great Czech born German Jewish novelist, wrote of his interest in secular Jewish culture and Zionism, which provided a counter-Jewish identity for many middle class Jewish youth of his day.

You see what can be learned just by reading these brief comments on each of these important Jewish personalities? Imagine how much more can be learned by going to the above-mentioned places.

As a kid, visiting the Washington, Jefferson and Lincoln Memorials, I was prompted to read these men's works and to learn respectively about the importance of democracy, the essence of freedom and the value of equality. So too can a Jew, by visiting the Budapest birthplace of Theodor Herzl (1860-1904), the father of modern political Zionism, understand the meaning of the Jewish People's return to its ancient homeland. By walking through the Spanish-Portuguese synagogue in Amsterdam, a Jew can encounter the Jewish philosopher, Baruch Spinoza (1632-1677), who was excommunicated for daring to reject the synthesis of reason and revelation that had been the goal of medieval philosophy, especially that of Maimonides. By discounting the notion that the Bible should be reconciled with philosophy, he became the forerunner of biblical criticism. There is much to be learned.

So when you go on your next trip abroad: in Germany, stop off at Leipzig, Cologne, Frankfort and Berlin; in France, follow a route from Alsace to Paris; in Austria, travel from Moravia to Vienna. This may not be as powerful or as impressive as Big Ben, the Eiffel Tower, Red Square, the Vatican and Dam Square, but how much follow-up identity building can you do regarding clocks, erector sets, failed revolutions, Jesus worship and drug abuse? You're better off adding some Jewish sites to your European excursions. Yes, **the third way to be Jewish is to be a Jewish tourist.**

YOUR LANGUAGE[1]

or:

You're a Royal Pain in the Ass!

Man (*in a telephone booth*): Is this Ms. Jones, the first-grade teacher?

Ms. Jones: Yes, it is.

Man: This is an obscene phone call: Ca-ca, duty, sissy, tushy, pee-pee, boom-boom!

The English language is fairly bizarre. Some expressions, while rather benign, are completely inane, like: "He's as smart as a whip." Or: "Have you lost your marbles?" Other sayings are rather creative, though still meaningless, like: "He's a chip off the old block" or "I'll take a rain check." Speaking of rain, what about: "It's raining cats and dogs?" And one of my all-time favorites: "I have a

1. See **Way #1 — Your Name**, footnote 2.

frog in my throat." Still others are graphically descriptive, although on close examination they make little sense. For instance: "Don't get caught with your pants down" or "Let's kill him with kindness." How about these oxymorons: "I'll give you even odds" or "It's the same difference." Or this improbable request: "Bite the bullet."

Unfortunately, the English language has been abused over the years. Teenagers, particularly, are pretty gross when it comes to conversing. Every other word out of their mouths seems to relate to some organ of the human body. When it comes to verbal articulation, jazz pianist Mose Allison's lament about his friend is most applicable to many of today's youth: "Your mind is on vacation, but your mouth is working overtime!"

And rap music? It is often racist and sometimes blatantly anti-Semitic. What does it tell you about the cultural values of a society if its language is so readily devalued? It tells you that these kids' language "sucks!" And that is just the point. Verbiage cannot suck. But who cares about making linguistic sense? Nowadays, if you say "that's bad," you mean something is quite good. If you are into demeaning women, a guy might refer to his girlfriend as "one mean babe," which is translated as a good-looking lady. With the advent of the Internet generation, half the time it is impossible to know what someone is talking about. When I overheard my thirteen-year-old daughter's girlfriend tell her how she prefers a hard disc to a floppy one, I almost flipped out! Don't ask me about cruising the web, trashing a font, or bulleting a template. It all sounds terribly criminal to me.

And, English idioms like those aforementioned, if taken literally could actually paralyze an individual. Just imagine someone "holding his tongue," or "grabbing hold of herself."

English is an impractical language to learn. There is little rhyme or reason to it. There are too many exceptions to the rules, and it is phonetically impossible to decipher. Why are shoot and foot not pronounced alike? Why are the vowels in science and friend pronounced differently? Who can possibly figure out why psychology and xenophobia are spelled the way they are?

By contrast, Hebrew is an orderly, systematic and sensible language to learn. The rules of grammar are consistent. Also, it is phonetic. A word sounds as it is printed. In addition, one is spared the wasted effort of adding vowels to one's written work; they simply are omitted, making Hebrew far more economical than the over-abundant and word-weary English language.

Also, Hebrew is devoid of curse words. This is not to say that the modern guardians of the Hebrew language, Israelis, are incapable of insulting one another. But their spicy use of Hebrew requires creativity and ingenuity, not a litany of filthy, deleted expletives. Sadly, English swear words have entered the Hebrew lexicon in Israel. But even here, the use of imported dirty language does not have such a great impact because anything in translation loses its power. Further, one must remember that Hebrew is considered a "holy tongue."

The Jewish People have been expelled, persecuted, scattered and killed for centuries. Yet throughout their simultaneously tortured and glorious history, they held onto their language. Italians do not speak Latin, and ancient Greek has little resemblance to modern Greek. Chaucer's English sounds nothing like a Texan's English. The very fact that the Jews have survived for hundreds of years and eventually established a state in ancient Israel has much to do with the durability of the Hebrew language. Holding on to this "holy writ" gave them the spiritual will to survive.

It has also unified Jews throughout the centuries and across the seas. I had just finished participating in High Holy Day services in a synagogue in a small town in the deep South of the United States. During the course of the prayers, I was moved by the confessional chant *Avinu Malkeinu* (Our Father, Our King). A few weeks later I found myself visiting the Jewish museum in Prague where I saw an 11th century *Prayerbook* opened up to this same chant. Hebrew is the universal language of the Jewish People. The Hebrew of today is basically the same as the Hebrew of our ancestors. Therefore, there is value in a language that represents such longevity.

While Americans want to believe that everyone understands English, reality contradicts such megalomania. If a Jew wants to communicate with other Jews outside of North America, particularly with the one hundred ethnic composites of the Jewish People who live in Israel, then Hebrew is the language of communication. In addition, knowing Hebrew not only ties one to the history of the Jewish People, but it also opens up a world of great literature that has served as a moral force for much of the world's sense of social and ethical behavior (the Bible, for instance). It also helps one understand the Hebrew prayers rather than depending on sanitized and paraphrased English translations.

So for those of you who suffered through Hebrew school and Bar or Bat Mitzvah preparations, know that if you learn this Jewish language now, you will be greatly enriched, and complimented... because it is relatively easy to learn. Also, imagine the bragging worth of speaking a language that is so old and holy, not to mention the delicious possibility of speaking behind someone's back while being right in front of the person. Just think, instead of telling someone to "go screw yourself" or worse, you could quote the first commandment that appears in the Bible and tell the son-of-a-bitch the same thing, but only more subtly: "Be fruitful and multiply!"

It also might be helpful along the way to learn a few "Yiddishisms," the once popular and highly inventive language of the Jews of Central and Eastern Europe that is a combination of Hebrew and German. Instead of telling your foul-mouthed kid that he or she is "a royal pain in the ass," you could threaten to provide him or her with "a patsch in tuches," which translates to a far more effective "swift kick in the butt!"

A fourth way to be Jewish? Learn the Jewish people's language — Hebrew.

Asa Yoelson/Al Jolson

Robert Zimmerman/Bob Dylan

YOUR SINGERS

or:

With a Song in my Heart[1]

In the Introduction, I stated that this book was geared toward middle-aged Jews and their offsprings. While just turning fifty-seven, and therefore technically beyond those years when some men go through a mid-life crisis and buy a Corvette stick-shift, I consider myself, in the words of that seminal crooner Frank Sinatra, "young at heart," which raises a question. When my friends and I were teenagers, we put on Sinatra albums, like *Songs for Swingin' Lovers* or *Only the Lonely*, as we slow-danced in our living room, thinking that we were ever so cool. I have always wondered, as did Johnny Carson when he broached this question to "Ole Blue Eyes"

---

1. Song by Richard Rogers and Lorenz Hart.

on his *Tonight Show*: Whom did Sinatra listen to on the "phonograph" when <u>he</u> wanted to make out?

The answer: the soft sounds of Benny Goodman's clarinet, and in his "more mature years," Barbra Streisand. (In my advanced stage in life, I still listen to Sinatra. Unfortunately it is to one of his most famous albums, *September of my Years!*) Yes, Sinatra listened to Jews (see **Way #49 — Your Sinatra**).

From Klezmer to Gershwin, Jews love music. The ancient Temple was filled with harps, horns, lutes, pipes, loud-clashing cymbals and songs of praise (see *Psalm* 150). In traditional Judaism, it is the cantor who occupies the central role in the synagogue. Although my father did not know Yiddish melodies with which to serenade me, he still would take me on his lap, and purposefully <u>not</u> sing me to sleep with songs of Bing Crosby or Nat King Cole. I suspect the reason was that they respectively sang *White Christmas* and *The Christmas Song*, even though White Christmas was written by a Jew, Irving Berlin. He even passed over the sentimental songs of Jimmy Durante, who has become fashionable of late thanks to the soundtrack to Nora Ephron's successful movie, *Sleepless in Seattle*. Durante, Perry Como, Fred Astaire, Rosemary Clooney and later Tony Bennett, Andy Williams and Jack Jones — all these popular entertainers were just too *goyish* (pejorative term for Christians) for him. Instead, he would hold my head close against his shoulder, and sing the haunting lyrics from Al Jolson's *Sonny Boy*[1]:

> Climb upon my knee, sonny boy. Though you're only three, sonny boy.
> You came from heaven and I know your worth.
> You've made a heaven, right here for me on earth.
> And when there are gray skies. I don't mind the gray skies.
> You make them blue, sonny boy.

---

1. From the film *The Singing Fool* (1928), written by Lew Brown, BG DeSylva, Ron Henderson and Al Jolson.

It is amazing that some fifty years later, I remember every word. What son could not feel the total and unconditional love **of** his father who sang such beautiful words to him as a child? What son could not remember the total and unconditional love **for** his father long after he died, because he sang such beautiful words to him when he was young? And for my father, singing songs of Al Jolson, a cantor's son, was an expression of a Jewish musical tradition.

When I was a little older — no longer so cute, on the fringe socially, a bit nerdy, not academically adept — my father turned to the more "hip" Eddie Fisher to encourage me with Richard Adler and Jerry Ross' song from the Boradway musical *Damn Yankees*:

> You've gotta have heart. All you really need is heart.
> When the odds are saying you'll never win, that's when the grin should start.
> You gotta have hope, musn't sit around and mope.
> Nothing's half as bad as it may appear, so wait 'til next year and hope.
> If your luck is battin' zero, keep that chin up off the floor.
> Sister, you can be a hero, you can open any door.
> There's nothin' to it, but to do it.
> You've gotta have heart, miles and miles and miles of heart.
> Oh, it's fine to be a genius of course, but keep that old horse before the cart.
> First you've gotta have heart.

In many ways, this song is the antithesis of the Jewish parents' attitude toward achieving, that is, to do well in school and get good grades. But recognizing that their child was no Albert Einstein, they took pride in the fact that I was a "good kid." My parents and Eddie Fisher taught me something about my own parenting: love your kid for who he or she is, not for what you would like him or her to be.

Tradition is important in building family closeness. I am proud to say that all my children know every word to Jolson's *Toot Toot Tootsie* and *Swanee*, and most importantly, *Sonny Boy*. And I plan to hit the next generation with the same songs. After all, that is what

Judaism is all about, handing traditions down from one generation to the next.

For those of you who are my age, perhaps a little younger or a little older, and may feel a bit disheartened because you missed developing a certain closeness with your kids that living a full Jewish life can provide, well it is not too late. There are the grand-children. If you did not have the advantage of having a parent peppering your childhood with songs of Sophie Tucker or Eddie Cantor, then you can turn to Bette Midler and Barbra Streisand. Even Bob Dylan (Robert Zimmerman: see **Way #1 — Your Name**) might do, although it is advised to skip his Christian phase. And of course, there are the twosome that don the cover of this book, Paul Simon and Art Garfunkel. One good thing about Dylan, Simon & Garfunkel is that many of their songs have a social message that is in keeping with the Jewish prophetic tradition of social justice and equality (see **Way #18 — Your Social Activism**). Also their words are genuinely memorable, as were the words to those Al Jolson songs.

I might add that, just as Jolson's life served as a reflection of the conflict between tradition and modernity as protrayed in the movie of his life, *The Jazz Singer*,[1] so too do the lives of Dylan, Simon & Garfunkel reflect new dilemmas on the American scene, like mixed marriage and assimilation — so readily displayed by the intermarried singing duo from my era, Steve Lawrence and Edie Gorme, whose songs my father refused to sing to me. (He sang me Eddie Fisher songs prior to his marriage to Debbie Reynolds.) I am not sure that he would be happy with Ms. Streisand for marrying James Brolin. But Streisand is a perfect example of the challenge of navigating a Jewish existence in a homogenous American society.

---

1. *The Jazz Singer* protrays Jolson's life story. His father wanted him to follow in his footsteps and become a cantor, but Jolson bolted the family tradition and became an entertainer. When his father was approaching death, Jolson returned to his family's synagogue to sing the beautiful *Kol Nidre* prayer on Yom Kippur.

Can one be a committed Jew, serving to guarantee Jewish perpetuity when being mixed married? Many American Jews would answer yes, as I am sure Ms. Streisand would. But one must ask, does her singing of the traditional High Holiday chant *Avinu Malkeinu*, her directing Isaac Bashevis Singer's *Yentl*, and her donations to Israel offset her singing of *Ave Maria* or her Christmas album?

Finally, this entry is not about Jewish music or Jewish songs. **This fifth way to be Jewish is about singing songs sung by Jews.** Behind each Jewish singer there is a Jewish story, and therefore, there is something Jewish to be learned; and anything Jewishly learned is Jewishly worthwhile.

WAY #6

YOUR HOME

or:

Any Place I Hang my Hat is Home[1]

W ay #6 could be a never-ending Jewish subject. That being the case, I will limit the sixth step to being Jewish to the symbols that characterize a Jewish home. I will concentrate on obvious Jewish ritual and cultural objects, but first, let me ask a simple question. If you were forced to leave your home, as was the case with so many Jews throughout the centuries, would the memorabilia that you would choose to pack in the one suitcase you would be allowed to take on your journey indicate that you came from a Jewish home? If not, then we have some work to do.

The following suggestions may be well known ones. For a start, a *mezuza* on your front door is an absolute necessity, for within the

---

1. Song by Johnny Mercer and Harold Arlen.

mezuza are inscribed the words from *Deuteronomy* (as well as the reason for putting it there[1]): "Hear, O' Israel, the Lord our God, the Lord is One. And you shall love the Lord, your God, with all your heart, with all your soul and with all your might" (6:4-5). But, most importantly, you are also implored to: "teach these (commandments) to your children" (6:7). Judaism is not just a faith where one declares his or her belief in God, it is a commitment to action. Such intimate engagement with our children will necessarily set a Jewish tone to our house. And, if we are commanded to teach elements of the Jewish tradition to our children, then we don't want our kids stumping us with questions like: "Hey, Mom and Dad, explain to me again about the thing you stick in the *mezuza*. What does it say, where is it from, how come it has to be written on special paper, who decided this stuff in the first place? Is it sacrilegious to put a *mezuza* on the dog-house?" In order to pass something on to our children, we have to know something ourself.

Hard as it is to believe, only about fifty percent of the American Jewish population has a *mezuza* on their house. Many of the other half probably knows little of what is written inside the *mezuza*, and those who do know may have little understanding of what is its meaning. But a *mezuza* is a beginning. Yet one must not just settle for only religious symbols like Sabbath candlesticks, a *menorah*,[2] a *kiddush*[3] cup and a *seder*[4] plate. There have to be some cultural accoutenments.

Those Jolson, Fisher and Dylan albums from **Way #5 — Your**

---

1. "And you shall write them upon the doorposts of your house and your gates." (*Deuteronomy* 6:9)
2. A seven-branched candelabrum used in the days of the First and Second Temple, but colloquially referred to as the candelabrum used for Chanukah, which has eight branches.
3. A cup used for the blessing of wine on Jewish holidays and the Sabbath. The word *kiddush* means sanctification.
4. A reference to the food plate of historical gastronomical symbols that are used on Passover.

Singers would certainly be helpful. But also what will be needed is a coffee-table book on *The Jews of Boston* (only if you're from New England); the *Bernard Malamud Reader* (see **Way #14 — Your Book Shelf**); a video of *Life is Beautiful* (see **Ways #36 — Your Holocaust Awareness**); some painting of either an ultra-Orthodox rabbi with his flowing beard and side-curls, dressed in his full religious regalia, or a scene of a Jerusalem sunset; and finally, a picture of one's great-grandparents eating in their *sukkah*[1] in Minsk.

Now there can be no cheating here. Irving Berlin, Robert Wise and Philip Roth may all be Jewish, but owning a copy of Berlin's Christian masterpiece *White Christmas,* or Wise's convent movie classic, *Sound of Music,* or Roth's self-hating romantic novel, *Goodbye Columbus* should not be seen as definitive hallmarks of a Jewish household. A Jewish home cannot be clouded with cultural syncretism. Still one might argue that a Statue of Liberty paper-weight has some Jewish worth to it, since the Jewish poetess Emma Lazarus wrote the words inscribed on the "Lady" which served as a beckoning call to freedom for so many Jews who immigrated to America's shores from Europe in the latter half of the 19th century.

While this step to be Jewish opened with a hypothetical question, the fact of the matter is that most Americans, among them Jews, move on the average of three to four times in their adult lives. It can be assumed that, with each relocation, some things are left behind, unless you are a member of my family where every little item has some sentimental value, like a headless cabbage-patch doll or a puzzle with half of the pieces missing. I might have been willing to save both, had the doll been named Leah instead of Kimberly and had the puzzle been of the Old City of Jerusalem rather than the Baptist youth-group-looking cast from *Dawson's Creek.*

Because of the unsettling aspect of uprooting oneself and the

---

1. A booth in which Jews were commanded to live for seven days so as to remember the Israelites who lived in temporary shelters during their exodus from Egypt.

uncertainty of adjusting to a new environment, it is emotionally essential when making each new transfer to retain elements in one's life that symbolize continuity, assure familial stability and provide a sense of security. This is especially important in an age where there is so much divorce, and where the children of broken marriages desperately need a sense of belonging. Since Jewish religious and cultural objects, symbols and habits have been mainstays of the Jewish People for centuries, safeguarding Jewish continuity, stability and security — wherever Jews were scattered and no matter how difficult circumstances may have been — it would stand to reason that they would help a family acclimate to a new situation. A Jewish tradition at home can bring comfort and unity to a transitional stage in a family's life, just as it has done for the Jewish People as a whole.

The sixth way to be Jewish is to establish a Jewish home, replete with Jewish physical evidence. It should be that "any place you hang your hat (or rather your *mezuza*) is home."

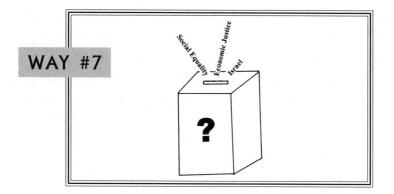

YOUR VOTE

or:

Sectarian and Non-Sectarian

For certain, the American presidential election of the year 2000 demonstrated the importance of every citizen's vote. Participating in the democratic process is a sacred task. Jews have always outstripped the general population when it comes to the percentage of votes cast. In the last national elections, only about fifty percent of Americans cast their votes, while close to seventy-five percent of Jews fulfilled their civic duty. (However, one must keep in mind that Jews make up a little less than two-and-a-half percent of the population.)

Why do American Jews take their voting responsibility so seriously? Why do they seem to have a greater vested interest than their non-Jewish fellow citizens in who gets elected to political office? The answer could lie in the proverbial "Elephant and the

Jewish Question," that is: Is it good for the Jews? Where does Jesse Ventura stand on Israel? What is Richard Gephart's view on parochial schools? What is Trent Lott's attitude toward school prayer? But does such secularism still play a role for today's Jew? Should Jews adopt a parochial view of politics? (However, it should be noted that there is a certain legitimacy in Jewish politicians advancing Jewish interests, in the same way that African-American or Hispanic politicians advocate for their concerns. Lobbying is the "American way" of political maneuvering, and addressing sectarian matters does not necessarily contradict what might be best for the country.)

Well, if you want to be Jewish in your voting habits, the answer is a resounding "Yes." A vote for a liberal candidate is a protective vote for all Jews. As a minority, Jews have to protect other minority interests in order to guarantee their own. Since consistently over eighty percent of the Jewish population votes democratic, and since Democrats mostly take up the cudgel of the "little guy," then there must be something of Jewish worth to Jews casting in their lot with the Democratic Party.

So should a Jew vote for a Republican? For certain, many do. But, let's take the Israel quotient, but not from a traditional perspective. When considering Israel, a vote for a Republican should be problematic for Jews, as most Republicans cater to the oil industries, which necessarily are dependent upon Arab fuel.

During the Gulf War, President George W. Bush Sr. held a press conference that smacked of anti-Semitic rhetoric: "We went to war against Saddam Hussein to defend Israel, as much as American interests" (Jews can't fight their own battles); "Americans give Israel the equivalent of $1,000 for every Israeli citizen" (Jews want to take your money); "The Jewish lobby is sure powerful" (Jews work insidiously behind the scenes). All of these statements are tried and true anti-Semitic canards. But anyone with any sense knows that the United States did not go to war with Iraq for Israel's sake, that the Arab oil lobby is far more powerful than AIPAC,[1] and that no Israeli has ever taken $1,000 designated for some family in Des Moines, Iowa.

The point here is that too many Republicans have a tendency to harbor subtle discriminatory views. And if many Republicans are against gays and lesbians, affirmative action and a social welfare system, they may very well try to enact laws that could have a concomitant detrimental effect on Jews. Being a persecuted minority for so many years should sensitize Jews to the suffering of others. So while a Jew may vote for a Republican, he or she should be certain that the individual politician reflects a world-view that is commensurate with the prophetic values of social justice and equality.

Of course, the real challenge is to avoid a knee-jerk reaction whereby every politico with a "Jewish" name gets our vote. Three recent secretaries of defense, William Cohen, James Schlesinger and Casper Weinberger, none of whom are Jewish, all have Jewish last names. The one who was perceived as the most hostile to Israel was Weinberger, but with a first name of "Casper," we Jews should have known that we wouldn't stand a "ghost of a chance" with him at the head of the defense establishment.

But let's take Joe Lieberman, the seemingly quintessential Jewish politician. Does a Jew vote for him because he seems to embody the perfect synthesis of Americanism and Judaism? After all, many of his social and educational stances contradict traditional Jewish stances. (Here the word traditional should be understood as liberal.) Could he be a closet Republican in democratic drag?

Whom one votes for tells much about an individual. For example, a vote for George W. Bush Jr. could indicate an inadvertent vote against two important Jewish values: respect for life and reverence for old age. (I realize that this may be overstating my case, but it is necessary to make a point.) Mr. Bush supports capital

---

1. The American-Israel Public Affairs Committee, which is the chief lobbying arm for Israel in the United States.

punishment. While capital punishment is permitted in the Bible, subsequent interpretive Jewish sources make it virtually impossible to institute the death penalty. Therefore, it is no accident that in Israel, the Jewish state, the death penalty is outlawed, except for Nazi war criminals. (In fact, it has been carried out only once, against Adolf Eichmann.) This is quite amazing when one considers the terrorist attacks perpetrated against Israel over the years. Also, Bush's seeming general distrust of the Social Security system makes him suspect regarding the elderly, and therefore may very well contradict Judaism's positive attitude toward the aged (see **Way #35 — Your Aging**).

To return to Israel: Since Israeli and American interests are generally the same, conflicts of dual loyalty rarely arise. Yet it cannot be automatically assumed that Israel will always maintain itself as a strategic asset to the United States. No manner of Jewish lobbying will affect US government policy if America sees support for Israel as hurting its national interests. Moreover, American Jews have to contend with a new demographic reality, an Arab-American one.

Even though Arab-Americans have been stigmatized with a negative image in wake of Islamic fundamentalism that has unleashed its ugly scourge of international terrorism, their influence in the voting booth will still be felt. The rapid growth in the number of Moslems in America is proportionally matched by the steady decline in Jewishly identified Americans. In addition, those African-Americans who have taken on Islam as their religious identification increase the numbers of those who would sympathize with the pan-Arab side of the Israel-Arab conflict. Their overall loyalty to Arab causes, even in the face of monstrous acts of collective murder committed by radical Moslems, is unyielding. More than American Jews, Arab-Americans vote with a singular voice.

With this new reality, American Jews will need to protect

Israel's interests. Since in some states, senators and congresspeople are dependent upon Jewish support, it becomes critical that Jews vote for candidates who are both positively inclined toward Israel and liberal-minded. So far this combination has not been all that rare.

Every political decision has its moral equation. Voting reflects one's ideological world-view. **Therefore, the seventh way to be Jewish requires Jews to cast a Jewish vote:** for those who support causes of social justice, who promote equality and who advocate for Israel.

WAY #8

YOUR CLOTHES[1]

or:

An Itsy-Bitsy, Teeny-Weeny, Yellow Polka-Dot Bikini[2]

In the Fifties, I wore a black turtle-neck, tight black jeans and black desert boots (I was a beatnik). In the early Sixties, I wore overalls, a plaid shirt and light tan hiking boots (I was a civil rights activist). In the late Sixties and early Seventies, I wore purple bell-bottoms, a torn tie-dye T-shirt, a bandana and sandals (I was a hippie). In the Eighties, I wore a herring-bone sport jacket with elbow patches, chinos and hush-puppies (I was a yuppie). In the Nineties, I wore a tie, wool pants and black alligator shoes (I was a rabbi). Today I wear Levis, Rockport shoes and either a flannel shirt

1. See **Way #1 — Your Name**, footnote 2.
2. Brian Hyland's popular song of the Fifties.

or a banlon short-sleeve pullover, depending on the season; and always a Ralph Lifschitz, now Ralph Lauren. I guess he has yet to read **Way #1 — Your Name.** (I am now semi-retired.)

There is nothing intrinsically Jewish about turtle-necks, overalls, hush puppies or a flannel shirt. But the small, round item on top of my head, crocheted of yarn, that remained constant throughout four decades of ever-changing political dress was a giveaway. No, it was not a beanie that a college freshman rushing a fraternity is humiliatingly forced to wear. It was a *yarmulke*, or what is known as a skullcap, in Hebrew, a Jewish head covering that shows deference to God.

Not every Jew wears a *yarmulke* all the time. Orthodox Jews do. Conservative Jews do when they are involved in any sort of religious event. Reform Jews may or may not wear a *yarmulke*. And here is where Jewish dress is critical. Just as a Jewish name and the Hebrew language were instrumental in maintaining Judaism throughout the ages, so too were Jewish garments. The very fact that many Reform Jews opt not to wear a *yarmulke* in their synagogues may help to explain why they are the most assimilated of the religiously affiliated Jews in America.

Now some Jewish dress seems outlandish. Philip Roth's short story, *Eli, the Fanatic*, tells of the ultra-Orthodox Jew who moves into a community where Jews feel quite comfortable and accepted, primarily because they do not "stand out." And here comes Eli, with his flowing beard, his prominent black *yarmulke*, and his all black attire that sees his pants neatly folded below the knee so as to expose his knickers. Suddenly the other Jews feel threatened. It is as if, once their Judaism is exposed, they will lose their social standing in the general community. (A good twist to Roth's story would have been to let these overly self-conscious Jews pretend that Eli was really Amish.)

There is no expressly Divine dictate to wear such garb, but it is interesting to note that the present Orthodox community has the lowest attrition rate of self-defined religious Jews. Such uniformity of dress most certainly is a contributing factor, not only to their staying power, but also to their commitment to establish a full Jewish lifestyle.

But one does not need to go to extremes. For, example, in Israel, a "Modesty Squad" has been established in some Orthodox neighborhoods. A woman who attempts to shop in a local grocery store without the proper attire, that is, not being covered from her neck to her ankles, is provided a full-length robe.

Yet, on the other hand, modesty is considered a Jewish value: modesty in dress, modesty in outward behavior, and modesty in self-evaluation. Does that mean that women should not wear "itsy-bitsy, teeny-weeny, yellow polka-dot bikinis" and men should not wear tight underwear-looking bathing suits? Well, maybe at the beach, but most certainly not low cut dresses or open-buttoned shirts in synagogue. Such attire can only detract one from his or her worshipful intent, thereby serving an individual's social inclinations, not one's religious needs.

In fact, there is a Jewish dress code for most synagogues that has been maintained for hundreds of years: the *yarmulke* and the *talit*, a prayer shawl that is mandated from biblical times. Even on certain Jewish holidays there is a dress code suggested. On Yom Kippur, one is to wear white to symbolize the purification that one is supposed to undergo during the Day of Atonement. On Passover, at the *Seder* table, one dons a robe so as to feel the total relaxation of a person of freedom, the theme that the holiday expresses.

And then there is that statement of Jewish pride, the gold *chai* (life) necklace or the wedding ring with a Hebrew quote or the Jewish Star earrings. The only problem is that those men who wear those golden *chai* necklaces almost always violate the modesty code, as they unbutton their shirts not only to show off the *chai*, but also what they almost always mistakenly believe is their impressive physique.

I once overheard this conversation between two female rabbinical students. One asked the other: "I noticed that you wore a *talit* for the first time. Did you think about putting on *tefillin?*"[1] To which she replied: "No, I don't look good in *tefillin!*" Wearing a *talit*, *yarmulke* or *tefillin* should not be considered a fashion statement. At a convention I attended, a prominent lay member of the Jewish community was about to participate in Sabbath morning services. Before ascending the pulpit, he turned to me and said: "I will wear a *talit*, but not a *yarmulke.*" I inquired as to his reasoning, and he replied: "I am going to make a statement." I was curious to know if he intended to light only one Sabbath candle from now on or put up a *mezuza* without the scroll inside. The only statement he seemed to be making was one of arbitrary foolishness.

In fact, there is little that is arbitrary within Judaism. Many of its laws make good practical sense. Most were laid down to preserve Jewish life. Given Judaism's longevity, their value has been well proven. Even Jewish dress serves as a contributing factor to the maintenance of Judaism. And so, **the eighth way to be Jewish is to dress like a Jew.** This does not mean wearing an 18th century Polish overcoat, or a *shtreimal* (a wide-rimmed fur hat), or a *babushka* (a head covering for a woman). It does not necessarily mean wearing a *yarmulke* all the time or a substitute baseball cap. It means being sensitive to the continuity and unity of the Jewish people by donning such Jewish paraphernalia when in a Jewish setting — around the Sabbath table, at the Passover *Seder,* or in synagogue.

---

1. Hebrew for phylacteries. *Tefillin* consist of two black leather boxes, containing the biblical injunctions for their use, worn by adult male Jews at morning prayers (except for the Sabbath and festivals). One is worn on the forehead and the other on the arm, both affixed by black leather straps.

YOUR CAR

or:

Cars are Cars[1]

"Cars are cars all over the world... similarly made and similarly sold..." So writes Paul Simon. Well, anyone with a heightened Jewish consciousness knows that this is not quite accurate. Since the advent of the Model-T Ford, the choice of a car often gives a hint of the owner's personality and even of his or her values.

This is very true for Israel. For example, a person who drives a Russian Lada probably is a recent Russian immigrant, suggesting a certain nostalgia despite his or her adoption of a new home. Almost all station wagons and vans are owned by Orthodox Jews because of their large families. Those Israelis who tend to be liberal usually

---

1. Paul Simon's song in his *Hearts and Bones* album.

drive the yuppie Mazda or Honda. A BMW or a Chrysler would indicate someone who leans ideologically to the right This is because the right-wing Likud party was out of power for the first twenty-nine years of the state's existence, and suffered an inferiority complex. The purchase of a BMW or an American car was seen as a status symbol — a way to restore one's pride.

What cars should American Jews own? Well let's start by employing a process of elimination. This might fall under the category of "negative theology," the philosophical process that Maimonides went through in order to define God by first establishing what God is not. Jews should not drive a German car. I know I just mentioned that Israelis drive BMWs (as well Audis, Opels and Volkswagens). Also the majority of the taxis in Israel are Mercedes-Benz. When the country began importing German cars, there was a tremendous battle about the decision to do so. Yet Israel, as the Jewish state, is surrounded by so many elements of Jewish living, that driving a German car does not necessarily injure an Israeli's Jewish identity. This is not the case with the American Jewish reality.

Americans are very good at forgiving and forgetting. But there are some aspects of one's history that are so terribly painful that the act of remembering is a positive statement of affirmation. Ferdinand Posche, the designer of the first Volkswagen, found his original Beetle getting its push when Adolf Hitler's crony Robert Ley built the huge Wolfsburg plant for the car. The factory also served as the chief contractor for the jet-powered V-1 flying bomb, the world's first successful cruise missile. The Volkswagen was considered the Nazi car.

To further pursue Maimonides' theory of "negative theology," a Jew should avoid buying a Ford as well. Henry Ford has been accused of being an anti-Semite who harbored Nazi sympathies. Indeed, Ford had an interest in the VW factory built by Ley. Far from rejecting the plant, Ford proposed that it be merged with

Ford's existing German operations. Only a failure on the part of a Ford executive prevented the merger from taking place.

As for the Mercedes-Benz, one could argue for some understanding in purchasing one. After all, when Israeli commandos rescued the Entebbe hostages,[1] they brought with them a Mercedes, made to resemble the one that Idi Amin, the Ugandan president at the time of the hijacking, would drive. They dressed someone up to look like Amin and rode right to the airport terminal where the hostages were being held. This guise was sufficient to fool the Ugandan soldiers, making it possible for the Israelis to bring in their crack sharp-shooters to rescue the captives.

Jews should probably put on their hit list most Japanese cars. Honda, Toyota, Mitsubishi and Mazda honored the Arab boycott against Israel. The worst thing would be to drive in one of these cars drinking a Pepsi, for Pepsi also observed the Arab boycott. As far as Cadillacs are concerned? They're out. Jews generally bought them as a status symbol to show off their wealth (or perceived riches), in order to prove that they had "made it" in America.

A sure sign of one's positive Jewish identity would be to cruise on the highway in a Peugeot with a Coca-Cola in hand, for neither of them heeded the Arab boycott. The purchase of a Swedish Volvo or Saab would also be a positive Jewish statement, because the Swedish diplomat, Raul Wallenberg, saved thousands of Jews during the Holocaust.

Now all of this may seem rather silly or even inane. But it really is not. One of the surest signs of being Jewish is to look at things through a Jewish prism. If we relate to the Divine mandate of the central statement of Jewish theology contained in the *Shema*, then we have to take its words seriously: "You shall speak of them when

---

1. On June 27, 1976, an Air France plane carrying 200 passengers, the majority of whom were Israelis and French Jews, was hijacked by Palestinian and German terrorists to Entebbe, Uganda. One week later, on July 4, an Israel army commando unit flew to Uganda to rescue the hostages.

you are sitting in your house, when you are walking on your way, when you lie down and when you get up" (see **Way #2 — Your Neighborhood**). We might amend this prayer to include: "…and when you drive along the highway!"

Whenever I purchase a car, I am asked why I bought the car I did. Admittedly, the reason I bought a Czechoslovakian Skoda is that the particular model happened to be called a "Forman." Usually, when asked why we chose one car over another, we answer that price, size, reputation, resale value, etc. were some of the reasons. Just imagine throwing in a Jewish rationale: I bought a Chevy because General Motors has no history of anti-Semitism; it has fair union practices for its workers; it never paid heed to the Arab boycott of Israel; and "what's good for General Motors is good for America." But most importantly, we could say with pride that the late Dinah Shore, a Jew, sang that wonderful theme song: "Drive your Chevrolet, through the USA — America, the greatest land of all." If we can combine the singer of this song with the words of this song, then sitting behind the wheel of an Impala would be the ultimate healthy fusion of Americanism and Judaism. Yes, **the ninth way to be Jewish is to buy a car in a consciously Jewish manner.**

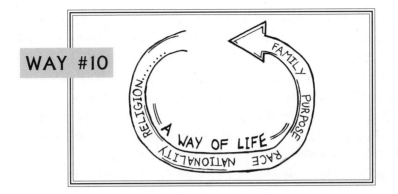

YOUR CULTURE

or:

A Way of Life

You should not begin reading **Way #10** with an eye toward a presentation of some "cutesy" homilies on the quirks of the Jewish People. For certain, we Jews do have some interesting cultural habits. No, we do not eat our soup with a fork or our mashed potatoes with chopsticks. But we do operate soup kitchens and provide hot meals of meat and potatoes to the homeless. Why the latter? Because we have a tradition of aiding the poor, which finds its articulation in our literature and in our historical experiences. So as you read on, be prepared for a quasi-sociological peek into the cultural heritage of the Jewish People. Brace yourselves for a brief historical journey.

Culture is the sum total way of living, built up by a group of human beings and transmitted from one generation to another. It reflects an organic mosaic of arts, manners, letters, religion, folk-traditions, language, scholarly pursuits, politics, economics and ethical conduct. It determines moral standards and values. It sets goals, hopes and aspirations. It establishes patterns of behavior in a society that is a reflection of the individual member of a larger collective. Culture sets the rhythm of one's life, giving the person self-definition and providing him or her with a particular identity.

Rarely is one given the opportunity to choose his or her culture. One is born into it. Unlike a Christian, who, for the most part, defines his or her Christianity in religious terms, a Jew defines him- or herself in national and cultural terms, as well as religious ones. According to the late, great Jewish thinker, Mordecai Kaplan (1881-1983), the only name that adequately describes the Jewish heritage is civilization or culture. He defines Judaism as such because it fits all the above cultural categories. To belong to the Jewish People is not only to belong to a religion, but also to be part of grand culture. Wherever Jews live, in addition to their own country's cultural peculiarities, they can be part of a Jewish culture, for Jewish culture spans continents and centuries. Culture defines a people. It establishes a way of life.

There is no intention here to respond to each of the categories above and recount the numerous cultural contributions Jews have made to the societies of which they have found themselves to be a part. I have no interest in parading before you the contributions to the world of arts and sciences of the Einsteins (Albert), the Rubinsteins (Arthur), the Bernsteins (Leonard), the Hammersteins (Oscar), or the Spielbergs (Steven), the Goldbergs (Molly), the Greenbergs (Hank), or for that matter a combination of the two: the Steinbergs (Bernie, my good friend, who is the Director of Harvard Hillel House[1]). Instead, I would like to outline some of the cultural characteristics of the Jewish People from its earliest stages as a

---

1. The Jewish student organization on many university and college campuses.

nomadic tribe in the ancient Near East to the present. I admit to a certain presumptuousness in attempting to present such a historical panorama within the confines of **Way #10**. But perhaps that is one of the cultural manifestations of at least this Jew: to presume to achieve more than is humanly possible. Or maybe not, considering the resilience of the Jewish People throughout their long, five-thousand-year dramatic history.

Judaism is an extraordinary way of life. It has successfully kept pace with the evolution and development of western civilization. Born as a religion of semi-nomads in the ancient Near East, it is still applicable today in a technological age. Along the way it spawned two other world religions: Christianity and Islam. It was sustained by an elitist group, which only briefly enjoyed independence. There may have been other religions that have persisted longer, but there is no other religion that has mastered the complex art of survival through every phase of western civilization, subsequent to its emergence at some unknown time in the ancient Near East.

Its attachment to land contributed to its staying power. Yet even though an eventual return would be fulfilled, most Jewish history has been one of dispersion. Having to overcome the most insidious and inventive ways to destroy it, remarkably Judaism has survived until today.

How does one account for this miracle-like experience? The explanation is found in a people who has derived its strength from a belief that God was involved in the life of the Jews, collectively and individually. I will not discuss concepts of God here. That will have to wait until **Way #15 — Your God**. What happened at the incipient stages of Jewish life — from the particular formation of a Jewish character as exemplified by Abraham, the first Jew, to the fashioning of a national persona as experienced by the Jewish People at Mount Sinai — is that a consistent culture of behavior and attitudes was fixed, one that would last throughout the centuries.

What are the elements of this culture? Some have already been hinted at in previous **Ways**. For example, we could add to **Way #1 — Your name** that when a Jew is given a Hebrew name, he or she is referred to as the son or daughter of...This is the same tradition that existed in biblical times. Such identification ties one to his or her most immediate culture: the family. **Way #4 — Your Language** and **Way #8 — Your Clothes**, both reflect one's cultural ties. But Jewish culture is far more inclusive.

Just as one's name and language have been passed on from one generation to another, so too is the Jewish heritage, which finds its cultural embodiment in its rich literature. The Jewish literary tradition is built on stepping-stones. The Bible begot the *Mishnah*,[1] which gave birth to the *Talmud*,[2] which in turn spawned a wealth of *Commentaries*[3] that ushered in a genre of *Responsa* literature,[4] which later gave way to modern Jewish writers (particularly Israeli authors) who call upon these traditional sources to enhance their social and artistic message for today.

The thread that runs through the generations of this literary adventure is divided into two categories: legal codes and moral guidelines. Both serve as the grounding for Jewish culture. Simply put: There are binding laws, that, while introduced by a Divine Being, are applied to the realities of every day existence; these laws lend themselves to determining an ethical code of conduct. That ethical code of conduct (see **Way #18 — Your Social Activism** and **Way #23 — Your Moral Mitzvot**) bore the Ten Commandments.

---

1. Codification of Jewish law compiled by Judah HaNasi around 200 CE. It contains the basis for the *Oral Law* (*Talmud* — see footnote 2), traditionally given to Moses at Mount Sinai and handed down, side by side with the *Written Law* (*Torah*), from generation to generation.
2. Comprehensive designation of the *Mishnah* and the *Gemara* as a single unit. The *Gemara* interprets the *Mishnah*. There were two *Talmuds* — *Jerusalem* (3rd century) and *Babylonian* (3rd to 5th century). Unless otherwise indicated, quotes from the *Talmud* in this book will be from the *Babylonian Talmud*.
3. Body of literature written by the leading commentators throughout the centuries, such as Rashi and the Rambam (see **Way #3 — Your Trips Abroad**).
4. Answers to questions that arise in rabbinic literature.

To be heir to such a powerful social message, which has stood the test of time, not only for the Jewish People, but for western civilization, is only one aspect of the culture of Judaism. When such high standards are set, they affect all aspects of one's cultural life. And so, Marc Chagall can use biblical motifs in his art and Saul Bellow can quote from Hasidic[1] sources, lending a Jewish cultural authenticity that surely enhances their work.

The desire of the Jewish People to fulfill the biblical mandate to be a "light unto the nations" does not only relate to Israel, but to all Jews. This may explain why so many Jews, far beyond their numerical proportion in any given society, have assumed roles of leadership in so many social causes. Whether it be a Jew who denies his Judaism, like Karl Marx or Leon Trotsky, or places his Judaism on a back burner, like Sigmund Freud, or abrogates his Judaism, like Jesus himself, it is no accident that their influence on the world seemed to grow out of a Jewish culture that always tried to adapt itself to changing realities, even as it held on to the cultural contiguities in a common history that kept Judaism alive.

The standards of social behavior, which are the very essence of culture, stem from a commitment to a prophetic longing for justice and equality that found American Jews at the forefront of the struggle for equal rights for African-Americans, and at the center of the flower-child revolution of the Sixties. Jewish luminaries like Abraham Joshua Heschel, Stephen S. Wise, Kivie Kaplan, and uninformed Jews like Abbie Hoffman, Jerry Rubin and Mark Rudd all seemed to want to bring about a social change that turned out to be reflective of the Jewish historical experience. Our own Dylan and Simon & Garfunkel sang about social revolution. After all, the obligation to help "the other" has its roots in biblical texts and in

---

1. A religious movement founded by the Baal Shem Tov in Volhynia and Podalia in the eighteenth century. It was primarily an Eastern European religious ecstatic movement, which spread to nearly all parts of the world. The word Hasid means "pious one."

the subsequent literature that expounds on those biblical texts. But it first finds its expression in coming to the aid of one's own community, which explains the organizational ingenuity of the Jewish People in helping one another.

One's culture sets the paradigm for human interaction. In Judaism, this pattern is clearly delineated. First comes the immediate group, the family, or the "nature" group — the group you were naturally born into. The second group might be best defined as a "purpose" group — the group with which you find common cause. A third group is a "racial" group — the group where you may find similar physical features or genetic links. A fourth group could be a "national" group — the group with which you share a common history. A fifth group is a "religious" group — the group where your ritual customs and spiritual yearnings find communal comfort.[1]

I would dare say that most Jews would have a difficult time harmonizing all these groups in the American milieu. While emotionally they may feel more comfortable in their identification with the home where they have grown up, intellectually and spiritually they may have an easier time placing all these groups in a unique whole under a Jewish umbrella. Family (united by lineage), purpose (contained in the social message of the prophets), race (certain physical resemblances), nationality (expressed by a two-thousand year longing for return, ultimately realized) and religion (practiced through observance of ritual and moral commandments). All five of these groups constitute one's culture.

Jewish culture is far more instructive than sitting around the table, eating knishes, telling Jewish jokes, reading a Chaim Potok novel, wringing your hands about the latest developments in Israel, and seeing which Jewish senators voted for gun control legislature.

---

1. *Modern Jewish Problems*, Roland B. Gittelsohn, UAHC Press, 1964 (published at the beginning of Simon & Garfunkel's debut, at the height of the volatile Sixties).

All these are outward manifestations of Jewishness. They pale in comparison to the identification with a cultural heritage that would have us study our sources, which serve as a guideline for ethical conduct. Or that would see us take up the cause of a people who are trying to establish a society in Israel that will be likened to a "holy nation" (even if it has yet to become one), and of which all Jews might one day be proud. Jewish culture would have us set up philanthropic institutions that aid others as well as ourselves. Jewish culture would mandate us to practice a religion that not only sets ritual customs uniting all Jews throughout all lands and ages, but also that dictates a moral code of conduct, which is succinctly embodied in the Ten Commandments — that universal guideline given by the Jews to the world.

The tenth way to be Jewish is to bring Jewish culture into your hearts and minds. There is no conflict here with living out your life in Boston, Philadelphia or Phoenix. (Well, maybe Phoenix if you read **Way #2 — Your Neighborhood**.) The Jewish People enjoyed a Golden Age in Spain and an Enlightenment in Europe (until they were either expelled or liquidated). Your life can be enriched immeasurably by a world of literature, folk-ways, social standards and ethical choices. If you can expand your horizons, both qualitatively (in terms of values) and quantitatively (in terms of history), by adopting a way of life that is already part of your cultural heritage, then "go for it."

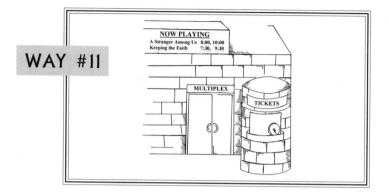

WAY #11

NOW PLAYING
A Stranger Among Us 8:00, 10:00
Keeping the Faith   7:30, 9:30

MULTIPLEX

TICKETS

YOUR FLICKS

or:

That's Why God Made the Movies[1]

As I kid, I used to love going to double features at my neighborhood single-screen movie house. I do admit that today there is an advantage to watching a flick in the new twenty-two multiplex movie theaters, and that is: in addition to watching the movie you chose to see, you can hear the movies in the theaters on each side of you!

Having parents who would sing to me (see **Way #5 — Your Singers**), I loved going to musicals. One of my favorite double features was the 1955 release of *Oklahoma*, with Gordon McCrae and Shirley Jones, and of *Love Me or Leave Me*, with Doris Day and James Cagney. As I moved out of this rather frivolous stage and

---

1. Paul Simon's song on his *One Trick Pony* album.

entered the socially conscious Sixties, I chose as my double feature the 1962 films: *To Kill a Mockingbird*, with Gregory Peck, and *The Days of Wine and Roses*, with Jack Lemmon. It was not until later that the Vietnam War movies appeared, and I could watch the 1970's *Coming Home*, with Jane Fonda and Jon Voight, and *The Deer Hunter*, with Robert DeNiro and Meryl Streep. As part of my Jewish upbringing, *Gentleman's Agreement* (a story of anti-Semitism in the United States at the close of World War II) and *Exodus* (the story of the birth of Israel) were mandatory viewing. What was so attractive about these latter two films was the drawing power of the stars, Gregory Peck and Paul Newman, respectively.

Oftentimes one goes to a movie for sheer escapism. Many people are not interested in attending a film that is a graphic reminder of the social ills of society or the multifaceted problems of a family. Yet there are some masochistic individuals who enjoy seeing an image of their own suffering portrayed on a large screen, and even more so, of the woes of others. This all falls under the category of "entertainment" (although I have always been baffled as to why people attend movies that are scary, tense or violent; there are more than enough of these manifestations of emotions and behavior to go around in real life).

For many, a movie can be a great learning tool. After all, I often waited for the movie version of a book to come out, so that, when writing my literary analysis of *Oliver Twist* or *The Great Gatsby* for school, I could pretend that I read the book. Watching movies is an easy way to access a subject of concern. Some films can be emotionally engaging, socially alarming and historically compelling. Since most Jews know so little about their Judaism, attending a film with a Jewish theme can be one of the simplest ways to become Jewishly aware. Here is a list of films that I would subjectively suggest to see. The movies are according to categories.

Animation: *American Tail — Feivel Goes West, An American Tail, Moses — Prince of Egypt.* **Anti-Semitism:** *Gentleman's Agreement,*

The Fixer. **Biblical**: *King David, Samson and Delilah* (just for fun), *The Ten Commandments*. **Comedy**: *Bye-Bye Braverman, Cemetery Club, Enter Laughing, Goodbye Columbus, Keeping the Faith, The Frisco Kid, The Producers, To Be or Not to Be*. **Documentaries**: *A Life Apart: Hasidism in America, Chicken Soup, The Brian Epstein Story, The Jew in the Lotus, The Life and Times of Allen Ginsburg, Wild Man Blues*. **Drama**: *A Stranger Among us, Avalon, A Walk on the Moon, Compulsion, Crossing Delancey, Driving Miss Daisy, Enemies — A Love Story, Hester Street, Homicide, Shine, The Chosen, The Front, The Marathon Man, The Price of Rubies, The Way We Were, Unstrung Heroes*. **Gangster**: *Bugsy*. **Holocaust**: *A Shop on Main Street, Europa Europa, Friendship in Vienna, Left Luggage, Life is Beautiful, Night and Fog, Schindler's List, Shoah, Sophie's Choice, Sunshine, The Diary of Anne Frank, The Eighty-First Blow, The Garden of the Finzi Contini, The Last Wave, The Pawnbroker, Voyage of the St. Louis*. **Israel**: *Afula Express, Beyond the Walls, Cast a Giant Shadow, Exodus, Judith, Kadosh, My Michael, Sallah Shabbati, Siege, The Little Drummer Girl, Under the Domim Tree*. **Musicals**: *Fiddler on the Roof, Kazablan, Milk and Honey, Oliver, Sound of Music, Yentl*.

Of course, a more complete listing of Jewish films can be readily perused on the Internet. In addition, almost every major city in the United States sponsors a Jewish Film Festival and some have special Israeli Film Festivals. Also, there are directors whose films have a Jewish theme running through them: Woody Allen, Mel Brooks and Carl Reiner. While many of their films deal with Jewish neurotic tendencies, stereotypically so, they nevertheless are instructive. A Jew should stay away from films that feature either Maurice Chevalier or Errol Flynn, both known for their anti-Semitic tendencies.

The one constant I found in all the films mentioned here is that they are absorbing. They engage the viewer in a world of Jewish living that many Jews on the periphery might find fascinating, if not compelling. A particular film may also reveal entry points for identifying with a particular character or situation. And then again, there is nothing wrong with adopting Paul Newman or Kirk Douglas as Jewish heroes (see **Way #20 — Your Heroes**).

During the McCarthy witch-hunt of the late 1940s and early 1950s, Hollywood was singled out. Many Jews occupied high positions in the film industry, and some became household names: Bernstein, Kahn, Ornitz, Maltz, Biberman. Labeled the "Hollywood Ten," they were dragged before the House on Un-American Activities Committee (HUAC), accused of Communist sympathies and subversive acts against the United States. They had to resume their writing under pen-names, never getting the credit due them. Many had their lives destroyed. Two of the best movies that deal with this period are *The Front*, with Zero Mostel, who himself was blacklisted during that dark time, and *Guilty by Suspicion*, with Robert DeNiro. Whenever my family complains that I go to the movies too often, I cite my moral obligation to support the film industry, which was once so mercilessly maligned — Jews in Hollywood being the most abused.

In the Introduction to this guidebook on how to be and feel Jewish, I mentioned that I had hoped to produce a primer of "fifty easy steps to be Jewish." It is a relatively painless step to take in a movie. In fact, many of these films are out on video and/or DVD. So sit back, relax, kick off your shoes, take out some cranberry juice and a Chewy Granola Bar, and enjoy **the eleventh way to be Jewish by slipping a Jewish flick into your video machine**.

WAY #12

YOUR SYNAGOGUE

or:

The Need for Community

and Introspection

Note: A disclaimer. **Way #12** will only deal with the synagogue as a "House of Worship." There will be no discussion of the synagogue as an educational center or as a Bar/Bat Mitzvah training center. These subjects will crop up in other **Ways** of this book.

I used to hate going to "shul" (Yiddish for synagogue). As a child, I found it boring. As a teenager, I found it insufferable. As a university student, I found it false. As a young adult, I found it tiring. Through all these stages of my life, I found it basically meaningless, a bunch of mumbo-jumbo uttered to a God, in whom, yes, I did believe; but not much beyond a Supreme Being who created the world, because I could not come up with any other reason for a human being's existence. The synagogue was the institutional embodiment of religion, which I found intrusive. John Lennon's song *Imagine*[1] expressed my generation's view on religion better than any rabbi I knew did: "Imagine no religion."

I am now older, with an abundance of children, and I attend shul regularly. But it is not for them that I go, but rather for me, although I do believe in the notion of that overworked cliche: "A family that prays together, stays together." However, as soon as we do something only "for the kids," a child's keen instincts hone in on our lack of authenticity.

So what is the reason that I now feel cozy in synagogue, not bored, not suffering, not feeling hypocritical, not tired, and sensing something meaningful is taking place? I do not want to discuss here my belief in God, although clearly to understand my comfort level in a religious setting would require some theological explanation. But "God talk," I will save for **Way #15 — Your God**. I wish to address two other major elements: community and introspection.

Community

> **Friend #1**: Tell me, why do you go to synagogue? You don't believe in God.
>
> **Friend #2**: Jews go to shul for different reasons. You see my friend over there, Rachmiel? (From **Way #1 — Your Name**.) He goes to shul to talk to God. I go to shul to talk to Rachmiel.

Jews are defined as a people, which suggests community, that in turn demands a *minyan*, a group of at least ten people — the minimum requirement of individuals to constitute a quorum for synagogue prayer. A Jew prays in the plural, asking for the blessings

---

1. From John Lennon's album *The John Lennon Collection*.

of peace and health to be granted to others as well to him- or
herself. Judaism is basically an unselfish religion. And given the
present realities, when books like *Looking Out for Number One* are
still bestsellers, and when twenty thousand people can gather at the
Cow Palace in San Francisco for an EST session whose sole purpose
is to concentrate on the "me," it is a relief to think that others
beyond oneself actually do exist out there.

Now it is true that I finally found a synagogue that meets my
social needs. Oftentimes I sit in my synagogue, which is set up like a
theater-in-the-round in order to create intimacy, and am totally
entertained by the people around me. There is the couple who, arm-
in-arm, seem to be doing a "two-step" to the *Shema*. There is the
fellow across the way, who, whenever a spirited *nigun* (a song
without words) is sung, begins howling, featuring himself as some
sort of Luciano Pavarotti. There is the lesbian couple next to me,
one of whom is nursing their baby, and the gay man who is chasing
his surrogate-born kid around the shul. I especially like the guy who
bows so low during one of the prayers that he virtually prostrates
himself on the ground. There are the holier-than-now members
who sway back and forth with such intensity that I am certain their
heads are going to fly off. Then there is the divorced father who has
his arms around his two teenage children as they nestle into his
comfortable and comforting arms, and the family with four sons
who sits opposite the family with four daughters, each child eyeing
the other with a mixture of shyness and flirtation. There is the
mourner who just lost a parent and the parents who are celebrating
the birth of a child. The rabbi often has three or four kids sitting on
his lap. And then there are the mentally challenged adults whom
the shul adopted. It is a true panoply of personalities.

Coming of age in the rebellious Sixties, this is the perfect
spiritual environment for me, because it stretches the limits of my
social tolerance. Ultimately it determines whether I am indeed a
true liberal and a basically all-embracing and loving human being.

Because I thoroughly enjoy what happens in synagogue, I guess I have passed the test. This is my community. And I find myself being pulled along, participating fully and singing to the rafters — and hopefully beyond.

Introspection

This serves as a good segueway for the second reason that a synagogue can be an important part of a Jew's life. As I sit among this community of people, I am prompted to turn inward. Our rabbi provides some quiet moments for each person to reflect on the past week and to ponder how he or she prepared for the Sabbath. (For someone of my age, this is quite unsettling. While my long-term memory is still intact, my short-term memory is showing signs of lapses. As I move up the week to the morning of the Sabbath, my memory seems to fade. Maybe this is just as well, because my Sabbath preparations usually consist of me running around like a madman doing last minute errands.) And yet, I find the soft, yet ecstatic melodies propelling me to examine myself, to reach deep inside of me, to pray for certain things — some abstract, some concrete. And because the setting is so communal, I find my prayers to be inclusive.

Most people need to identify with a group, as outlined in **Way #10 — Your Culture**. A certain alienation has taken hold of the American reality, and too many people get lost. A community is very much needed, and a synagogue can serve this need. In biblical times, we read of Moses addressing the "community of Israel" or the "children of Israel" or the "people of Israel." The prophets too stood before the "household of Israel," urging them to consider their behavior and actions, especially in relation to the larger community. This concept of shared responsibility found its expression throughout the ages in the *minyan*.

The question is whether one can find an eclectic synagogue like mine, or if one is even interested in such a place. Since I am writing this manual for those like me, I will egotistically take "Yes" for an answer. And if the answer is indeed "Yes," then I can assume that, like me, you regard most synagogues as dreary places of worship. Like me, you would prefer to bypass the painful ordeal of dressing up and then being "prayed at" — all the while being continually harangued by a rabbi who can never seem to make up his (or her) mind: "Now stand up, sit down, stand up, sit down," *ad nauseam*. As for those temples that still play musical instruments, attending synagogue can be a frightening experience, especially for a young child, as the organ's introduction to the "Call to Worship" may sound more like the overture of *Phantom of the Opera*! So what to do?

Well, many synagogues, recognizing the need for more intimate, informal and participatory services, have set up *havurot*, small groups of people who can get together at convenient times to pray and study. Many major cities have well established *havurot* — Boston, New York, Philadelphia, San Francisco, Chicago, Baltimore, and more. Jewishly less populated metropolitan areas like Buffalo, Wilmington, Dallas and St. Louis also are experimenting with *havurot*. This *havurot* movement is growing independently. Its most attractive feature is that it is a welcoming community.

If you live on either Coast, there is the chance to join some synagogues whose jubilant services literally rock. B'nai Yeshurun Synagogue in New York draws thousands to its Friday evening services because of the music and ecstatic dancing that takes place. And of course there are the "Friday Night Live" services in Los Angeles that host an eight piece band. In each case the rabbi gives a "hip" ten minute sermon, and then the young Jewish singles mix and date. Rent the movie *Keeping the Faith*, starring Ben Stiller, to get an idea of what type of rabbi serves these congregations and why they are so attractive.

After a long week, while some people need to seek out quiet

time, others crave the envelopment of a community. In both situations, rarely does one find him- or herself engaging in any kind of self-examination. Most people do not do yoga on their own or any other form of meditation or relaxation. Rarely does one go off to a lake or a forest to contemplate the measure of one's life, even on a short-term basis. A community, which has behind it a long history of a rich literature and ritual practices, creates the ambience and environment for some sort of introspection that is a necessary additive to one's life and can lead to self-improvement. If one is already Jewish, then why not look to one's own resources? **The twelfth way to be Jewish is to attend synagogue in some form or another,** in order to be part of a community, a community that will coax you into a weekly regimen of obligatory "soul-searching," so that you can cleanse yourself and thus be an even more pleasant participant in different communal settings.

YOUR LEISURE TIME

or:

"Dootin-Doo-Doo, Feelin' Groovy"[1]

"Slow down, you move too fast. You got to make the morning last. Just kickin' down the cobblestones, lookin' for fun and feelin' groovy." So sing Simon & Garfunkel whimsically. But if we take seriously the words of the Jerusalem scribe and sage Simeon Ben Sira[2] (2nd century BCE): "The wisdom of a learned man comes through leisure, and he who has little business shall become wise" (*Apocrypha: Ben Sira* 38:24), then there is an element of truth to Simon & Garfunkel's song.

Ben Sira's view contradicts the stereotype of the Jew who needs

1. *The 59th Street Bridge Song (Feelin' Groovy)* from the Simon & Garfunkel album *Parsley, Sage and Rosemary and Thyme.*
2. Ben Sira collected his wise sayings and aphorisms in his well-known book *The Wisdom of Ben Sira,* which was translated into Greek and included in the *Apocrypha* (body of Jewish literature written in later Second Temple times).

to "get ahead" and is particularly adept in business. After all, we know, that "all work and no play," makes Rachmiel a "royal pain in the ass" (see **Way #4 — Your Language**). Recently, I met a rabbinincal couple. He worked as a rabbi for a large national Jewish organization and she was a rabbi of a sizable synagogue. I asked them if they found time to be together, and they responded that their work schedules made it difficult.

I inquired about their young children. They said that they had a "live-in" (a Puerto Rican Catholic). They then proudly claimed that when they do find time to be with each other and their kids, it is "quality time." With great restraint, I replied: "Give me a break. Who are you kidding? An ethnic Catholic is raising your future."

Whenever someone throws at me the phrase "quality time," I hear: "My family, my kids, my friends, my hobbies, my relaxation, my political and social involvement are all of secondary importance." Why? Because "quality time" inevitably means a lack of "quantity time," that which is required to add genuine "quality" to one's life. This is not to say that someone should fudge his or her work ethic, rather that one must order priorities in such a way that the words "quality time" are not denuded of their essence: time to read, travel, visit, play, walk, talk and most of all — to spend time with family, friends and be active in the community.

The first Jew, Abraham, in addition to founding a religion, leaving his home, handling a difficult family situation, almost sacrificing his child, arranging a peace agreement, and purchasing land to guarantee his and his people's perpetuity,[1] managed to find time to entertain such a wonderful leisurely concept as

---

1. In *Genesis*, we read of Abraham: leaving his father's home to go to "a land that I (God) will show you" (12:1), having a child, Ishmael, with his handmaiden Hagar because his wife Sarah is barren, only to father Isaac with Sarah a little later and having to force Hagar and Ishmael to leave (21:1-21), almost sacrificing his son Isaac to prove his absolute faith in God (22:1-19), striking a compromise with the Philistine Avimelech over a dispute of water rights (21:22-34), buying the Cave of Makhpela in Hebron (23:1-20).

"hospitality" (*Genesis* 18:1-13). This tradition is formally enshrined in the Passover *Seder*, as a Jew is commanded to invite all those in need to join in this festival of freedom. If one cannot find time to be with his or her child because of the demands of work, then freeing oneself to engage in the leisurely activity of visiting with friends will never be realized. Since the notion of *minyan*, which reflects a sense of community, is central to Judaism (as outlined in **Way #12 — Your Synagogue**), then finding time to spend with friends is a prized Jewish value.

We should not be so wrapped up in our work that when one of our children taps us on the shoulder, we tell the kid "to take a hike;" instead of going on a hike with him or her. We need to find time to play Scrabble with our kids, toss around a ball, go to a movie or show, take a bike ride. Further, leisure time accords us the opportunity to pursue any hobbies that we have, or to renew the ones we so enjoyed when we were kids.

Throughout Jewish literature we read of the great rabbis insisting on leisure time in order to provide for further study. Also many are the rabbis who took time off from their work in order to meditate, as was the case with the great "Kabbalists," medieval Jewish mystics who saw a communion of the soul with the Divine. In order to realize this fusion, leisure time was needed. It was essential for the nourishment of the soul, which provided for a calm disposition. Leisure accorded one the time to appreciate all of God's handiwork.

The basic component of Yom Kippur is soul-searching, to evaluate one's relationship with God through one's relationship with family, friends and community. According to Jewish theology, an individual can only be granted Divine forgiveness if the person confronts the errors that he or she committed in his or her dealings with family, friends and community, and personally acknowledges them (see **Way #27 — Your Holidays**). Such an act requires time — time that was not found during one's busy schedule over the past year. And so family was neglected, friends ignored, and activism with the community and for social causes disregarded.

It is significant to note that all the Jewish holidays are family and/or community oriented. One needs to make time to exploit the natural warmth these holidays exude. Maimonides held that a person should release him- or herself from daily chores in order to allow time to enjoy the pleasures of Creation.

The thirteenth way to be Jewish is to find the proper balance between work and play. For Jews (and for others as well), leisure time, in addition to providing an opportunity to read a good book, go to a ball game, watch a movie, pig out at a local restaurant (regarding "pig out," see **Way #33 — Your Food**), and just hang out, must be primarily used to develop closer family ties, deepen friendships and make the world a little better, through social activism and integration with the wider community.

So:

> Slow down, you move too fast.
> You got to make the morning last.
> Just kickin' down the cobblestone,
> lookin' for fun and feelin' groovy.
> Hello lamp post, what you knowin'?
> Come to watch your flowers growin'.
> Ain't you got no rhymes for me?
> Dootin-Doo-Doo, feelin' groovy.

YOUR BOOK SHELF

or:

Reading is Believing

The Jews are often referred to as the "People of the Book (*Torah/Five Books of Moses/Pentateuch*)." This stems from the account in the *Torah* and the ensuing biblical works of the dramatic story of the Jewish People. The *Torah* and the entire Bible has been interpreted over the years and incorporated into a vast wealth of written commentary that serves to maintain and perpetuate Judaism and Jewish life. Jews are supposed to "live by the Book."

Because Jewish literature is so vast and all encompassing, as a people, Jews have always placed great emphasis on learning. Reading Jewish texts has always been a primary goal within the Jewish community. The well-read and learned individual was highly respected. As Jews integrated into the modern world, they extended this seemingly ingrained passion for reading.

Despite the fact that the English language is difficult (see **Way #4 — Your Language**), there is a multitude of reading material in English on any number of Jewish subjects that can greatly enhance one's Jewish knowledge and commitment. As with **Way #11 — Your Flicks**, I will provide a varied list of books, by no means exhaustive, yet most certainly subjective. I will stay away from "Sacred Texts," like the Bible, Commentaries, *Mishnah*, *Talmud*, *Kabbalah*, as these will find their expression in **Way #29 — Your Jewish Education**, along with basic texts on Judaism, also not included in this **Way**. With the exception of those books that deal with theology, "God books" are not included (see **Way #15 — Your God**) — the emphasis here being more on ethnic, cultural and historical forms of literature. As with movies, one can look to the Internet for a list of Jewish books. In addition, every major Jewish community sponsors a Jewish Book Week (or month), and most Jewish community centers and synagogues have extensive libraries.

Many Jewish magazines have extensive book review sections: *Commentary, Jerusalem Report, Jewish Spectator, Midstream, Moment, Tikkun*, among others. And of course reading these magazines will increase one's Jewish knowledge. *Ha'Aretz* (English version of the leading Israeli Hebrew paper: **haaretz.co.il**) and *The Jerusalem Post* (**jpost.com**) have book review departments.

Now, in this **Way**, I am not suggesting that you forgo Stephen King when riding the commuter train to and from work, rather that you opt for Saul Bellow now and then. If you do that, you can take the former to bed with you at night. Or you can do the opposite. Read Danielle Steel on the train and take Cynthia Ozick to bed. As far as the bathroom is concerned, it would be a good idea to stick with Jackie Collins or Tom Clancy. Of course, reading requires that you accept the thesis of **Way #13 — Your Leisure Time**. You need to build into your schedule the leisure hours to imbibe a good book.

To understand Judaism, one has to be Jewishly literate. In order to gain some semblance of Jewish knowledge, I intend to concentrate on "popular" Jewish books. The emphasis will be on books that are readable and enjoyable, not intrusive or didactic. Therefore, most of the books suggested will be novels, some historical fiction, and a few books of historical and spiritual interest. I will also include a list of authors whose books have predominantly Jewish themes or Jewish characters. Finally, I will subscribe to the notion that a book should be written so that "man can read it swiftly," (*Habakkuk*, 2:2). The following books and authors fit the prophet Habbakuk's insightful comment.

Here is a very partial list of authors, writers and poets, around whom you can build a Jewish library: S.Y. Agnon, Shalom Aleichem, Yehuda Amichai, Saul Bellow, Haim Nachman Bialik, Stephen Birmingham, E.M. Broner, Ze'ev Chafets, E.L Doctorow, Martin Gilbert, David Grossman, Stanley Elkin, Emil Fackenheim, Haim Guri, Joseph Heller, Abraham Joshua Heschel, Irving Howe, Harry Kemelman, Lawrence Kushner, PrimoLevi, Meyer Levin, Bernard Malamud, Amos Oz, Cynthia Ozick, Chaim Potok, Mordecai Richler, Anne Roiphe, Philip Roth, Howard Morley Sachar, Nelly Sachs, Isaac Bashevis Singer, Art Spiegelman, Leon Uris, Joseph Telushkin, Elie Wiesel, Herman Wouk, A.B. Yehoshua and Israel Zangwill.

Some of the books mentioned below were written by those in the above list. **Anti-Semitism**: *Anti-Semite and Jew* (Sartre), *Focus* (Miller), *Hollywood on Trial* (Kahn), *The Fixer* (Malamud), *The Reader* (Schlink). **American Judaism**: *An Orphan in History* (Cowan), *Chutzpah* (Dershowitz), *Does the World Need the Jews* (Gordis), *Faith or Fear* (Abrams), *Generation without Memory* (Roiphe), *Israel on Broadway; America: Off-Broadway — Jews in the New Millennium* (Forman), *Jewish Baby Boomers* (Waxman), *Jew vs. Jew* (Freedman), *Lost in America* (Singer), *Members of the Tribe* (Chafets), *Mixed Blessings* (Cowan), *Our Crowd* (Birmingham), *The Color of Water* (McBride), *The Vanishing American Jew* (Dershowitz), *World of Our Fathers* (Howe). **Biography**: *Begin* (Katz), *Eban* (St.

John), *Fear No Evil* (autobiography of Natan Sharnasky), *My Life: Golda Meir* (autobiography), *Herzl* (Bein or Elon)), *Moses* (Buber), *Rabin* (Slater), *Moshe Dayan: The Story of my Life* (Autobiography). **Fiction (American Jewish Literature):** *Acts of Faith* (Segal), *A Malamud Reader* (Malamud), *Beach Music* (Conroy), *City Boy* (Wouk), *Call it Sleep* (Roth), *Daniel Deronda* (Eliot), *Enemies — A Love Story* (Singer), *Friday — the Rabbi Slept Late* (Kemelman), *Goodbye Columbus* (Roth), *Herzog* (Bellow), *Inside-Outside* (Wouk), *Jewish American Literature* (Chametzky, Felstiner, Flanzbaum and Hellerstein), *My Name is Asher Lev* (Potok), *Portnoy's Complaint* (Roth), *Snow in August* (Hamill), *The Apprenticeship of Duddy Kravitz* (Richler), *The Assistant* (Malamud), *The Brothers Ashkenazi* (Singer), *The Chosen* (Potok), *The Promise* (Potok), *The Rise of David Levinsky* (Cahan), *Zuckerman Bound* (Roth). **Historical and Sociological Novels:** *As a Driven Leaf* (Steinberg), *Life is with People* (Zborowski and Herzog), *The Last Jew* (Gordon), *The Last Trial* (Spiegel), *The Red Tent* (Diamant), *The Slave* (Singer), *The Source* (Michener). **Historical Fiction (On Israel):** *Exodus* (Uris), *Little Drummer Girl* (Le Carre), *The Harvest* (Levin), *The Settlers* (Levin). **History:** *A History of the Jews* (Johnson), *Jewish People — Jewish Thought* (Seltzer), *Jews of Silence* (Wiesel), *The Gift of the Jews* (Cahill), *The Jew in the Modern World* (Mendes-Flohr and Reinharz), *World's Religion* (Smith). **Holocaust:** *Justice in Jerusalem* (Hausner), *Mein Kampf* (Hitler), *Notes from the Warsaw Ghetto* (Ringelblum), *The Banality of Evil* (Arendt), *The Black Box* (Ehrenberg and Grossman), *The Final Solution* (Reitlinger), *The Holocaust* (Gilbert), *Inside the Third Reich* (Speer), *Murderers Among Us* (Wiesenthal), *Survival at Auschwitz* (Levi), *War of the Jews* (Davidowitz), *While Six Million Died* (Morse). **Holocaust Drama:** *After the Fall* (Miller), *Andorra* (Frisch), *Diary of Anne Frank* (adaptation by Goodrich and Hackett), *Incidents at Vichy* (Miller), *Judgment at Nuremberg* (Mann), *Man in the Glass Booth* (Shaw), *The Condemned of Altona* (Frisch), *The Deputy* (Hochhuth), *The Investigation* (Weiss), *The Wall*

(Lampell), *Watch on the Rhine* (Hellman). **Holocaust Literature**: *A Bag of Marbles* (Joffo), *Babi Yar* (Kuznetsov), *Dawn* (Wiesel), *Eva* (Levin), *Fragments of Memory* (Greenfield), *Gates of the Forest* (Wiesel), *House of Dolls* (Ka-Tzetnik), *Last of the Just* (Schwarz-Bart), *Night* (Wiesel), *Oppermans* (Fuchtwanger), *Out of the Whirlwind* (Freedlander), *Sophie's Choice* (Styron), *Stones from the River* (Hegi), *To See You Again* (Schimmel), *Treblinka* (Steiner). **Humor**: *A Treasury of Jewish Humor* (Ausubel), *Big Book of Jewish Humor* (Novak and Waldoks), *Side Effects* (Allen), *The King of the Schnorrers* (Zangwill), *The 2000 Year Old Man* (Brooks-Reiner), *Without Feathers* (Allen). **Israel**: *A History of Zionism* (Laquer), *A Jewish State* (Herzl), *Old-New Land* (Herzl), *Arab and Jew: Wounded Spirits in a Promised Land* (Shipler), *From Beirut to Jerusalem* (Friedman), *Genesis 1948* (Kurzman), *Guni* (Harnik), *Here and There in the Land of Israel — 1982* (Oz), *Heroes and Hustlers, Hard Hats and Holy Men* (Chafets), *Israel* (Gilbert), *Israel — an Echo of Eternity* (Heschel), *Israel in the Middle East* (Rabinovich and Reinharz), *Jewish Schizophrenia in the Land of Israel* (Forman), *Oh Jerusalem* (Lapierre and Collins), *The Children of the Dream* (Bettelheim), *The Seventh Day* (Shapira), *The Zionist Idea* (Hertzberg), *To Jerusalem and Back* (Bellow). **Israeli Literature**: *Mr. Mani* (A.B. Yehoshua), *My Michael* (Oz), *The Black Box* (Oz), *The Blue Mountain* (Shalev), *The Lover* (A.B. Yehoshua), *The Yellow Wind* (Grossman). **Plays**: *Enter Laughing* (Reiner), *JB* (MacLeish), *Merchant of Venice* (Shakespeare), *The Collected Plays of Neil Simon* (Simon), *The Dybbuk* (Ansky), *Years Ago* (Gordon). **Poetry**: See the works of Yehuda Amichai, Haim Nachman Bialik, Nelly Sachs and Haim Guri. **Spirituality**: *Honey from the Rock* (Kushner), *I and Thou* (Buber), *Satan in Goray* (Singer), *The Book of Letters* (Kushner), *The Golem* (Meyrink), *The Jew in the Lotus* (Kamenetz), *The Sabbath* (Heschel).

My suggestion: Do a little mixing and matching. Read a book of poetry along with an historical novel. As an alternative approach, you could pick one author and focus on his or her work, or concentrate on a specific subject or a particular historical epoch. You should surround yourself with Jewish books. Yehuda Ibn Tibbon[1] tells us: "Make books your friends." During the Golden Age of Spain, Jewish literature soared. Great Spanish-Jewish intellectual thinkers, like Maimonides, Ibn Tibbon, Moshe Ibn Ezra,[2] who held that "books are pouches of wisdom embroidered with words of pearls" (*Shirat Yisrael*), helped keep Jewish life vibrant and creative. Such was the case throughout all the dispersions of the Jewish People.

The fourteenth way to be Jewish is to read Jewish books. "A book is the most pleasant of friends. If you wish, its proverbs will amuse you, or if you wish, its advice will gladden you. It contains words of the old and the new, the past and the present. It speaks of the dead and tells much of life. It is a friend that enhances your talent. There is no friend in the world more faithful...There is no better teacher..." (Avraham Ibn Ezra).[3]

---

1. Spanish-Hebrew translator (1120-1190).
2. Spanish poet and scholar (1055-1135).
3. Spanish scholar and poet, (1089-1164).

YOUR GOD

or:

"Jesus Loves you <u>less</u> than you will Know"[2]

Where to start? Well, did you hear the one about the agnostic dyslexic insomniac who stayed up all night contemplating whether there is a Dog? Theology is a hard nut to crack. But I begin with an overall assumption that most Jews believe in God, it is just that many have yet to define that belief and understand how they might integrate a faith-system into their everyday lives. Scratched into the washroom stall at Cronin's Bar in Harvard Square (circa 1962) were the words: "God is dead," signed Nietzsche. The clever

1. The number 15 in Hebrew is an abbreviation for God's name.
2. Paul Simon and Art Garfunkel's song, *Mrs. Robinson* (written by Paul Simon), from the movie *The Graduate*.

ivy-leaguer who scribbled that graffiti was a bit too confident. One could probably assert with a greater degree of certainty: "Nietzsche is dead," signed God. The truth is, in regard to a belief in a Higher Being, most of us fall into the lap of the agnostic, not really knowing. Yet, unlike the insomniac, we don't really care enough to lose sleep over it. Colloquially speaking, we are indeed dyslexic when it comes to God — that is, terribly confused.

Yet God occupies center stage in Jewish life. God is central to the Jewish religion and contained in its most powerful Divine affirmation of faith, the *Shema*: "Hear, O' Israel, the Lord our God, the Lord is One" (*Deuteronomy* 6:4). But Judaism is an activist religion, for this singular statement of faith is immediately followed by what is described in the Introduction to this book: "To Jew it!" We recite in the same theological breath that we have to teach Judaism to our children, and that we must carry out moral and ritual commandments in order to concretize our belief in God. Faith and follow-up, belief and action, creed and deed go hand and hand.

Now, you will have to indulge me a bit, because what follows may sound a bit cerebral. But I have to be somewhat presumptuous in order to place God into the framework of the Jewish historical experience. In all likelihood, God could place me wherever He/She chose to. But I wish to avoid any presentation of a male chauvinist God sitting atop a throne on high (as is the intention of using the He/She appellation), pulling strings for us mortals below. I also wish to disavow the reader of a Christian notion that all one has to do is close one's eyes and open one's heart to Jesus. Jews reject the notion of Jesus because there is only one God, and that God does not need an intermediary to do either His/Her bidding or our bidding in opening a Divine conversation, however we may define that dialogue between two unequal partners. For Jews: "Jesus loves you <u>less</u> than you will know."

As outlined in **Way #10 — Your Culture**, there may have been other religions that existed longer than Judaism, but there is no other religion, which has mastered the complex art of survival through every phase of Western civilization, subsequent to its emergence at some unknown time in the ancient Near East. Having had to overcome the most inventive means to destroy it, remarkably Judaism has survived until today.

This was essentially achieved by commitment to a unity principle, i.e., the determination to cope with the diversity of the natural order and the variegation of historical experience as evidence of unity. All novel phenomena, be they natural or historical, were affirmed as further proof that the God of our ancestors was indeed omnipotent, omniscient and omnipresent. The powers and the functions of one God were always expanded to include new experiences, new understandings and new knowledge. This has meant that Judaism has not been committed to a single concept of God, but to a single principle: God must be adequate to deal with natural phenomena, scientific advancement and historical growth. Since Jewish awareness and experience constantly underwent change, concepts of God expanded so that God might remain adequate. The idea of one God grew and developed because of a tenacious commitment to a unity principle — historical monotheism.

Judaism satisfied this historical belief in one God through episodic and creative syncretism. Exposed to radical shifts in history, Judaism demonstrated its power to reshape itself without relinquishing its basic identity. Committed to the unity principle, Judaism became simultaneously absorbed, creatively innovative and thus able to persevere. The outcome was always a varied form of Judaism, but still tied to the past. It may not always seem to have been a logical outgrowth of previous forms of Jewish religious expression, but rather the historical consequence of actively mastering complex problems of survival through a commitment to unity.

The modern Jew needs to ask if a commitment to God, adequate to envelop the evolution of history, can take precedence over traditional concepts of God: that is, a God who determines for the individual, and indeed the world, what will be, because of some Divine plan that we lowly creatures could not possibly fathom. If we adopt such a traditional view, we will find ourselves impotent in the face of change. Judaism cannot surrender its **traditional** paradigm of ideological growth and historical development for **tradition**. Judaism never sought to create a religion that was so absolute that progress and change would be perceived as a threat. To guarantee a constant dynamism in Judaism, God must continue to be defined as adequate to cope with change.

Such an approach to belief in God helps a Jew understand the machinations of a world that too often seems Godless. For a Jew there are questions that are acute in defining God. I do not here refer to personal confrontations or disappointments, but rather to universal questions, like: Why six million Jews? And of course one can extrapolate and apply this to many areas: Why Biafra, why the Armenians, why Bosnia, why the Crusades (done in the name of God)? And: Why slavery, why poverty, why hunger, why disease, why natural disasters — drought, floods, fire?

But when we blame God for what is wrong, do we in equal measure thank God for what is right? Perhaps we can find the answer in Harold Kushner's book, *When Bad Things Happen to Good People*. But how do we respond "when good things happen to bad people?" According to Judaism, God is intimately involved in the history of the Jewish People, as the biblical narrative most graphically demonstrates. That being the case, with God being the object of worship, how can we pray to a God who allows incredible cruelty to be inflicted on His/Her creatures — for Jews (and the world), the slaughter of six million Jews being the tragic example? If, on the other hand, we reject the notion that God is intimately involved in the life of the Jewish People, then why pray to Him/Her?

When confronted with such confusion, does a Jew throw up his or her hands and exclaim in frustration: "God Almighty, for God's sake, as God is my witness, I do not know who in God's name can answer these questions, so help me God?"

Well, before we violate one of the Ten Commandments and invoke God's name in vain, let us return to our cerebral discussion above, to which the answer lies within us. We behave in such a way as to make God inadequate to cope with the explosive contortions of history and the unpredictable intrigues of the human mind. And so we must blame ourselves for what has gone wrong or accept certain events as happenstance. Any other alternative would limit our free will. One should imagine a game of chess. God sets before us all the possible options that each player could choose, but allows us to ultimately make the choice — some good and some bad.

Does this then rule out a God? Not for Jews. The world was created in one miraculous moment, and this in no way contradicts theories of evolution or big bangs. It simply helps explain the unexplainable in human terms, and comforts us that not all is random. And so, we see a God who trails us through our early history, by pure empiricism, not by some involved or complicated philosophical argument. Jews today believe in the same God of Abraham, Isaac and Jacob. In allegorical terms, God interacts with us, coaxing us to do right, and chastising us when we do wrong.

Even as Abraham pleaded with God and Moses argued with God, so too does a Jew dialogue with his or her Divine conscience (see **Way #43 — Your Dreams**). But more than that, Jewish theology is not just a statement of "I believe." Dialogue must lead to action, as outlined in the definitive theological declaration of faith, the *Shema*, when, as aforementioned, a Jew is told not only to believe, but also to act. This is consistent with the first prayer a Jew is commanded to say when waking up in the morning: "Thank you God for returning the breath of life to me." When asleep, it is as if we are in the dark world of pre-creation. And upon seeing the first light, it is as if the world is being created anew with us; as if God breathed the same breath of air into us that was breathed into Adam.

Therefore, belief in God is the fifteenth way to be Jewish. Faith in God has both a spiritual thrust and a practical implication. It elevates our lives so that we feel a Divine spark dwelling within us, thus prompting us to cultivate that Divine spark so that we can follow the positive dictates when faced with choices, as dramatized in their polarity in chapter thirty of *Deuteronomy*, where moral and practical choices are clearly defined: "I have set before you this day life and good, or death and evil...I have set before you life or death, a blessing or a curse; choose life, therefore, that you and your descendants may live..." (30:15-20).

❖ ❖ ❖

Selected Bibliography: *After Auschwitz* (Richard Rubenstein), *Finding God* (Rifat Sonsino and Daniel Syme), *God and Me* (Heller), *God's Grace* (Bernard Malamud), *God's Phallus* (Elberg and Schwartz), *God Was in this Place, and I did not Know* (Lawrence Kushner), *I and Thou* (Martin Buber), *Man in Search of God* (Abraham Joshua Heschel), *Seek My Face, Speak My Name* (Arthur Green), *Science of God* (Gerald Schroeder), *The God I Believe In* (Joshua Haberman), *This is for Everyone* (Douglas Goldhamer and Melinda Stengel), *When Children Ask about God* (Harold S. Kushner) **AND** the Bible (God).

YOUR ANIMALS[1]

or:

Man Gave Names to All the Animals[2]

"**M**an gave names to all the animals, long time ago," so writes Bob Dylan. I often ask myself, why was this privilege bestowed upon human beings? I know what the biblical account says. In one creation story it is written: "And out of the ground the Lord God formed every beast of the field, and every fowl of the air; and brought them before Adam to see what he would call them: and whatsoever Adam called every living creature, that was the name. And Adam gave names to all cattle, and to the fowl of the air, and to every beast..." (*Genesis* 2:19-20). In the alternative creation story we read: "And God said: Let us make man in our image, after our likeness, and let him have dominion over the fish of the sea, over

---

1. This **Way** is dedicated to my grand-dog.
2. Bob Dylan's song from his album *Slow Train Coming*.

the fowl of the air, and over the cattle, and over all the earth, and over every creeping thing that creeps upon the earth" (*Genesis* 1:26). Well, I know some people who are real "creeps," and I wouldn't trust them to have dominion over my pet hamster.

In the allegorical (or factual, depending on your theological bent) beginning of the world as recorded in the Bible, the human being is the last of God's creations. Whether one opts to believe the first creation story or the second one as it appears in *Genesis*, in both renderings of the tradition, animals are created before those who would rule over them. This actually should be fairly humbling, for God is telling us that even the lowly ant came on the scene before us humans. So the statement "Go to the ant, you lazy one. Consider her ways and be wise" (*Proverbs* 6:6) makes perfect sense. Jewish sources tell us that we can learn from the ant two morally compelling lessons: 1) "Had not the *Torah* been given us, the ant would have taught us how not to steal" (*Talmud Eruvin* 100b), and 2) "The ants are not a mighty people, yet they make ready their food in the summer (*Proverbs* 30:25). So any creep who likes to torture ants with a lit cigarette or simply gets off on crushing them under a shoe, remember, at the miraculous moment of the Creation, that little ant was higher on God's priority list than we were.[1]

Indeed, respect for animals is well ingrained in the Jewish tradition: "A righteous man takes heed for the life of his beast" (*Proverbs* 12:10). This biblical dictate is followed by the talmudic entreaty, which lends force to the prior notion that the creation of the animals before human beings is indeed significant: "A man should not eat before he feeds his livestock" (*Talmud Brachot* 30a). This contradicts the stewardess' instruction that tells us air

---

1. Frank Sinatra's song *High Hopes*, from the 1959 movie *A Hole in the Head*, speaks to this issue: "Just what makes that little old ant think he'll move a rubber tree plant. Anyone knows an ant can't move a rubber tree plant. But he's got high hopes, he's got high hopes. He's got high apple pie in the sky hopes. So anytime you're gettin' low, 'stead of lettin' go, just remember that ant. Whoops, there goes another rubber tree plant" (Sammy Cahn and Jimmy Van Heusen).

travelers "to place the oxygen mask first over your own mouths and only afterwards over your children's."

For certain, all the above sources clearly indicate that respect for animals is paramount within the Judaism. We see this in the story of Noah and the ark, where he carefully protects all animals, guaranteeing their procreation (*Genesis* 6:9-9:29). And so, Jews should necessarily support the Society against Cruelty to Animals. There also should be little question that a Jew should not view being a dog-catcher as his or her professional goal. I still feel guilty when I recall the need to remove a cat from our home because of the intense allergic reaction that my children had to her. I drove in the pouring rain to the only shelter for cats and dogs in greater Jerusalem, which happened to be in the heart of the West Bank, north of the furthest Jewish Jerusalem suburbs. It was during the first Intifada[1] when violence was at a peak, as Israelis and Palestinians fought each other in the streets every day. When I got to the shelter, it was closed. After waiting for over two hours with my furry companion running amok in my car, I decided to return to the safety of the outskirts of Jerusalem. Not knowing what to do, I dropped the cat off in an upscale neighborhood (truly upper middle-class), reasoning that the garbage there would be of a high quality, and our little feline friend would survive well. While my children did not hurl Jewish quotes at me to decry my behavior, their disapproval was such that I felt what I did was indeed anti-Jewish, if not anti-Semitic, given the fact that our cat was named after Moses' mother, Yocheved (see **Way #1 — Your Name**)!

In addition to not being a dog-catcher, a Jew should not aspire to be a hunter. In fact, I often wonder how a Jew could become a *shochet* (ritual slaughterer). Of course, if one is destined to eat meat,

---

1. Palestinian uprising against Israeli occupation of the West Bank and the Gaza Strip that began December 9, 1987, and continued until September 13, 1993, when Israel and the Palestinian Liberation Organization agreed to mutual recognition.

then the *Talmud* is indeed instructive when it tells us: "The end of man is to die, and of an animal to be slaughtered" (*Talmud Brachot* 17b). Yet, the simple fact is that the laws of *kashrut* (see **Way #33 — Your Food**) demand that any slaughtering of animals be done in the most humane fashion possible.

Further, since the fall of the Second Temple almost two thousand years ago, animal sacrifice as a form of worship was eliminated from Judaism. Just as prayer developed and became more civilized, so too did the treatment of animals. So, the question arises, if a Jew is to show respect for animals, should he or she maintain some of them as pets? Certainly not a dog in a fifth floor walk-up. And what about a family of vegetarians? What would that poor dog eat? And what is it with all those canine owners who after a very short period of time begin to look like their dogs or wear spotted coats when they walk their cross-braded mutts?

But the real moral dilemma is whether to allow a relatively domesticated animal to be free to enjoy the companionship of its own kind or to confine the species to a basically unnatural, yet warm home environment. Jewish tradition has no definitive answer, except to require kindness, which would rule out "choke collars" for discipline usage. But what of goldfish, hamsters, rabbits, guinea pigs, et. al.? For certain a seeing-eye dog is permissible because we are warned: "Do not place a stumbling block before the blind" (*Leviticus* 19:14).

Circus animals are clearly an abuse, as is hunting and fishing purely for sport. For some, alligator shoes, fur coats, sheepskin rugs and leather belts are out. Experimentation with animals is a gray area, as some experimentation, especially in cancer research with mice, may very well fall under the category of *pikuach nefesh* (saving a life), a general talmudic legal dictum that supersedes all other Jewish laws. **The underlying Jewish rule of thumb is that respect and kindness for animals is commanded and thus qualifies as the sixteenth way to be Jewish.** As a natural corollary to this: If you must have a pet, then treat it with TLC (tender-loving care), but don't let it sit on the living room couch. A shedding dog is the pits, and "dehairing" the furniture takes forever.

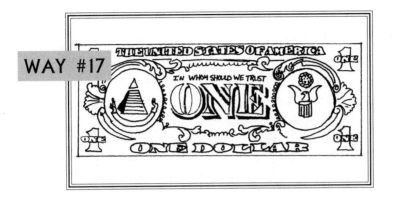

YOUR MONEY

or:

"Your Money or your Life"[1]

"Can't buy me love…Money can't buy me love;"[2] so sang the Beatles. It is a truism that wealth can grant much to an individual, but ultimately it cannot buy love. With money, you can bestow lots of wonderful things upon someone you love, and who loves you in return. But money will never be a replacement for love: "He who loves money will never be content," says that eternal optimist, Kohelet (*Ecclesiastes* 5:10). However, let it be clear that in **Way #17**, I do not intend to discuss the integration between love and money, although this could be quite interesting and attention-

---

1. A traditional comedy sketch of Jack Benny. Invariably, a gangster would threaten to rob him, and say: "Your money or your life?" Benny would pause, gaze out at the audience with a deadpan expression, look back at the robbers, and reply: "Give me a few minutes."
2. From the Beatles' song *Can't Buy Me Love* on the album *The Beatles/1962-1966*.

grabbing. Indeed, what one does with his or her money could generate the love of a person, but not in the traditional sense of the Beatle song: "I'll buy you a diamond ring, my friend, if it makes you feel alright." Rather, this **Way** will put forth the thesis that how one spends his or her money is a reflection of that person's values. And values that are positive and "giving" do indeed forge respect and love.

In the *Torah*, we are taught that a Jew should leave one tenth of his or her field for the needy: "a tithe…to the stranger, the orphan, and to the widow" (*Deuteronomy* 26:12). Already, one can see in this biblically ordained commandment a hint of what was to be regarding the overall attitude of the Jewish People to charitable organizations, not only within their own confines, but also within the wider community. Charity in Hebrew is rooted in the Hebrew word *tzedeka*, which means: righteous deeds. How one actually spends his or her money is of prime importance in the Jewish mindset. It is a reflection of the role charity plays in one's life. Among the many talmudic quotes that deal with charity, none is more poignant than: "Charity outweighs all other religious precepts" (*Talmud Baba Batra* 9b). For a fuller understanding of the role of charity in the Jewish tradition, one should read Maimonides' "Ladder of Giving" in his monumental work, *Mishnah Torah*.

Now most of you reading this book are probably upper middle-class. That must be the case because, in all likelihood, you have purchased this guidebook at a Barnes & Noble or similar upscale bookstore. This means that you had to shell out $19.95. You may have decided, after reading this handbook, that there really are better ways to spend your well-earned salary. However, if you divide the fifty ways to be Jewish presented here into $19.95, you're paying approximately forty cents for each Jewish way. If you ask me, that's a pretty good bargain. But enough of this sycophantic fodder. The point here is that you spent your money on a book, a Jewish one at that. And buying Jewish books is a worthwhile use of your funds.

Every family has to make choices on how to budget its earnings.

Does one send his or her child to a private school rather than to a public school? Does one choose a state university over a private college? Does one go on a trip to France instead of sending a kid to a summer camp? A Jewish approach would warrant one not to create a situation whereby a family overextends itself; after all, "money can drive its owner frantic" (*Talmud Shabbat* 117b). For certain, when making a decision of this kind, prestige and pretense must not play a part. Choices such as these usually affect those who have limited financial resources and live on a tight budget. But they should be comforted by the dictum: "Who is rich? He who is content with his portion" (*Sayings of the Fathers* 4:1).

More significantly: Do you choose always to go to the movies instead of giving twenty-five dollars to the *United Way*? Do you invest a couple of thousand more dollars in Nasdaq and never contribute an approximate amount of money to a local community project to help the homeless (unless you intend to donate at least a small part of the interest of your stocks to a social cause). In short do you "leave one tenth of your field (your income) to the stranger, the orphan and the widow" or do you buy a Jacuzzi for your third bathroom? The Jewish answer is self-evident. While Judaism does not preach asceticism, it does emphasize generosity.

Then there is the matter of hedonism. While most people like to indulge themselves, the question remains, how much "spoiling" is permitted? Undue displays of wealth, exaggerated acquisitions, and a basic flaunting of one's riches must be considered nothing less than pure selfishness. Most people who get caught up in the frenzy of ambition and who flaunt their materialistic possessions are unaware of their possible folly. There is the story of a Jewish couple in Long Island who were embroiled in a bitter litigation with the Village Council of Southampton over the violation of the building code. The couple set out to build the most expensive house in the history of New York, a twenty-five million dollar castle by the sea, with sixty-three rooms, gothic towers and a thirty-foot waterfall cascading into an indoor pool. Among the medieval decorations in this palace was one suit of armor, purchased for over three million dollars. The home, which many would call a true monstrosity, was fittingly named "Dragon Head."

True, this couple could afford everything they did, including the purchase of a fleet of seven Rolls Royces. What a pity that the husband, an obvious business genius, who made his fortune of three hundred million dollars in less than ten years, could find nothing better to do with his cleverness and his wealth. I wonder what I would say to him if I met him face-to-face. Probably: "Imagine you had one more year to live, would you really give all your money to 'Dragon Head?' After your death, in all likelihood, everything you put into this mansion will be disposed of in a public auction at maybe one-tenth of the price. Instead of filling your house with expensive junk, should you not furnish your mind with a philosophy of life? Think of the good things you could be doing. Don't you want to be remembered as a benefactor? After all, Jewish tradition teaches: 'How can riches be made beautiful? By performing acts of righteousness' (Tahkemoni),[1] not by gross and ostentatious displays of wealth."

Now, what should we say to "those who love their money more than their lives" (Talmud Brachot 61a)? This seems to be the case with too many of those who work in such high-powered professions as law, stocks and bonds and the high-tech world. Their overly long work hours can too readily warp their priorities. This also can apply to doctors, teachers, rabbis and a host of other professionals. Abraham Joshua Heschel[2] tells the story of a father who was so busy earning a buck, that he was away on a business trip when his wife gave birth. Returning home, he rushed into the bedroom where his

---

1. *Book of Narratives* in rhymed prose by Jewish-Spanish poet Yehuda Al-Harizi (1170-1235).
2. Jewish theologian and scholar, who synthesized mystical tradition with modern existentialism (1907-1972). See **Way #14 — Your Book Shelf**.

newborn child was sleeping, and remarked: "What a beautiful crib. And to think it only cost $99.50!"

So: "Just as money can purify the bastard, so too can it bastardize the pure" (*Alcalay*).[1] We need to think about the absolute essentials without which we could not live. They are very few: health, shelter, food, clothes, and a living income — and a few people we care about and who care about us. Everything else is of a much lower priority. I am not suggesting that people provide the bare minimum to get by. As already stated, the Jewish tradition does not preach self-denial. But if we cannot strive for monetary idealism, we should consider financial altruism. **Yes, the manner in which a person spends his or her money is the seventeenth way of being Jewish.** Wealth should be shared with those who are less fortunate, to be contributed to causes for the "common good." It should be showered on projects and materials for self-improvement. A Jew must leave a "tithe," a tenth of his or her money for those less fortunate. We must never get to the point whereby we "love money more than our lives," or give off the impression that we do. At the end of the day, how "one distributes wealth is a criterion for judging whether its owner is good or bad" (*Mishle Yehoshua*).[2]

---

1. Reuven Alcalay (1907-), a Hebrew lexicographer and editor. Author of *The Complete Hebrew-English Dictionary*.
2. A book of proverbs compiled by Hebrew fabulist Yehoshua Steinberg (1825-1908).

YOUR SOCIAL ACTIVISM

or:

The "Sixties" Revisited

Okay, all of you who are about my age, that is those of you in your middle to late fifties, this **Way** is your **Way**. It is time to recall those heroic days of our youth when we believed that we were on a sacred mission to change the world, when we were part of those too great "Movements:" the struggle for civil rights and the fight to end the war in Vietnam. How glorious that moment in time was, although in retrospect it was a truly sad era, as African-Americans were often brutally victimized, both physically and psy-

---

1. The number eighteen (18) in Hebrew has great social implication. It equals the numerical value of the letters composing the Hebrew word for "life" (*chai*). So it is most appropriate that this **Way #18** should concentrate on social activism, which breathes life into an individual and should invigorate one.

chologically, and US soldiers, as well as Vietnamese, North and South, were dying in a war considered both futile and immoral.

What was the reason that so many Jews took the lead and so many Jews were active in these two struggles, particularly in numerical comparison to the general American population? Why is it that a disproportionate number of Jews concern themselves with issues of social justice and equality? There are two basic answers, one rooted in the history of the Jewish People and the other grounded in its theology — the two are intimately intertwined.

As the nascent stages of Jewish history unfold, we read in *Exodus* how Jewish national identity was forged on the anvil of the Egyptian experience of slavery. It was against the background of collective suffering and disenfranchisement that Jews were born as a people, and charged with the mandate of becoming a "kingdom of priests." In that Sinaitic somewhere of Jewish wonderment, our sages and prophets interpreted the legend of our escape to freedom as the authoritative rejection of the social model of power and its abuse, as symbolized by ancient Egypt. Likewise, our ancestors conceptualized a new world order whose origins could be best understood in the perspective of our communal experience.

Jews are reminded continually throughout their literature: "Remember, you were slaves in Egypt." As a result we are admonished to heed the reason for the fast of Yom Kippur: "Is not this the fast that I have chosen? To loose the fetters of wickedness, to undo the bands of the yoke, and to let the oppressed go free, to share your bread with the hungry, to bring the poor into your house, and to clothe the naked" (*Isaiah* 58:6-7)? This message is reinforced throughout our history, and its literary expression is: social injustice is evil, and the abuse of power is the greatest of social evils. In codifying a new moral code, our ancestors established the historical and theological principle: "In every generation a person is obligated to see himself as though he personally had gone forth from Egypt" (*Passover Haggadah*).[1]

It was in this way that Judaism subordinated the use of power to the will of God. However one interprets the concept of Divinity, Jews are taught to understand that the use of power must be morally restrained. (For certain, the relevance of this principle to Israel's present social and political reality is profound.) Of course, the cynic will say that in the world of "realpolitik" it is not morality that counts, but power. In response, ought we not to say that the unrestrained use of power will inevitably lead to anarchy and totalitarianism? This is precisely the reason that Jews have tried to establish for themselves moral and ethical standards of conduct. "Justice, justice, you are to pursue" (*Deuteronomy* 16:20). The rabbis ask, why is the word justice repeated? In order to show that one must seek justice justly. Lofty goals do not justify corrupting the means to achieve them.

If the universal application of the belief that "God created man and woman in His (Her) own image" (*Genesis* 1:27) is not taken seriously, then all manner of discriminatory behavior will be unleashed. In response to this verse, the rabbis asked: "Why was but a single man created? It was for the sake of peace, that none would say to his fellow, 'my father is greater than your father'" (*Mishnah Sanhedrin* 4:5). To make certain that this was understood in terms of race as well, the rabbis taught: "God formed Adam from the dust from all over the world — yellow clay and white sand, black loam and red soil. Therefore the earth can declare to no race or color of man/woman that you do not belong here, that this soil is not your home" (*Yalkut Shimoni* 1:3).[2]

---

1. *Haggaddah* literally means narration. It is the name of the book that is read during the *Seder* (Passover meal) in which the story of the exodus from Egypt is included.
2. A 13th century anthology containing midrashic (allegorical literature) interpretations of biblical versus.

In the creation story, Adam and Eve's first-born child, Cain, kills his brother Abel. According to the narrative, God asks Cain what has become of his brother. Cain responds with the rhetorical and famous question: "Am I my brother's keeper?" God replies: "What have you done? The voice of your brother's blood cries out from the ground" (*Genesis* 4:9-10). Thus, we are taught at the very beginning of Jewish awareness, not of the literal history of the world, but of the intellectual history of the Jewish value heritage, that "we are our brother's keeper." Life is indeed precious: "If one destroys a single person, it is as if he has destroyed the entire world...if one saves a single person, it is as if he has preserved the entire world" (*Avot de Rabbi Natan* 31).[1]

And so, in matters of moral and ethical behavior, Jews must be cognizant of the sacredness of life and of the obligation to strive to protect it. Both our literature and our long history instruct us accordingly. Jews define themselves through social acts of human affirmation and holiness. As outlined in **Way #17 — Your Money**, Jews understand their moral responsibility to the "poor, the widow and the oppressed" because of the larger sense of the sacred quality of life.

Therefore the bounds of Jewish moral responsibility are clearly defined: "Whosoever has the capacity to prevent his household from committing a crime and does not, is accountable for the sins of his household; if for his fellow citizens, he is accountable for the crimes of his fellow citizens; if for the whole world, he is accountable for the whole world" (*Talmud Shabbat* 54b). When it comes to matters of equality, social justice and human rights, a Jew is responsible.

All a Jew must do is turn to the prophets of old to be galvanized into social action, the cry of Micah being the most definitive example: "He has told you, O man, what is good, and what the Lord

---

1. A collection of early rabbinic sayings (from the 1st century BCE to the 2nd century CE) collected between the 6th to 13th century CE.

requires of you — only to do justice, love mercy and walk humbly with your God. Then will your name achieve wisdom" (*Micah* 6:8-9). Further, this call to activism is reinforced with wonderful statements like: "Study is not the chief thing, but action" (*Sayings of the Fathers* 1:17). "Everyone whose deeds are more than his wisdom, his wisdom endures. And everyone whose wisdom is more than his deeds, his wisdom does not endure" (*Ibid.* 3:12). "The day is short and the work is great... and it is not incumbent upon you to finish the task, but neither are you free to desist from doing it" (*Ibid.* 2:21-22).

What gives further force to these compelling religious commands is the too often long-suffering of the Jewish People throughout history. Cast out by the nations of the world, subject to abject anti-Semitism, which reached its zenith during those awful days of the Holocaust, a Jew must be incredibly aware of the suffering of others. Knowing prejudice and experiencing discrimination throughout the generations must sensitize Jews to oppression wherever and however it occurs.

The biblical notion of becoming a "light unto the nations" should not only apply to Jews wherever they live, but should find its utopian realization in Israel. Yet the Jewish state has yet to fulfill its historical and theological mission to become that "holy nation:" a country based on the prophetic ideals of social justice and equality (see **Way #21 — Your Israel Quotient**).

In the words of that one character in our youth who, among too many others, served as the antithetical personality to all our attempts to right the wrongs of our society, Richard Milhous Nixon: "Let me make this perfectly clear" — **the eighteenth way to be Jewish is to be involved in causes of social and ethical import.** We have to feel ourselves "accountable" for the ills of society. In short, the words of Abraham Joshua Heschel again speak to us: "If we are not all guilty, we are all responsible." For those, for example, who, in the heady days of the Sixties, were participants in those struggles to guarantee equal rights for African-Americans or protested against America's involvement in the Vietnam War, when their children ask: "What did you do during those terrible days?" they can say: "We tried to change things. We were accountable." The activism of our youth must guide us throughout our lives. Being able to respond with "I was accountable" gives meaning to the theological will and historical drama of the Jewish People. Being able to say "I was responsible" means that our children will look at us and declare: "Good deeds are done by good people" (*Talmud Shabbat* 32a).

WAY #19

YOUR SPORTS

or:

Is there such a Thing as a Jewish Jock?

This **Way** is a tricky one (and should be distinguished from **Way #37 — Your Body**, which primarily will deal with health). Now, I do not intend to fall into the easy role of asking a Jew to identify with other Jews who have "made it" in certain athletic disciplines. That would be demeaning, although many Jews do indeed "root" for another Jew — no matter what the sport and no matter for whose team he or she plays.[1] Those of my generation were certainly reared on this attitude, but there are dilemmas that can arise from such a parochial outlook on life. (Although, the massacre of the eleven Israelis by Palestinian terrorists at the 1972

---

1. Israel's Maccabiah games, a Jewish Olympics, most certainly provide an outlet for full Jewish identification with Jewish sportsmen and women.

Munich Olympics most certainly justified a Jewish identity with those young athletes.)

For example, my parents raised me on the singular philosophical tenet: Is it good for the Jews? Hank Greenberg was their baseball idol. Being from Boston, we were loyal Red Sox fans. So for whom was I to cheer when Greenberg's Detroit Tigers came to town? When the Cleveland Indians lost to the New York Giants in the 1954 World Series in four games, partly because its heralded Jewish third baseman, Al Rosen, barely hit the ball out of the infield, I fully expected an outbreak of anti-Semitism in all of Ohio. And then again, my folks held up Sandy Koufax, the star pitcher for the Dodgers, as an example of a "good Jew" because he refused to pitch on Yom Kippur — even if it meant not appearing in a World Series game. (I promised my parents that I too would never pitch on Yom Kippur when I reached the major leagues!)

In America, many minorities tried to find their acceptance through sports. Boxing was one of the foremost activities that gave a Jewish male relatively easy access to the larger community. They were fairly dominant in the sport between the two World Wars. Allen Bodner's *When Boxing was a Jewish Sport* (Praeger Trade, 1997) catalogues the activity of Jews in this profession during the 1920's and 1930's, when Maximilian Baer was the World Heavyweight Champion (1934) and Barney Ross was the reigning Welterweight World Champion (1924-1937). But it would seem to me that becoming a pugilist would be forbidden to a Jew, because the sole purpose of the boxer is to **beat** his opponent into submission and to spare him no mercy. There are simply too many sources within Jewish literature that speak out against such cruelty, especially when executed for entertainment purposes: "And they shall **beat** their swords into ploughshares (*not into someone's chin*), and their spears into pruning-hooks (*not into someone's kidney*)" (*Micah* 4:3).

Too many athletes with potentially debilitating injuries

continue to compete, not only because of their work ethic, but because management wants to guarantee victory, which increases revenues and profits. Reggie Lewis of the Boston Celtics suffered from an irregular heartbeat. Collapsing once during the course of a game was not a sufficient reason for him to stop playing. The right doctor had to be found who would give a medical okay for him to continue to play the game — until he finally collapsed again in a routine practice and died. Paul Simon writes of this phenomenon to push someone to the edge in his song *Night Game*: "There were two men down and the score tied in the bottom of the eighth when the pitcher died."[1]

For certain, this attitude is most prevalent in the field of boxing, which, as aforementioned, attracted many Jews at one point. Folk singer Pete Seeger immortalized Featherweight Champion Davey Moore when he sang Bob Dylan's song *Who Killed Davey Moore*.[2] Moore succumbed to brain injuries after being knocked out in the tenth round by Sugar Ramos in 1963.

> Who killed Davey Moore? How come he died, and what's the reason for?
> Not I, says the referee, don't point your little finger at me.
> Sure I could have stopped it in the eighth and saved him from his terrible fate.
> But the crowd would have booed I'm sure, not getting their money's worth.
> Too bad he had to go, but there's pressure on me, you know.
> No, it wasn't me that made him fall. You can't blame me at all.
>
> Who killed Davey Moore? How come he died, and what's the reason for?
> Not I, says the angry crowd, whose screams filled the ring aloud.
> Says too bad he died that night, but we just like to see a good fight.
> You can't blame us for his death, we just like to see some sweat.
> There ain't nothing wrong in that.
> No, it wasn't us that made him fall. You can't blame us at all.

1. From Paul Simon's album *Still Crazy after all these Years*.
2. This song appears on Dylan's album: *The Bootleg Series*. Pete Seeger made it famous in his 1963 Carnegie Hall Concert, which was recorded in his album: *We Shall Overcome*.

Who killed Davey Moore? How come he died, and what's the reason for?
Not I, says his manager, puffing on his big cigar.
It's hard to say, it's hard to tell. All was thought that he was well.
Too bad for his wife and kids he's dead. But if he was sick, he should have said.
No, you can't blame me at all. It wasn't me that made him fall.

Who killed Davey Moore? How come he died, and what's the reason for?
Not I, says the boxing writer, pounding his print on his old typewriter.
Says boxing ain't to blame, there's just as much danger in a football game.
Says boxing is here to stay. It's just the old American way.
No, it wasn't me that made him fall. You can't blame me at all.

Who killed Davey Moore? How come he died, and what's the reason for?
Not I, says the man whose fists laid him low in a cloud of mist,
Who came here from Cuba's door where boxing ain't aloud no more.
I hit him, yes it's true. But that's what I was paid to do.
Don't say murder, don't say kill. It was destiny, it was God's will.

Who killed Davey Moore? How come he died, and what's the reason for?

Too many boxers have been killed in the ring. A Jew must have no part in what can only be labeled as "legally sanctioned murder."

Syllogistically, this should warrant a Jew to refrain from participating in any sport that involves hard-core contact. I know this is an extreme disappointment for many men, especially for all those football fans. It is not that I would encourage Jews to engage in purely cerebral sports like chess. I would hate to see anyone become a hopeless recluse like Bobby Fischer as a result. But here we can distinguish between being a participant and being a spectator. One should look at this entire issue as the ancient rabbis did. They were not even around during the time the *Torah* was written. Moreover, since the rabbinic commentators believed in Divine Revelation, whereby God on Mount Sinai gave the *Torah* at one moment to Moses, their absence was truly problematic. They should be considered the original Monday-morning quarterbacks. Their commentaries on the *Five Books of Moses* became legendary (and eternal, like the Bible). They were not participants. They were spectators, and great ones at that.

It is also interesting to note the sociological reasons that Jews have not been active in certain sports over the years: for example, tennis, golf or polo. These sports were often confined to an exclusive country club set, which once banned Jews from membership. So Jews, like other minorities, availed themselves of the public facilities for sports: playgrounds, primarily for baseball and basketball. But, as Jews moved up the economic and social ladder, not only did they join what was once "Gentile" country clubs, they also established their own. Additionally, it should be noted that most Jews feel fully accepted in the American milieu as equal citizens. They find no need to "prove themselves," as was the case when they were part of an immigrant generation or the children of an immigrant group. So showing that a Jew can pulverize someone to near death in fifteen rounds of fisticuffs is no longer a Jewish obligation.

In short, Jews play ping-pong and badminton, go skiing and surfing, ride horses and broncos, shoot rifles and arrows. Yet traditionally, they have not and are still not perceived as "jocks." It is not that they necessarily tend to the managerial side of sports either. Jews are not particularly prevalent in sports because they are numerically an insignificant minority in the world.

There is only one sport that I can say for certain a Jew should not play, and that is Lacrosse. And most definitely a Jew must not engage in its newly derivative game, Intercrosse — at least not until marriage (see **Way #34 — Your Sex Life**).

Most importantly, sports should be an enjoyable pastime, not an obligatory professional goal. A Jew should relate to sports as a wonderful leisure activity; and the Jewish benefits of leisure were outlined in **Way #13 — Your Leisure Time**. One must add, that contrary to the Leo Durocher philosophy that "nice guys finish last" and the Vince Lombardi ideology that "winning is everything," the Jewish view is that such notions can create "a dangerous intoxication, which sometimes betrays victors..." (Ahad Ha'am).[1] Competitiveness, which is inherent in all sports, when applied to the athletic arena, too often brings out the *yeitzar hara* (evil inclination) of an individual, whereby the ultimate goal of winning gets lost in the means and methods to attain the victory. After all: "The character of the end depends on the character and functions of the means employed" (M.H. Luzzatto, *Mesillat Yesharim*, chapter 1, page 17).[2]

Sports can test one's character. I remember being tested on the football field when I was in high school. After completing a successful first-down run, getting up from the tackle, a six-foot, five-inch guard whispered in my ear: "Next time, Forman, you're dead meat!" Being a vegetarian at the time, my tolerance level for such a possibility was rather limited. And if sports builds character, then it took courage on my part to march over to the coach and tell him that I valued my liver more than the game. (After all, it took a lot for me to get over handling a football made of "pigskin," both from a vegetarian and Jewish standpoint.) Yes, it indeed took guts, that overrated commodity in the sports world, to quit on the spot. (Some accusingly claimed that though I might be a Reform Jew, deep down, I was really an Orthodox coward!)

However, being involved in athletics does build character, discipline and sportsmanship. Peter, Paul and Mary's song *Right Field*, from their album *No Easy Walk to Freedom*, traces the transition from baseball "klutz" to baseball "hero." Sports helps develop coordination, not only physically, but humanly, in that one

---

1. In Hebrew, "one of the people," this was a pseudonym for Asher Ginsberg (1856-1927), Zionist thinker and essayist, who expounded the theory of "cultural Zionism." He envisioned Israel as being the spiritual homeland for all Jews.
2. Italian poet (1707-1746) and Kabbalist.

has to learn the essence of teamwork, which by definition requires one to help the other, and to work for the common good. This is why the bunt or the sacrifice fly in baseball, the assist in basketball, hockey and soccer, and the pass in football are such wonderful ideas. They reinforce the notion that to give oneself over for the good of the whole is a positive value. Such cooperation creates unselfishness and reinforces the essential reasons for the establishment of the *minyan* in Jewish life (see **Way #12 — Your Synagogue**), which, by definition, takes into consideration the other members of the Jewish community or "team." **Yes, the nineteenth way to be Jewish is to participate in some capacity in sports,** not for the sole satisfaction of winning, but rather for the higher spiritual purpose of reaping the rewards of its side benefits: loyalty, dependability, dedication, teamwork and collective responsibility.

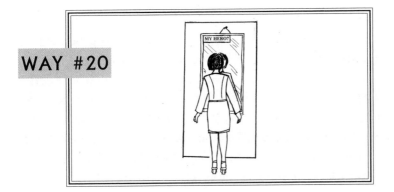

YOUR HEROES

or:

Reality versus Ideal

While all of us have adopted heroes through different stages of our life, it is rare for us to define the essential characteristics that go into the making of a hero. We basically choose to emulate or idolize those individuals in a myriad of professional fields whom we view as "successful." Usually our understanding of that person is one-dimensional, having little knowledge of what his or her personality is like beyond a public persona.

When I was younger, virtually every one of my heroes was a sports star. I would parade around the house jumping in midair, shooting jump-shots in the style of Celtic's great Bob Cousy. Often, I would take anything that resembled a bat, and stand in front of the mirror for hours at a time hitting an imaginary ninth inning home run in the style of Red Sox hall-of-famer Ted Williams (and once the antique vase in the living room). I was particularly adept at scoring a last minute touchdown, bobbing and weaving even better than Cleveland Brown's superstar Jim Brown. When Brown later became a movie star, I pictured myself being one of the "dirty dozen,"[1] battling arm-and-arm with him as we killed one Nazi after the other.

This need, when we are kids, to identify with celebrities is apparently universal. Having four daughters, I am always witness to a child either moon-walking like Michael Jackson or gyrating like Britney Spears. That my daughters also took such loving care of their cabbage patch dolls and their Barbies in a similar fashion to the way my wife and I tended to them never struck me as a possible identification with their parents.

It is interesting that, contrary to the traditional forms of hero identification, Judaism has a specific approach to the notion of heroism. It does not center around a person, but rather concentrates on a type of personality. It is also not parochial whereby a Jew is expected to model him or herself after a particular Jewish personage, like Abraham, Moses and Samson; or Maimonides, Rashi and Shalom Aleichem; or Freud, Einstein and Kafka; or Isaac Stern, Vladimir Horowitz and Yitzhak Perlman.

For Judaism, the true hero is oneself. "Who is a hero? He who conquers his evil impulses" (*Sayings of the Fathers* 4:1). "Who is a hero? He who turns his enemy into a friend" (*Avot deRabbi Natan* 23).[2] Indeed, the story of Rabbi Zushya referred to in **Way #1 — Your Name**, where Zushya fears that God will ask him after his death, not why he was not like Moses, but rather why he was not like Zushya, is Jewishly poignant. For example, have we subdued our will to build ourselves up on the backs of others' failures? Have

---

1. World War II film, *The Dirty Dozen*, about twelve American military convicts sent on a commando mission just before D-Day to occupied France to thwart the Nazi war effort.
2. Sayings collected during the Gaonic period, defined as such because of the great learning that took place in the Jewish academies of the time (6th — 13th centuries).

we derailed our desire to get ahead at all cost? Have we sacrificed our oftentimes-selfish needs for the good of the community? In short: Have we conquered our wrongful inclinations? Jews must constantly ask themselves these questions. The measure of a Jewish hero is the one who can respond "Yes" to pursuing understanding instead of seeking revenge.

Therefore, does Martin Luther King Jr. satisfy the definition of a true hero? Only partially. While working for the common good, it is clear that he was unable to conquer his sexual urges. Most certainly this seems to be a pattern of too many leaders whom many consider worthy of emulation: from King David to Bill Clinton. On the other hand, was the late Israeli prime minister, Yitzhak Rabin, a hero? On the surface it would seem that he was, as he tried to turn the perceived enemy of Israel, indeed of the entire Jewish People, Yasir Arafat, into a friend.

Judaism puts forth a cautionary note about the possible dangers in choosing a specific individual as a hero. A student of mine had hoped to spend his life following around Jerry Garcia and his rock group, the Grateful Dead. His unbridled ambition to commit himself to Garcia assumed obsequious proportions. He made an altar to Garcia in his dormitory room. His wardrobe consisted of "Dead" paraphernalia. His room was plastered with psychedelic skeletons and reeked of incense and marijuana. On a more dangerous note, those ecstatic religious Jews who deify their rabbis, blindly following their distorted dictates, can wind up assassinating a prime minister[1] or killing Arabs in a mosque.[2] When adulation becomes idol worship, a certain obsessive behavior sets in, whose influence can obviously be detrimental. And so, most significantly,

---

1. Yigal Amir, an Orthodox Jew, believed he was fulfilling a Divine command, articulated by some rabbis in Israel, to murder the one who would give back "holy land" to another people — and so killed Yitzhak Rabin.
2. Baruch Goldstein, an Orthodox Jew, on February 25, 1994, gunned down twenty-nine Moslem worshippers at the Cave of Machpela in Hebron.

idol worship is antithetical to Judaism. (This is the reason that synagogues do not have images of any Jewish personalities dotting their stained-glass windows.)

The notion that one can conquer his or her evil impulses as a Divine personality trait needs cultivation. No intermediaries are necessary. Jews do not call upon a Christ-like hero to atone for their sins. There is no possibility that "Jesus loves us more than we will know," for we willingly rejected Jesus as our religious hero, preferring to have direct access to God, our Divine hero. Even Moses, the number one Jew of all times, was knocked down a few pegs, so as to diminish his potential for hero worship.

Now, I hate to disappoint the reader by seemingly denying him or her the choice of a public personality to admire. There is little question that I was influenced by many people throughout my life. I would maintain that one is ultimately influenced more by personalities than by ideologies. My desire to become a rabbi was very much determined by my adoration for my own rabbi. (Although today, I am very much aware that one can practice "vicarious Judaism," by claiming to know a certain rabbi. A person can believe that such familiarity gives him or her some sort of instant Jewish credibility.) My involvement in what I considered were progressive causes was affected by the commitment of people such as Mahatma Ghandi and Martin Luther King Jr. to the principles of non-violence as a method for social change. Ironically, Paul Newman, who played the heroic Ari Ben Canaan in Otto Preminger's film *Exodus*,[1] propelled me to come to Israel to see if this was really the place for me to settle. But there are some people we consider heroes who, upon closer examination, turn out to be disappointments. This is especially acute when one becomes more committed to the individual than the ideas for which he or she stood. For me such a person was Natan Sharansky. This international hero of human rights advocates

---

1. Based on the book *Exodus*, by Leon Uris.

everywhere in the world, who, in standing up to the mighty Soviet Empire, gave hope to all those who suffered human rights abuses and national oppression, turned into a parochial politician upon gaining his ultimate freedom and settling in Israel. His deafening silence in the wake of alleged human rights abuses committed by Israelis against Palestinians and his continual denial to accord any recognition to the national aspirations of those same Palestinians, a national will that for himself he would not allow to be suppressed, frustrates me to no end. In choosing a hero, one must guard against going after false gods.

Therefore, the talmudic entreaty to nurture the potential hero within us is most appealing. And if we can find someone who seems to exemplify this ideal, then we are fortunate. There is the story of Guni Harnik who was killed in the Lebanese War in June, 1982 (euphemistically called "The Peace for Galilee Operation"). His mother, Raya, wrote a children's story about his life, simply titled, *Guni*:[1] "Guni was not killed because he hated Arabs, or because he wanted to be a hero. He was killed because of his love for this beautiful land...He wanted there to be 'peace upon you and all of Israel...' And if one day there is peace, and no more wars, then the story of Guni will be like a fairytale...Something you remember, like a dream or a song..." Guni was the paradigmatic example of a Jewish hero: selfless and devoted.

So now that it has been established that one must regard him or herself as a hero, how does one know if he or she has fulfilled the charge of being one? The best place to look is at your family, particularly at your children. My two oldest daughters recently gave birth to our first grandchildren (I mean their first kids). That each of them wants four children like their parents has provided my wife and me with great pride, because within that desire is the expressed view that there is something in our family constellation that they

1. Translated by Judith Haberman Forman, published by Carmel Press, 1999.

wish to emulate. And there is not a single parent in the world who does not want to consider him- or herself a hero in the eyes of his or her children — Oedipus and Electra be damned (see **Way #48 — Your Kids**).

The twentieth way to be Jewish is to adopt yourself as a hero. Overcome any nasty tendencies, try to see the good in others even against impossible odds, guard yourself against exaggerated "hero worship" (of yourself and others). Most importantly, you will know when you have succeeded in being your own hero when you can confidently say: "With little or much, I am content with myself" (*Apocrypha, Ben Sira* 29:23).

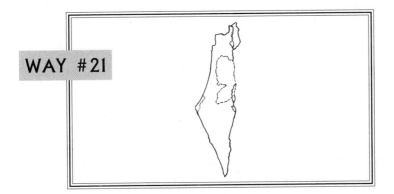

YOUR ISRAEL QUOTIENT

or:

A Jewish State or a State of Jews

There was a story making the rounds in diplomatic circles about the negotiations that took place at Camp David with American President Bill Clinton, Israeli Prime Minister Ehud Barak and Palestinian Authority Chairman Yasir Arafat. At one point in their conversation, Clinton blurted out in a moment of frustration: "I can't understand you Jews and you Moslems. Why can't you learn to live together in peace like good Christians?"

Northern Ireland aside, part of the answer may best be formulated with a question, for it has to do with the matter of Jewish self-definition. When referring to Israel, we must continually ask ourselves: What is a Jew and how should a Jew behave, and what constitutes Jewish commitment and knowledge?

I would maintain that whatever is done in Israel is done in the name of the Jewish People, for good and for bad. Israel is the only country in the world for which the Jews, as a particular people, are morally and politically responsible, which may explain why the image of the Jews and the perception of Judaism are often determined by what happens in the Jewish state. Most certainly, how Israel is viewed in terms of its response to the Palestinian struggle for statehood gives rise to all sorts of international reactions, which, in turn, have unleashed an increase in anti-Semitic incidents, particularly in Europe. Such an interdependent reality begs for an intimate relationship to ensue between the Diaspora and Israel. It prompted Saul Bellow to write: "Israel has become for the West what Switzerland is to the winter holidays — a moral resort area." Diaspora Jews cannot and should not take a moral vacation from Israel.

A number of years ago, I spent a sabbatical with my family in Washington, D.C. My children were enrolled in a suburban public school, and one of them, in the seventh grade at the time, had to study American Colonial history. Having been born and raised in Israel, she did not know the difference between a Pilgrim and a Native American. To help her get a feel for the era, I suggested that we visit the preserved colonial town of Williamsburg, Virginia. On one afternoon during our visit, we went to Carter's Grove, where a woman, dressed in colonial garb greeted us. She sat our touring group down in the living room of Carter's mansion, and, in a hushed dramatic tone, told us that we were going out the back door of the mansion to see an ancient Pilgrim enclave. She then asked if anyone could guess how old the village was. When no one responded, she confidently announced that it was a 17th century Colonial town. Then, with full bravado, she inquired: "Has anyone seen any site older than this?" My twelve-year old daughter raised her hand tentatively and said: "Where I live, my father and I sometimes go for walks to the grave of Samuel the prophet, who anointed Saul and David kings over Israel about three-thousand-and-five hundred years ago."

Our roots are in Israel, more than thirty-five hundred years of our history. It belongs to us. It is who we are. If it is not, then the prayers that we recite before God, where Israel is the focal point, not only of our history, but also of our spiritual longing, are rendered meaningless. It is no accident that at the close of the most significant historical holiday in the Jewish calendar, Passover, and at the close of the most significant theological holiday in the Jewish calendar, Yom Kippur, we say: "Next Year in Jerusalem." At the conclusion of a wedding ceremony, upon breaking a wine glass, traditionally the bride and groom recite: "If I forget you, O Jerusalem, let my right hand wither; let my tongue cleave to the roof of my tongue, if I cease to think of you — if I do not keep Jerusalem in my memory at my happiest hour" (*Psalm* 137:5-6). And when we remove from the Ark our sacred *Torah* that catalogues our history, our beliefs, our values, we sing: "Out of Zion will go forth the *Torah*, and the word of the Lord from Jerusalem." In our daily prayers, Israel comes in a close second to God. We Jews never gave up our spiritual longing to return to Israel, as we faced Jerusalem three times a day praying for restoration in our ancestral homeland.

If we pray it, then we should mean it, and God help us if we do not. We are theologically engaged with Israel. It is woven into the ideological fabric of our religious yearning. And if Diaspora Jews want to play a role in fashioning the ideals that sound forth from the Jewish state, as they are often forced to, then they, who define themselves mostly in religious terms, have to take this theology and make it their own, even as they define their Jewish self. But a strictly religious/theological definition of one's Judaism is not sufficient; for ultimately identification with Israel, and I would say with Judaism, can only come about when it is propelled by a self-definition that includes people, land, language, state, culture — as well as religion. Exclude one of these elements from our Jewish identity, and a severance between the Diaspora and Israel will develop. American Jews might very well find themselves creating a new brand of Judaism, legitimate in their own eyes, but unrecognizable to anything in our past that reflects the collective historical experiences and traditions of our people.

The relationship of Israel and the Diaspora is based on a symbiosis: the living together of two dissimilar but closely bound organisms, especially when the association is beneficial. There is a recognition that the national parameters of a Jewish state are mutually conducive to an increased Jewish identity. (Such a reality has prompted two Jewish multi-millionaires to sponsor ten-day free trips to Israel for an unlimited number of unaffiliated North American Jewish college-age students.)

When Israel sends an army rescue team to Entebbe, Uganda (see **Way #9 — Your Car**), flies Ethiopian Jews out of war-torn Addis Ababa, or absorbs hundreds of thousands of Russian Jews, it does so for the sake of the Jewish People. When Israel is engaged in wars of survival, when it combats terrorism, and makes real geographical sacrifices for peace, it does so not only to maintain its own existence, but also to guarantee that the Jews of the Diaspora can come to Israel to replenish their Jewish batteries.

Commitment to a Jewish state must not be determined by the policies of a particular Israeli government. Diaspora Jews must be certain to see a wider picture than their own self-portrait. Too often, Diaspora Jews tear Israel to shreds over the fact that non-Orthodox Jews are not accorded equal rights, which indeed, is a blight on Israel's democracy.

But one must be careful in the stridency of pressing this case. We must keep things in perspective. Israel is an "old-new" nation. It takes time to institute some of the more obvious freedoms that America enjoys. Although comparatively, and considering the real physical threat to Israel's existence that is ever present, Israel fares quite well. In fact, American Jews seem to embrace a certain amount of self-righteousness, not to mention selectivity, when transferring democratic demands to Israel.

Growing up in the United States in the Fifties and Sixties, for me America was characterized by McCarthyism, whose resultant hysteria saw two alleged second-rate spies, the Rosenbergs, put to death; a brutal oppression of African-Americans; an aggressive war in Southeast Asia; the Cuban missile crisis; and one political and racial assassination after another.

By comparison, Israel looks like a paragon of virtue. I do not want to sound Pollyannaish, but one has to consider whether the cup is half-empty or half-full. For example, it is a mark of Israel's freedom that there is no capital punishment (except for Nazi war criminals). This is truly amazing when one considers that terrorists can gun down twenty-six school children on a class trip or blow up buses or set off bombs in public places. Communists and Israeli Arabs who call for a secular democratic state in all of historical Palestine sit in the parliament. And while we can bewail the Orthodox monopoly in the country, one must understand that the reason ultra-Orthodox Jews often take to the streets to demonstrate is because Israel's High Court of Justice has been cutting down one ruling after another that favors Orthodoxy.

After all, it was the United States Supreme Court that forced integration, and it was not until the civil rights bill of 1964 was enacted and the voting rights bill of 1965 legislated that African-Americans were finally accorded their full democratic rights.

And while we may bemoan the slow pace of peace, if someone had asked me when I moved to Israel in 1972 what I thought about the prospects for some sort of reconciliation with our Arab neighbors, I would never have imagined that we would have a peace agreement with our ancient enemy, Egypt, or with Jordan, or that Benjamin Netanyahu, the spiritual descendant of the right-wing ideologue Ze'ev Jabotinsky, would shake Yasir Arafat's hand, let alone relinquish most of Hebron, one of Israel's sacred cities, to the Palestinian Authority.

The sacrifices that Israel has made in the face of implacable enemies is truly praiseworthy, yet oftentimes these prideful achievements get lost in an avalanche of Diaspora criticism. This is not to say that Diaspora Jews should give uncritical support to all that Israel does. Israel has yet to fulfill its role of becoming a Jewish state, of becoming a "holy people." It still is in the state of becoming, and so remains a state of Jews.

And yet, we Jews have managed to sustain the longest living national liberation movement in human history. From the time of the destruction of the Second Temple in 70 CE, Jews never lost the hope of reestablishing their nation-state. Roman conquerors, Crusaders, Inquisitors, Cossacks, Czars and Pogromists, Nazis, Arabs and terrorists could not thwart our national resolve. And so, our history should teach us two important lessons: one ideological and one practical. Ideologically, our suffering should sensitize us to the suffering of others. Our need to fulfill our national expression should help us understand the need of other peoples to do the same (not at the expense of our own national movement). While no other nation or religion can match our historical claims to Jerusalem, this should not in any way permit us to disregard the emotional and spiritual attachments to the Holy City of the two other great monotheistic religions, Islam and Christianity. Practically, just as no one could halt our continued march toward national liberation, so too will we be unable to forestall the ultimate national goals of the Palestinians.

While Israel must acknowledge this reality, it also must deal with moral questions that define its very essence as a "chosen" people, as two nations are locked in battle to maintain two independent states on one piece of land. And that struggle fashions real ethical challenges for Jews. For example: how do Israelis respond when Palestinians, in their attempt to achieve their national aspirations, use children to form a front-line defense for Palestinian gunmen to fire at Israeli soldiers and settlers? What should Israelis do when Palestinians hide in homes, health clinics, schools and churches in the Palestinian Christian town of Beit Jala, adjacent to Bethlehem, and fire upon a Jewish suburb of Jerusalem (considered part of greater Jerusalem by Israel, and as a settlement by the Palestinians)? How should we understand Palestinian denial of our historical rights to this land, and their murderous attacks on civilians (ours as well as their own)? And of course, the larger question remains: What if the Palestinians believe some of their own rhetoric, and do intend eventually to displace us?

These are moral dilemmas of great significance. If the resultant behavior turns Israel into a country that routinely violates others' human rights and tries to abrogate legitimate Palestinian national claims, then the very essence of Israel as a "light unto the nations" will be seriously compromised. It helps little to compare ourselves to other nations of the world. For certain, in relative terms, Israel is a cut above most other countries. We are a good country in a bad neighborhood. But we Jews should not be in the business of comparative shopping, for this will only invite invidious comparisons. We must guard against employing the lowest common denominator as the yardstick to measure or justify our behavior.

And so, Israel is not only the lightening rod by which Jews throughout the world are judged, it is against Israel that one can examine one's own Jewish commitment, particularly in times of stress. No one expects Diaspora Jews to rescue Jewish hostages, Ethiopians and Russians. But one can conservatively expect Diaspora Jews to cling to their Judaism. And one way to demonstrate Jewish continuity is, at times of tension, to be engaged with Israel. Such engagement requires intimacy, which provides a basis for knowledge, which is a prerequisite for commitment.

Israel can cognitively serve the North American Jewish

community. Elder hostels, synagogue groups, national and local missions, student programs need to come to Israel, not to engage in political lobbying, but to learn. To travel through the hills of Jerusalem with a Bible in hand, or to visit the Galilee with a *Mishnah* open to see how Jews in the ancient town of Tzippori managed to codify a set of laws that would help them maintain their Jewish life in spite of the encroachment of a Greco-Roman culture. Personal interfacing with Israel helps a Jew understand where he or she fits into the continuum of Jewish history, and what his or her obligations are to guarantee the perpetuation of the Jewish People. It also builds credibility when one wishes to extend his or her influence over what happens in Israel, which is essential, since, as stated, all Jews are affected in some way by what happens in the Jewish state.

This overall interaction must shape the relationship between Diaspora Jewry and Israel. After all, when we recite the central theological tenet of our faith, *Shema Yisrael* — "Hear O Israel, the Lord our God, the Lord is One" (*Deuteronomy* 6:4), which virtually every Jew in the world knows, we are essentially committing ourselves to join in the unfolding history of the Jewish People. **The twenty-first way to be Jewish is to learn the Jewish drama being acted out in Israel — to claim it, to participate in it, and finally to help write the next great act**. As the only self-contained Jewish community in the world, Israel, perhaps more than any other aspect of our Jewish lives, challenges our very Jewish being.

YOUR RITUAL MITZVOT[1]

or:

A Gateway to Family Unity

Today's average nuclear family sees both parents working. Their children are fully programmed. There is little time to sit down to dinner together, let alone spend an evening in familial harmony. Often weekends do not alter the hectic pace, as each one goes his or her own way. Then, all of a sudden, one of the parents gets totally unreasonable and starts haranguing everyone how no one respects anyone anymore, how there is a complete lack of order in "our" lives, how "we" never have a family meal, a family outing, a family "anything" together. Everyone agrees, and responds: "You're right Dad. Next week, we promise."

Maimonides, one of our most celebrated Jewish philosopher/

---

1. The Hebrew word for commandments. Colloquially it means "good deeds."

theologians, to whom I referred a number of times in previous **Ways**, understood this dilemma almost one thousand years ago. He held that it was crucial to "bracket everything in the empirical world for one moment, and try to remain alone — with our families and immediate surroundings." The man knew what he was talking about.

Now this **Way's** approach to rituals in Judaism will differ from a traditional Jewish concept, which maintains that ritual commandments are observed because they are mandated by God. This leads us to the notion of Revelation in Jewish thought. It is believed that at one dramatic moment, God revealed the Written Law (*Torah*) and the Oral Law (*Talmud*) in one fell swoop at Mount Sinai. Moses sat atop the mountain, while the people of Israel were gathered below, and, like a stenographer, wrote down every word and commandment that God dictated. There were no less than six hundred and thirteen commandments. Some negative, like "Thou shall not do this or that," and some positive, like "Take a bath every morning and a shower every evening" (Oh wait, that's one of the commandments in my house). A much better example of a positive commandment is: "Love your neighbor as you love yourself" (a powerful psychological statement, as it presumes that one truly likes him- or herself).

Further, the commandments are divided into moral ones (see **Way #23 — Your Moral Mitzvot**) and ritual ones. Neither precludes the other. In fact, each one serves the other, and together they form a single package. Of course, the primary reason for obeying these commandments is that they are Divinely ordained. According to a traditional understanding of Revelation, any side-benefits are of secondary or tertiary importance. But for you and me, who wittingly or unwittingly do not abide by every one of God's entreaties, therefore basically rejecting the theory of Divine Revelation, to the extent that we want to put a little order in our lives, we would settle for the practical rewards of observing some, not all, ritual commandments.

I mentioned the word "order" because that is essentially what ritual brings to one's life: order. For example, the Passover *Seder* is filled with rituals. In Hebrew, the word *Seder* means "order." Almost all the Jewish holidays present the possibility not only for order, but also for family traditions, as Jewish holidays are, first and foremost, family oriented (see **Way #27 — Your Holidays**). And because the commandments were given to a people, collectively and not individually, they can provide for family or communal unity and harmony.

We are all aware of the family benefits of holidays. Take Thanksgiving, which virtually every American Jewish family celebrates. Thanksgiving has its own set of rituals. First there is the food: turkey, stuffing, cranberries, sweet potato and marshmallow "mush" and pumpkin pie. Then there is the song: "We gather together to hear the Lord's Prayer." Although to be honest, I never knew what the Lord's Prayer was, because we just sang about it, without ever actually getting to it. And of course, there is the well-established ritual of watching one of those great college football games on TV. If you are in high school, it means attending the game with your team's traditional rival.

Families revel in this unity, so centered on rituals. If it makes such good sense to enjoy one another on this day, and if it brings so much contentment to the family unit, why not adopt this form of ritual bonding every week. Judaism provides this possibility. One only has to look to the Sabbath and all the rituals that surround the Sabbath table, which encourage family participation, to strengthen the notion that a Thanksgiving type of family experience can be instituted weekly (see **Way #28 — Your Sabbath**).

Almost all Jewish rituals, because they are shared, provide for family unity. Jewish rituals surround all life-cycle events. They begin with birth and end with death. Interlaced are the holidays with their myriad ritual expressions that are directly related to the theme of the specific holiday. Add to this some simple rituals like reciting the *Shema* with your kid before he or she goes to bed. If it was good enough for Laura Engels on *Little House on the Prairie* to get on her knees, fold her hands neatly together and thank God for getting her through another day, then it has to be good enough for us. After all, the Engels were the perfect family!

Now I know that this is impractical when children reach a certain age. After all, I would not expect any of us to stay up all hours of the night until our kids get home to say a prayer with them before they turn in. On second thought, maybe it is practical, since, if you are like me, you stay up anyway worrying until your kid gets home. But Judaism provides for other rituals that bridge the age gap. For example, dialogue between parent and child is intrinsic to Passover. Passing the *Torah* from generation to generation during a Bar or Bat Mitzvah ceremony links a grandparent to a grandchild. In my house, I perform a weekly ritual, again centered around the Sabbath table. I bless my children every week, using the words that Moses' brother, Aaron, used to bless the children of Israel: "May the Lord bless you and keep you. May the Lord deal kindly and graciously with you. May the Lord bestow favor on you and grant you peace" (*Numbers* 6:24-26). My oldest daughters are married with children, and yet this ritual still maintains — and if for some reason I forget, they remind me.

For certain, observing Jewish ritual commandments can be overwhelming, and the undue emphasis on ritual on the part of some Jews, sometimes at the expense of keeping the moral commandments, can be frustrating. Once an Orthodox friend of mine was staying at our house for the Sabbath. Just prior to the Sabbath, he went around our house checking that the refrigerator light bulb was unscrewed so that it would not go on when someone opened the refrigerator door (thus violating the ritual commandment that forbids the activation of electricity on the

Sabbath), and making certain that toilet paper was torn into neatly shredded squares (thus not violating another ritual that forbids tearing things on the Sabbath). I stopped him in the midst of his Sabbath worries and warned him that he was so busy preparing for the Sabbath, that he would have little time to enjoy it! And then there are the Orthodox chaplains in the Israeli army whose major concern is whether there is enough wine for *Havdalah*,[1] and not the more significant concern of the soldier who is faced with a moral dilemma in the field of battle.

Clearly a balance between the two must be found. **But the benefits of some sort of ritual observance constitute the twenty-second way to be Jewish.** Certainly weekly, if not daily, rituals establish order, unity and consistency. They provide an opportunity for shared traditions, which can set in motion a chain of practices that will maintain a sense of continuity, linking one generation to the next. Rituals can help to guarantee a family's perpetuity, safeguarding family memories for years to come.

---

1. Literally translated as "separation," it is a brief home service, conducted on Saturday evenings (see **Way #28 — Your Sabbath**).

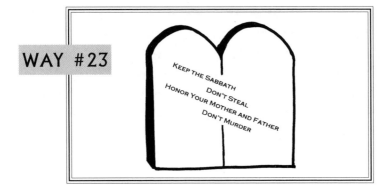

KEEP THE SABBATH
DON'T STEAL
HONOR YOUR MOTHER AND FATHER
DON'T MURDER

YOUR MORAL MITZVOT

or:

A Gateway to Individual Responsibility

That great Jewish theologian, Allen Konigsberg (better known as Woody Allen — see **Way #1 — Your Name**) said: "I was thrown out of college for cheating on my metaphysics exam. I was caught looking into the soul of the student sitting next to me." I know that many of us consider ourselves to be good, and basically moral. And hopefully, the reason that we act in ways that are ethically commendable is not for fear of getting caught, but because we intuitively know that certain behaviors are just not acceptable. In order to maintain a stable social order in our lives, we instinctively distinguish between right and wrong. Okay, so we tell white lies now and then, exaggerate a little bit, inflate our own ego every so often, cheat a bit in reporting our taxes, cover up some minor errors and blame others once in a while for our mistakes. We still tell ourselves, and our children, that these are insignificant moral lapses, of little consequence.

The story is told of a great Italian actress who obtained a contract from her manager before coming on tour to the United States, which guaranteed that every hotel room in which she stayed would be kept at seventy-two degrees. This was in the days before air-conditioning and automatic thermostats. The manager was in a quandary as to how to meet this provision, until someone suggested extracting mercury from the thermometer and filling the tube with red ink up to the marker for seventy-two degrees. The actress was tremendously impressed by the comforts of American hotels, but did remark on one occasion, how strange it was that seventy-two degrees in Chicago seemed so much colder than seventy-two degrees in Miami! There are no moral "degrees" in Judaism. A Jew is not permitted to blow "hot and cold" depending on the circumstance. This lends credence to Leo Baeck's[1] famous statement: "Judaism is not merely ethical, but ethics constitutes its essence" (*The Essence of Judaism*).

The division of the commandments into moral and ritual realms testifies to the underpinning of ethical standards within Judaism. Just as there are to be no compromises ritually, so too should there be no "bending" of the moral rules. As outlined in **Way #18 — Your Social Activism**, the Jewish People were born out of the antithetical expression of moral behavior as exemplified by ancient Egypt, a nation that enslaved the Jews. Yet while in **Way #18**, I dealt with moral issues as they affect the community, here I will refer to those moral *Mitzvot* that have a bearing on individual responsibility and behavior.

It would be too tedious to insist that we go through all the moral

---

1. Leo Baeck (1873-1956) was a German theologian and liberal Jewish leader. He was imprisoned during WWII in Theresienstadt concentration camp. After the war he settled in London, where he headed the World Union for Progressive Judaism.

Mitzvot that appear in the *Torah*. Instead, I will concentrate on those ethical commandments that tell us to hold in check some of the more destructive human emotions that lead to immoral behavior. It also is interesting to note that many *Mitzvot*, which seemingly come under the category of ritual commandments, actually have an ethical thrust to them. For example, many of the laws that relate to *kashrut* (see **Way #33 — Your Food**), address the issue of how one should slaughter an animal. While ritualistic in nature, they take into moral account the manner by which one kills an animal, in order to make certain that it is done as mercifully and painlessly as possible.

But first let me touch upon some of the "morals of the story" that are so dominant in the biblical narrative. Now, a Jew should not claim that because Judaism has a plethora of moral commandments, which are Divinely inspired, he or she has a lock on moral integrity. Neither as individuals nor as a people have we succeeded in living up to the ethical standards laid down for us. As discussed in **Way #21 — Your Israel Quotient**, the Jewish state has a considerable way to go before it approximates a nation based on the highest moral values. Yet, the very emphasis on moral *Mitzvot* in the most important of Jewish historical literature, the *Torah*, tells us that: "Moral action is the meeting-place between the human and the Divine" (*Is There a Jewish Philosophy?* Leon Roth[1]).

Here are a few "morals of the story." Some of these stories relate to the allegorical beginnings of the Jewish People, while others relate to the historical emergence of the Jewish People. The story of the generations of Adam and Eve is most instructive, because at the very inception of the human species, we basically see that our literature constitutes one extended morality play. Even after all the warnings to Adam and Eve to behave in certain ways, they and their

---

1. Brilliant English professor of philosophy (1886-1963). Roth was the first professor of philosophy at The Hebrew University in Jerusalem.

children quickly get caught up in a web of deceit. Through human weaknesses of wile, temptation and outright dishonesty, virtually each one commits a crime and then tries to cover his or her tracks. The best way to do that is to blame the next person for what happened. Adam blames Eve who in turn blames a snake (give me a break). Cain, incredibly jealous of Abel, kills him, and then when confronted by God, pretends that nothing ever happened.

The themes of uncontrolled jealously, deceit and avarice recur throughout the biblical narrative (see **Way #31 — Your Personality**). Among others, they play themselves out most dramatically in the stories of Noah and his children, the Tower of Babel, Jacob and Esau, Joseph and his brothers, King David and his son Absalom. Often there is no moral restraint on the part of the players, and the results of their unethical behavior is devastating, leading to dysfunctional families at best, to tragic consequences at worst.

It is interesting to note that the Ten Commandments, which comprise the minimal standards by which moral behavior, family unity and social order can be maintained, were probably set forth because of God's disappointment in the people that He/She fashioned. First God began with universal personalities, not specific Jewish ones, and each one of them proved a "lot lower than the angels." In fact, God tried to start the world anew after the passing of Noah, who was considered "righteous in his generation" (*Genesis* 6:9), which is to say that his moral behavior had a relative value attached to it.

Having recognized that this was not going to work, God determined to deal with particular personalities, hoping for a little better luck. So the next character appearing on the stage is Abraham, the first Jew. Not only did he become entangled with his son Ishmael born of his handmaiden Hagar, but also, at the obsessive insistence of his wife Sarah, he was forced to banish him and Hagar, so as not to corrupt her son, Isaac, born a little later (*Genesis* 21). While there is little question that Abraham possessed qualities that led to true moral behavior, he was overwhelmed by a surrounding family that continually compromised his integrity.

Perhaps the most devastating example of immoral behavior is the sibling rivalry between Jacob and Esau (*Genesis* 25:19-33:17), which involves deception, duplicity and trickery. The story culminates in the famous dream sequence in which Jacob wrestles with an angel. This has been interpreted to mean that he essentially struggled with his own conscience, thus admitting to his immoral actions at an earlier stage in life. In that battle with God's messenger, Jacob's name is changed to Israel. According to Rashi, the name Jacob means "deceit," and the name Israel means "honesty." The text relates that: "Jacob struggled honestly with beings, human and Divine, and prevailed" (*Genesis* 32:29) and so earned a new name, Israel (see **Way #1 — Your Name**).

After the fall of the generations of Abraham and Sarah, which ends with the Jews in Egypt, Moses arrives on the scene. While he often intuitively sensed what was right, his responses may have been exaggerated. Killing that Egyptian warlord for beating Jews compromised his moral integrity. Later, after heroically leading the Jews out of slavery, the people were not appreciative, began building a "golden calf" to worship, and actually longed for a return to Egypt. It was at that point that God threw up His/Her hands, and said: "Okay, apparently intuition doesn't work. I am going to have to devise a set of definitive commandments for people to live by." And so were born the Ten Commandments.

What these commandments deal with are human emotions. If one can control his or her inner feelings — of jealously, greed, suspicion and envy — then, in all likelihood, one's moral behavior will be guaranteed. (If not...well, just ask Bill Clinton or Richard Nixon.) The Ten Commandments are expanded upon throughout the *Torah*. At different stages throughout the Sinaitic experience, until entrance into "the Promised Land," the Jewish People are told in the book of *Leviticus*, which primarily outlines ritual observances, "not to steal, lie, act deceitfully. Not to oppress a neighbor, hold up the wages of a laborer, curse the deaf or put a stumbling block before the blind. Justice must never be perverted, neither by favoring the poor nor by deferring to the powerful. You must guard against slander (gossip), and must not stand idly by while your neighbor suffers. You can't hate your sister or brother in your heart, and you must reason with your family so as not to incur guilt on their behalf. You can't seek vengeance, bear a grudge, and most significantly, you must love your neighbor as you love yourself" (19:11-18). To obey these moral *Mitzvot* means to lead an ethically upright life.

Most of us attend High Holiday services and recount that long litany of sins we have committed during the past year, for which we are now sorry. I figure that I have committed too many of them numerous times, like: "passing judgment without the facts; deceiving myself with half-truths; condemning my kids for faults that I tolerate within myself; for gluttony (a big one for us overeaters); for being insolent and arrogant (*High Holiday Prayer Book*). All these characteristics point to foibles in my personality that led me to immoral acts. Had I abided by the moral *Mitzvot* outlined in the *Torah*, I would not sit in synagogue on Yom Kippur and feel like such a moral degenerate. What is so compelling about Judaism is that the holidays allow one to act with ethical correctness, but a discussion of the holidays will have to wait for **Way #27 — Your Holidays.**

Judaism tells us that morality is not a relative term. A Jew must not satisfy him or herself by comparative shopping at some ethical mall. There can be no sociological justification for immoral acts. There may be explanations, but there are no excuses. **The twenty-third way to be Jewish is to observe the moral *Mitzvot* in the *Torah*.** They help us to maintain our psychological equilibrium, so that we do not give in to deceit, jealousy, vengeance and selfishness. These are the human emotions that lead us to compromise our ethical standards, and to sacrifice our individual responsibility to be moral standard-bearers of decency and honesty to our family and community.

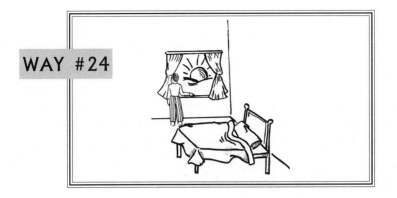

YOUR MIRACLES

or:

You can't be Serious

(A third-grade kid comes home from religious school.)

Mother: What did you learn today?

Kid: Nothing. Something about Moses and the Red Sea.

Mother: Well, tell me what the teacher said.

Kid: No big deal. I'd like to go play outside now.

Mother: Not until you tell me what the teacher taught you.

Kid: Okay. The Jews were running away from the Egyptians when they got to this huge sea. They then took some wood, bricks and chains, and built a humungous bridge. They quickly ran over the bridge to the other side. And when the Egyptians came after them and were on top of the bridge, the Jews blew it up, and all the Egyptians drowned.

Mother (*Aghast*): Is that what your teacher told you?

Kid: No. But if I told you what she said, you'd never believe me.

In Judaism, the Yiddish proverb "a Jew cannot live without miracles" is most applicable. Whether we attribute miracles to the work of God or to our own steadfastness matters little. That we Jews not only have survived exiles, crusades, inquisitions, pogroms, concentration camps, wars and terrorism, but managed to establish our own state after two thousand years of dispersion, must be certain proof of the occurrence of miracles.

Colloquially, none of us is above using the word miracle to describe what we consider are extraordinary events, such as the wonders of nature: the change of leaves in the autumn, a rainbow, the birth of a child. Other expressions of miracles include: "It is a miracle that I found you;" "what a miracle that we survived that storm;" "it is absolutely miraculous that she is alive after what she has been through." And: "The reestablishment of Israel after two thousand years is a modern-day miracle."

For me, anything to do with technology is a miracle: the cell phone, electricity, the TV, my CD player, my car, the computer on which I am writing this book. Saran wrap, frozen juices and Johnson & Johnson baby shampoo also make my list of incredible marvels. And if my beleagured Red Sox ever win a world series, that will most definitely be a miracle, not to mention the miracle should I live that long.

Yet, we all know that each one of the above miracles can give way to some sort of scientific explanation. (For me, to understand those explanations would be a miracle.) But, by definition, a miracle is that which cannot be explained. A miracle is inconceivable. One cannot comprehend a miraculous event by any manner of logic. One either believes in miracles or does not. Also, because of the very definition of miracles, one cannot pick and choose them. It is all or nothing — perhaps with the exception of the miracle of Creation. However, even here, given today's world of modern technology, when everything is verified either by CNN or the Internet, it is a **miracle** if we believe in the **miracle** of Creation. There was no one there to either film it or post it on a website.

Why do I say that one cannot pick and choose his or her miracles to believe in? According to the definition of a miracle as that which is unexplainable, one would have to acknowledge that the virgin birth was a miracle. Jesus walking on water was a miracle. The resurrection was a miracle. Naturally these definitively Christian miracles pose a challenge for the Jew. We simply do not believe in them. We say they did not occur because they cannot be explained. But, as pointed out, that is the very definition of a miracle. Belief in miracles requires a leap of faith.

So what do we do with Judaism's emphasis on the miraculous ways of God: Noah's ark, the parting of the Red Sea, the burning bush (a bush on fire that is not consumed), to name but a few? Indeed, the entire developing drama of the Jewish People as played out in the *Torah* is based on the supernatural interference of God. A Jew could say that the giving of the Ten Commandments, which fashioned the social agenda for the Jewish People for generations to come, was the greatest of all miracles. All these defy logic. So, in the same manner that we reject those Christian miracles, so too would we have to deny our own. But there is a way out of this seemingly troubling and contradictory Jewish dilemma. A Jew must recognize that all these "supernatural" events can indeed be explained either scientifically or allegorically.

Yet despite this, the one miracle that a Jew can confidently believe in is the miracle of Creation, which is renewed every time we witness the birth of a child. It is safe to assume that no one will ever be able to comprehend this one — no matter how many "big bang" theories scientists come up with. A Jew recognizes this when reciting his or her first prayer in the morning (see **Way #15 — Your God**). Upon awakening in the morning, we thank God for creating the world anew with us. For a Jew, every day that we are alive should be considered a miracle. We should look at ourselves in the morning as a continuation of the miracle of Creation, instead of concentrating on the foul taste in our mouths or the accumulated "gook" in our eyes. Such an approach to life elevates our worth as individuals and heightens our sensitivities and appreciation for the people with whom we interact and for the things and events which we encounter.

"A miracle cannot prove what is impossible; but is necessary to confirm what is possible" (Maimonides, *Guide to the Perplexed* 3:24). It is only natural to wish for a miracle when we are in trouble or when we are sick; or to a lesser degree, to succeed in our job or to do well in school. "In times of expectation, one must rely on a miracle" (*Talmud Yebamot* 39b). The very notion that a human being can attain what seems impossible is a driving force behind many of his or her achievements. There is no better example of this than the story of Helen Keller and her devoted teacher, Ann Sullivan. *The Miracle Worker* — how apt a choice of title for the wondrous movie describing the story of blind, deaf-mute Ms. Keller's life and Ms. Sullivan's heroic part in her achievements.

So, despite all our rational instincts, the twenty-fourth way to be Jewish is to believe in the efficacy of miracles, if not the actual inexplicable wonder of them. While we are cautioned to "not rely on miracles happening daily" (*Talmud Shabbat* 32a), thereby trying to absolve ourselves from being active partners in shaping our own lives and the lives of those around us, the belief in "a miracle…is necessary to confirm what is possible" — what we might ultimately achieve.

YOUR INTERNET

or:

I'm Caught in a Web---site

Jewish websites are set up almost daily on the Internet. There are few subjects that are not covered on the world-wide net, from the hidden secrets of the Kabbalah (Jewish mystical writings) to a Jewish gay bar in London. If you want to know what is happening in the Jewish world, or better yet, what Jews are thinking, then all you have to do is call up Yahoo, Webcrawler, Alta Vista and type in "Judaism." It is instant. You can look at it, bookmark it, maybe print it, and then shut down your computer.

Jewish organizations, institutions and synagogues are using the Internet to reach Jews otherwise unreachable. The Jewish web pages have become a Chinese menu — choose from column A, B, or C. And like Chinese food, no column will fill your stomach sufficiently, so you just scroll down a bit and order the next column of Jewish information. And of course, you become thirsty along the way, and then crave more and more. The problem is that Judaism can become impersonal and passive. It is taken in from a distance. Eventually it can turn into a computer game. Then, when you are away from your computer for any length of time, all that Jewish learning is at best sent to the recycle bin, at worst trashed.

So, is there any Jewish value in the Internet? Obviously, you won't find me quoting Jewish sources in this **Way**. But that is not to say that the Internet is hostile territory to a Jew. There are a numbers of ways that the Internet can serve Jews.

When someone has graduated from university and is in the work force, he or she may find it difficult to meet Jews on a social basis. Many single men and women who are older — in their forties and fifties — have a difficult time meeting potential partners. This is also true for widows, widowers and divorcees. There are countless reputable Internet sites that offer the possibility for Jewish dating. Although here I must offer a cautionary note, particularly to Israeli Jews. During the height of the second Intifada, called the Al Aqsa Intifada,[1] an Israeli high school student corresponded with a girl from the West Bank town of Ramallah via the Inernet. After several Internet conversations, they decided to rendezvous. Apparently, a trap was set for him. As soon as he arrived in Ramallah to meet his chat mate, he was kidnapped and killed by terrorists. Now rarely would something like this happen to you and me, but dealing with someone over the electronic wires does not guarantee the dream romance of a Tom Hanks and Meg Ryan, as depicted in the movie *You've Got Mail*.

For the busy professional who is interested in keeping up with what is happening in the Jewish world, the Internet provides all sorts of possibilities. The *Baltimore Jewish Times, Forward, Haaretz* (English edition), *Jerusalem Post, Jerusalem Report, Jewish Week*, all

---

1. Named for the holy mosque in the Moslem Quarter of the Old City of Jerusalem where the fighting originally broke out.

have websites. In addition, there are a number of Jewish journals that have web pages. *Commentary, Hadassah Magazine, Jewish Spectator, Judaism, Reform Judaism, Middle-East Affairs, Midstream, Tikkun,* are but a few.

If you are traveling anywhere (particularly abroad: see **Way #2 — Your Trips Abroad**), then the Internet is a great place to look, not only to find places of Jewish interest to visit, but also to find a family to spend the Sabbath with, where to go to services, where to meet other Jews, and as indicated at the beginning of this **Way**, where to find a Jewish gay bar in London. One can also find on the Internet a host of other Jewish sources: commentaries on the Bible, synopses of major Jewish works of literature, sociological data on all aspects of the Jewish community and Jewish life, biographical information on Jewish personalities, demographic trends in the Jewish community, Jewish studies departments at universities, Jewish libraries, Jewish museums, Jewish restaurants, Jewish art, public courses on Jewish topics. The list could go on and on.

However, one should not fool him- or herself into thinking that the Internet can satisfy any sort of real Jewish lifestyle. A Doonsberry cartoon shows two people conversing at a cocktail party. One asks the other if she has read a particular book. And she responds: "Not personally." Instead of taking the time to enjoy a beautiful site, we snap a picture of it. This fits in with our generation's obsession with instant gratification. If we are not immediately turned on by something, we hit the remote and search for an alternative. But being Jewish is not something that you can do impersonally, almost passively. You have to be directed. Judaism is a very personal way of life, but it is not private. It cannot be appreciated at a moment's notice, and certainly not by sitting alone in one's room opposite an IBM clone. Such an isolated approach bypasses a sense of community, so essential in Judaism. Being Jewish means having first-hand experiences. It cannot be filtered through a low radiation fifteen-inch diagonal screen.

The first Jewish Internet was the *Mishnah*, which catalogued the commandments of the *Torah* loosely according to subject matter. While the *Gemarah*[1] expanded upon them, other literary works consolidated Jewish law and practice: *Sefer HaChinuch*,[2] *Shulchan Aruch*,[3] *The Short Shulchan Aruch*,[4] *Sefer Aggada*.[5] Scholars such as Maimonides went further. He capsulated Jewish belief into thirteen basic principles of faith. However, these expressions of Internet were cumbersome. Today, one can buy a *Talmud* CD Rom, and according to the themes that interest an individual, with a few clicks of the mouse, he or she can access the information. Again, this lone venture is antithetical to the manner in which *Talmud* is supposed to be learned — in a *chevruta* (in pairs — literally in a friendly atmosphere). This allows for the possibility for the individual to share his or her ideas, interpretations, insights and questions with another person.

The twenty-fifth way to be Jewish is to go into the Internet, but to do so with an understanding of the limits of this new technology. A Jew must use the Internet in a very disciplined way in order to gain basic information. But the use of that information must serve as a basis for a live, creative interchange with other Jews. A Jew must not get caught in a web---site. To grow Jewishly, we need to learn from one another.

---

1. See **Way #10 — Your Culture**, footnote 2.
2. A highly popular work, translated into many European languages, it was compiled by Rabbi Aaron HaLevy of 13th and 14th century Barcelona. It is a catalogue of the commandments according to the weekly *Torah* reading, accompanied by much legal definition and moral edification.
3. Most widely used current code of Jewish law, prepared by Joseph Caro (1488-1575), and in use since the 16th century.
4. Abbreviated edition of the *Shulchan Aruch*.
5. Compilation of *Aggadic* material (homilies, folklore, legends and aphorisms) from the *Talmud* and *Midrash* (interpretations of *Bible* other than literary ones, instituted in order to better understand specific biblical demands and prohibitions) by Haim Nachman Bialik (1873-1934) and Yehoshua Hana Ravnitsky (1859-1944), compiled in Odessa between 1908-1911.

YOUR PROFESSION

or:

"I'd Rather be a Sparrow than a Snail"[1]

A teenage boy hurriedly ran into a drugstore to use the public telephone. Since the boy spoke rather loudly, the owner of the store could not help but overhear the conversation.

> **Boy**: Hello, is this 642-4189? May I talk to the director? Oh, you are the director? Well then, could you tell me, do you need a good office helper? You have one? Do you want to hire someone new? You don't want to make a change? That's fine. Thanks.

The young man was about to walk out when the owner stopped him.

---

1. From the Simon & Garfunkel song, *El Condor Pasa* (*If I Could*) on the album: *Bridge over Troubled Waters*.

Owner: I couldn't help but eavesdrop. I apologize. But I'm sorry you didn't get the job.

Boy: Thanks. I have the job anyhow.

Owner: What do you mean?

Boy: That was my boss I was talking to. I was just checking up on myself.

The issue for a Jew should less be his or her profession, rather than how he or she relates to the job, how satisfied he or she feels with the work done and what others think, and how well he or she performs his or her duties. A person has to harmonize the job with personal goals as much as with professional ones. An individual's status in the work place must not become an obsession. As stressed in **Way #13 — Your Leisure Time**, one has to guard against a job ruling the individual. While all of us want to achieve excellence in our chosen profession, we must not let the pursuit of excellence overwhelm us, coloring all other aspects of our lives.

Now, is there a profession that a Jew should choose which would be considered uniquely Jewish? Not unless he or she aspires to be a Kabbalist, a soothsayer or a prophet. As for myself, being a rabbi, I succeeded in doing so. But even here, there may be some question. After all, I am a Reform rabbi living in Israel. Given the Orthodox monopoly in the country, my status as a "Jewish spiritual leader" is officially rejected. The Israeli army refused to make me a chaplain, instead training me to be in the artillery corps. Now, on the American scene, there is a perception among many non-Orthodox Jews that the only way to maintain a full Jewish lifestyle, or to acquire Jewish knowledge, is to seek a specifically Jewish occupation such as that of rabbi, Jewish educator or cantor. Contrary to this notion, one can be a knowledgeable and committed Jew without necessarily being a "professional" one.

So how should a Jew go about deciding what to do professionally? No doubt, interest is as important as capability. And as my parents always stressed: "It never hurt to make a buck." But the true test for a Jew is to find a job that provides satisfaction and somehow serves to help others or helps the world to be a better place, even if indirectly. For those of you who do have prophetic aspirations, no doubt you would support the words that God said to our fellow prophet Jeremiah: "And do you seek great things for yourself? Seek them not" (*Jeremiah* 45:5). Reality would have it that virtually every job provides the possibility to do good for others. It is merely a matter of attitude. Speaking of attitude, how many of us know people who actually cannot stand their work, who are stuck in an unbearable job? Such people cannot help but bring home with them their professional frustrations. It is an art to separate one's home from one's work-place. The easy and best way to protect ourselves against such an unwelcome intrusion is to try to achieve this important goal: "Everyone's trade must seem fine in his own eyes" (*Talmud Brachot* 43b).

One day, I asked one of the people who works with me: "What's your professional goal?" He responded: "I want to be Number Two, but get paid like Number One!" I suspect that the staff member made this comment because he could not imagine becoming a slave to his job. But sometimes being at the top of the ladder, one can shape the collective personality of the work place, turning it into a nurturing and caring environment, as opposed to a dispassionate corporate entity. The head "honcho" must always remember: "Noble is the worker who honors his workmen" (*Talmud Gittin* 67b).

Now I apologize if you expected this **Way** to give you direction in finding a "Jewish job." For those of you who are gainfully employed as a doctor, lawyer, social worker, stockbroker, computer programmer, teacher, police officer, electrician, statistician, mathematician or mortician, I hope that you were not disappointed that these jobs were not singled out as good professions for a Jew, which they surely may be. (Indeed, no specific position is cited in this

Way.) Some of you may have thought I would suggest becoming a philosopher, a theologian or a palm reader, recognizing the spiritual implications of such employment. Sorry again. It is true that many Jews seek training in those jobs that serve the public sector, be it in the area of medicine, community work or the teaching profession. But certainly Jews do not hold exclusive rights to these types of employment, although it would be interesting to conduct a survey to see whether there was any Jewish motivation that prompted a Jew to choose such a profession.

The twenty-sixth way to be Jewish is to guarantee that whatever our profession may be, we not only perform our job to the best of our ability, but we also safeguard the human side of our work. It matters little if you are "a sparrow or a snail," a bricklayer or a nuclear physicist, a manager or a laborer, the important thing is to maintain your decency, sensitivity, dignity. When the tenth commandment closes with the statement "do not covet anything that is your neighbor's," in addition to the inclusion of "your neighbor's house, your neighbor's wife, his male or female slave, his ox or his mule," it can be readily assumed that one should also "not covet a neighbor's job" (*Exodus* 20:14). After all, the famous biblical quote, "Man does not live by bread alone" (*Deuteronomy* 8:3), was not uttered in a vacuum. It is presented as a work ethic. Its message is simple and direct: a job is performed well when one has an appreciation for all that surrounds him or her, for what came before and what will come after (based on *Deuteronomy* 8:4-10).

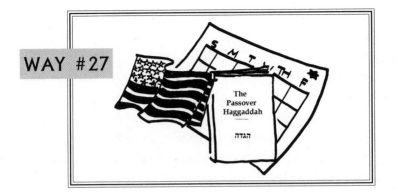

YOUR HOLIDAYS

or:

Living by a Jewish Calendar

Comedian Henny Youngman said: "I once was an atheist, but I gave it up — they have no holidays!"

In ideal terms, Judaism should be a twenty-four hour a day proposition. A Jew should live according to a Jewish calendar. Indeed there are many American Jews who do just that, but, for the most part, they belong to the Orthodox world. For the rest of us, we are fortunate that we can rely on Jewish holidays to set a Jewish rhythm to our lives.

Each Jewish holiday reflects a theme: historical, theological or agricultural. Further, attached to each of the holidays is a sub-theme that sets forth a social agenda. They are community-oriented, family-based, some particularly introspective, and each has its own unique customs. They provide a veritable crash course on Judaism. While they come but once a year, there is one holiday, the Sabbath, henceforth referred to as the Shabbat, which is celebrated every week, thus lending a unity throughout the year to all the holidays. The Shabbat will merit its own **Way (Way #28 — Your Sabbath)**.

So let's take a walking tour through the Jewish calendar. But first a warning: Do not expect to read of traditional approaches to the holidays. I am assuming that the basic elements of each holiday are familiar to the reader. While my comments will not necessarily be esoteric, they also may not be predictable.

Rosh HaShanah: Day of Sacrifice

It makes good sense that the Jewish year begins with Rosh HaShanah (literally translated as "the beginning of the year"), which has been referred to as the "birthday of the world." Apart from some of its quaint customs — wearing white to indicate starting the year in a pure manner, dipping apples in honey to begin the year on a sweet note, blowing the *shofar* (ram's horn) to awaken people out of their sleep "to consider their ways" (Maimonides) — the most startling aspect of Rosh HaShanah is the *Torah* readings chosen for the two days of the holiday.

The near sacrifice of Isaac (*Genesis* 22) sets forth the most dominant theme not only for the specific holiday, but also for the entire year. The backdrop for the dramatic account of Isaac almost being slain by his father is established in the preceding biblical chapter, read on the first day of Rosh HaShanah, which includes three stories: the birth of Isaac, the banishment of Ishmael (Abraham's son by his handmaiden, Hagar, who was also banished), and the peace treaty forged between Abraham and the Philistine leader, Avimelech (*Genesis* 21).

The story in brief is that Abraham is called upon to sacrifice his son to show his absolute faith in God. It is interesting to note that in the Orthodox tradition, one reads this passage every morning; a pretty heavy way to start off one's day. But the psychological force of this story is great. There is nothing more painful than the loss of a child. When one loses a parent, one loses the past. When one loses a child, one loses the future. Therefore, to sacrifice a child indeed would demonstrate a person's total belief in God. Since Rosh HaShanah sets the tone for the Jewish year, and since belief in God is central to the Jewish People, there is good sense in establishing the maximal parameters for one to express that belief, as extreme as they may seem.

But one should not fear, in the end, Abraham is stopped from offering up his son. His intent was sufficient to satisfy God. As uncomfortable as we may be with such a Divine command, the lesson for us is painfully direct. There will be times in our lives when we are called on to make choices, some minor and some major, when our dedication, loyalty and commitment will be tested. As we head into a new year, Rosh HaShanah forces us to ask ourselves what were the sacrifices we made in the past, and what are the ones we are willing to make, which leads into the next holiday: Yom Kippur.

Yom Kippur: Day of Introspection

Judaism is the only Western religion that institutes a full day of fasting and introspection. Aware that most people are simply too busy to take time out of their daily schedule to dedicate even a few minutes to meditation or self-examination, Judaism, already from biblical times, introduced Yom Kippur — a day of atonement.

If we had to think about the manner in which we conducted ourselves over the past twelve months in both our personal and professional lives, there is little doubt that we would find much to improve. There are simply too many acts we have carried out, or words we have uttered, which beg for forgiveness. One does not need a court of justice to determine the guilt we should feel for the people we have wronged by intent, neglect, misjudgment or miscalculation.

Yom Kippur gives real meaning to the role that guilt plays in our everyday life. As we plunge along during this day, we vacillate between self-flagellation and absolution. This dialectic, essential to Yom Kippur, is usually resolved by a synthesis of just the right amount of healthy and justified conscious guilt. Now, it may seem strange to hear of a Jewish approach to non-neurotic guilt, but as Stan Greenberg wrote in his book, *How to be a Jewish Mother*: "Let your child hear you sigh every day; if you don't know what he's done to make you suffer, he will."

This is the very essence of this day. We sit among the congregation, and are provided with people to look at, and who are looking at us, and sense: "Oh God, did I really put Stan down in order to build myself up?" "Dammit, why did I completely lose it with my kid over the bicycle thing?" If we allow ourselves to really get into it, we start to extrapolate and contemplate all aspects of our lives with a list of "shoulds and should nots:" "I should have given more time to my family; I shouldn't have been so consumed with my work; I should have been more patient; I shouldn't have procrastinated so damn much; I should have been more expressive about my love for my kids; I shouldn't have been so quick to draw conclusions," and so forth.

The dramatic tones of the day force us to deal with ourselves as we are told that the quality of our repentance will determine whether we are sealed in "the book of life" or "the book of death." While one obviously does not take such perorations literally, the imagery should be sufficiently powerful to prompt us to action, as we stand self-accused before the entire congregation. And that is the point: we do not direct our prayers to God to gain absolution, but we turn directly to those against whom we have committed indiscretions, and ask them for forgiveness. But this can only occur once we have pointed the finger at ourselves. Yom Kippur totally contradicts the Erich Segal view of the world as he boldly proclaimed it in his sappy novel, *Love Story*: "Love is never having to say your sorry," which became a mantra for many of us until we actually became serious about someone, falling truly "in love." Yom Kippur provides us with the opportunity to say: "We're sorry," which is a genuine declaration of love and respect for the person to whom we must express our sorrow because of the pain we may have caused him or her, "wittingly or unwittingly."[1]

So what is with this "fast" business, this bodily denial of a good corned beef sandwich, or rather in my household, of an avocado and alfalfa sprout salad? In the biblical account from the book of *Isaiah* that is read on the morning of Yom Kippur, we are cautioned: "Is this the fast I look for? A day of self-affliction? Bowing your head like a reed, and covering yourself with sackcloth and ashes? Is this what you call a fast, a day acceptable to the Lord? Rather, is this not the fast I look for: to unlock the shackles of injustice, to undo the fetters of bondage, to let the oppressed go free, and to break every cruel chain? Is it not to share your bread with the hungry, and to bring the homeless poor into your house? When you see the naked, to clothe them, and never to hide from your own kin? Then shall your light blaze forth like the dawn, and your wounds shall quickly heal; your righteousness will walk before you, the Presence of the Lord will be your rear guard. Then, when you call, the Lord will answer; when you cry, God will say: 'Here I am.' If you remove the chains of oppression, the menacing hand, the malicious word; if you make sacrifices for the hungry, and satisfy the needs of the afflicted; then shall your light shine in the darkness, and your night become bright as noon... (*Isaiah* 58:5-10).

---

1. The notion of doing something that would hurt someone, "wittingly or unwittingly," is part of the Yom Kippur liturgy.

Okay, try not to get stuck on words like sackcloth, shackles, fetters and kin. But if we want to feel guilty, just one quick read of the above passage should do the trick. The intent is obvious, allowing no time for self-indulgence. Since the majority of us have not met Isaiah's requirements, then it is obvious there is much room for self-improvement, not only in our individual family unit, but regarding our obligation to the general community. The purpose of the fast is not to serve as a substitute for "slim fast," but rather to force us to recognize the needs of others, and our need to help them.

Yom Kippur has it all: introspection, social action, forgiveness, and a promise of doing a better job the coming year. When my kid has an exam coming up, I tell her: "Review a little bit every day, so that when it's crunch time, you won't have to cram." It wouldn't hurt to absorb a little bit of Yom Kippur into our daily routine. It would make the actual day a little less overwhelming, and enrich our lives.

Sukkot, Simchat Torah and Shavuot: Honorable Mention

These three holidays get only honorable mention. This is not a reflection on the place of these holidays on the scale of Jewish importance. Indeed, Sukkot and Shavuot are considered two of the three pilgrimage festivals (Passover being the third), which should give them more significance than the more popular holidays of Chanukah and Purim. But since many of us seem to maintain the holidays "for the kids," these holidays may be less appealing than the quaint family customs that surround Chanukah and Purim.

Sukkot celebrates the completion of the harvest, just as Shavuot celebrates the gathering of the first fruits. Most significantly, Sukkot reminds Jews of the wanderings of their ancestors in the wilderness before entering the Promised Land, and Shavuot, which takes place seven weeks after Passover, commemorates the giving of the *Torah* at Mount Sinai. As a physical reminder of the Jews as "wanderers," on Sukkot a Jew is commanded to live in a booth (a *succah*) for seven days. (It should be noted that most Jewish holidays require some observance or statement that recalls the historical relevance of the holiday.)

Simchat Torah, which brings Sukkot to its formal end is like Shavuot, a festival on which we rejoice in the reading of the *Torah*. It is at this time that the yearly cycle of reading from the *Five Books of Moses* is concluded and begun anew. The day features singing and dancing with the Scrolls of the Law.

Because of the intensity of Rosh HaShanah and Yom Kippur, and the timing of Shavuot (often at the very beginning of the summer), the three holidays headlined here do not receive their rightful measure on the Jewish celebratory scale. Also, the agricultural attachments to Sukkot and Shavuot do not speak to a basically urban community. Yet, one would think that some of the elements of the holidays would be attractive, particularly the building of a *succah* and the expressions of ecstasy that surround Simchat Torah. Regarding Sukkot, we may feel a bit inhibited because the *succah* is built outside, and the wild frenzy of excitement that embraces Simchat Torah is heard outside. Other Jewish holidays seem to be more private, which is in keeping with the "American Way," whereby one's religious beliefs and practices are confined to one's private domain.

Chanukah: Light One Candle for the Maccabee Children[1]

Is this the Jewish substitute for Christmas? Not in my household.

---

1. Song from Peter, Paul & Mary's album, *No Easy Walk to Freedom*.

But that is because I live in Israel, and Christmas, let alone Christianity, does not get much of a play in the Jewish state. In fact, the first time my children encountered Jesus Christ was when I stubbed my toe!

Virtually every Jew knows the story of the miracle of the cruse of oil burning for eight days. After the Maccabees prevailed against the Greco-Syrian pagans, they found in the Holy Temple only one undefiled flask of oil with the seal of the high priest. The vial contained enough oil for only one day's lighting of the Temple's *menorah*. But miraculously, its oil lasted for eight days. The following year, the Maccabees designated these eight days for giving thanks to the Lord (*Talmud Shabbat* 21b). The Chanukah lights have come to symbolize the Jewish belief in the gradual progress of spiritual enlightenment. Starting with one light the first evening and increasing the number of lights by one each night, the Jewish People mark the slow but steady victory over violent storms, which have raged against them throughout the centuries.

While Chanukah is considered a minor holiday in the Jewish calendar, it has gained major importance in order to compete with the enticements of Christmas. The lesson to be culled from the Hasmonean[1] revolt is that Jews must always strive to overcome any attempts to delegitimize Judaism. The Hellenism that the Maccabees fought against had a devastating effect upon the moral life of Judea.[2] Observance of all religious precepts was prohibited. Copies of the *Torah* were destroyed, the Temple itself was converted to the worship of Zeus, harlots were brought within its sacred precincts and heathen altars set up in villages and towns. With such a list of outrageous violations against the precious ethical center of

---

1. Name of the priestly family, popularly know as the Maccabees, who organized the revolts against the Syrian-Greeks, leading to the cleansing and rededication of the Temple.
2. Reference to the name used for the south-central region of ancient Palestine, in which are found the Judean Hills and Judean Desert.

Judaism's faith-heritage, it is little wonder that the Maccabees went on a rampage to restore Judaism's dignity and integrity.

The Maccabees should serve as a shining example of people dedicated to fighting all who would threaten the very fabric of Jewish belief and practice. But as the tradition points out, the ultimate destruction of the Second Jewish Commonwealth was also prompted by internal conflicts as much as by external ones. And such is the reality today. We do not destroy our *Torah*, we just ignore it. We do not pray to Greek Gods, we just run after false ones (see **Way #17 — Your Money**).

The grammatical root of the word Chanukah means: "to educate." As we join in the wonderful family fare of lighting the *menorah*, singing songs of determination and victory, exchanging gifts (a real example of religious syncretism — the borrowing of a non-Jewish custom practiced by the majority culture and making it part of one's own tradition), and eating greasy potato pancakes and jelly doughnuts, we have to rededicate (another meaning of the word Chanukah) our efforts to upgrading our Jewish education (see **Way #29 — Your Jewish Education**), not letting it lapse into a state of disrepair. We cannot afford to finish the work of the Greeks by letting foreign elements overwhelm Jewish life because of our lack of interest and will. The heroism of the Maccabees cannot fall prey to indifference.

> Light one candle for the Maccabee children:
> give thanks their light didn't die.
> Light one candle for the Maccabee children:
> for the pain they endured
> when their right to exist was denied...
> Light one candle for the strength that we need
> to never become our own foe...

What is the memory that's valued so highly
that we keep it alive in that flame?
What's the commitment to those who have died
when we cry out: "They've not died in vain?"
We have come this far always believing
that justice will somehow prevail.
This is the burden and this is the promise,
and this is why we will not fail.

Don't let the light go out, it's lasted for so many years.
Don't let the light go out, let it shine through our love and our tears.

Purim: "Hey-Man," What's Going Down? (Or is it: Who's Going Down?)

Purim is a big favorite in the canon of Jewish holidays. It is the Jewish alternative to Halloween with a social-historical message. Instead of sticking razor blades in candy apples to ward off "tricking or treating" annoying goblins and witches, Jews don the costumes of queens and pirates, and celebrate the slitting of Haman's and his family's throats (via hanging) for their attempts to destroy the Jewish People. Even more so, we rejoice in glee at this prospect as we whistle and hoot, and twirl around that unbearable anti-Excedrin noisemaker — the grogger.

Got a problem with this holiday? You bet. Oh, it's a great day for kids, as they can legitimately act out their violent fantasies, all the while pretending that they are someone else. You guessed it. We should have a genuine difficulty with the story of Purim. While there is legitimacy in the satisfaction that we Jews were saved from Haman's wicked rule, the manner in which we express our feelings of relief seems almost schizophrenic: simultaneously there is exuberant joy and sinister hatred.

The joy is born out of the ultimate defeat of the enemy of the

Jewish People. But too easily that joy is turned into a vengeance that is embarrassing at best, mean-spirited at worst. The idea that at Purim we Jews rejoice with such fervor at the expense of someone else's misery may be natural enough, but it exposes a human frailty for which Jews were dramatically chastised at the moment of the greatest single event in Jewish history — the exodus from Egypt. After a narrow escape from Egyptian bondage, the Israelites, once safely ensconced on the other side of the Red Sea, danced with joy as they watched their Egyptian enemies drown. Tradition tells us that we were harshly admonished: "Are these people not part of My Creation? Are you to rejoice at the suffering of others" (*Talmud Sanhedrin* 39b)?

One of the signs of insecurity is the attempt to build oneself up on the back of someone else. Such an attitude ultimately fails to increase one's own self-worth, instead reinforcing delusions of self-importance. We Jews, who have been so downtrodden over the centuries, surely should recognize the inherent ill-will in such erratic forms of behavior.

I am not suggesting that the fun be taken out of Purim, or to strip kids of a chance to wear some creative costume. But we must be careful of the message that we transmit to our children as we send them into fits of ecstasy when they read of the public hangings of Haman, et. al. Indeed, the behavior we display on Purim contradicts the behavior patterns of other holidays on which we also commemorate the victory of the weak over the strong. Commemorating the defeat of the Greeks at Chanukah or the mortal blow encountered by the Egyptians at Passover is not accompanied by a parallel sense of excitement at their respective suffering. During the Passover *Seder*, ten drops of wine are taken from the wine cup, thus expressing our sense of remorse that the ten plagues had to be inflicted upon the Egyptians in order to secure our ultimate freedom.

It could very well be that one of the reasons we are commanded to get so drunk on Purim that we cannot distinguish between the two antagonists of the story, Mordecai (the good guy) and Haman (the bad guy), is because, as sober individuals, we would be truly ashamed that we take delight in capital punishment. Indeed, we are forewarned: "A drunkard praying is like an idolater" (*Talmud Brachot* 31b). How ironic. According to the tradition: "Of any sin spoken of in the *Torah*, if a man is told to commit it, and does, he will not die; save idolatry, incest and bloodshed" (*Talmud Sanhedrin* 74a). In short, to get drunk, pray and rejoice at the shedding of blood (even of one's enemy), is idolatrous and therefore worthy of death. So while in a drunken stupor, rejoicing at the death of one's enemy, one is really hastening one's own end. (This notion certainly has relevance for Israel.)

Perhaps it is for the above reason that the name of God is excluded from the Purim story. God must have felt uncomfortable with the brutal public hangings that took place. The fact that the hangings took place in front of such an enthusiastic crowd in all likelihood forced God to withdraw Divine sanction for such a blatant act of revenge. God seemed not to want any part of such a cynical charade. God prefers holidays where the positive is emphasized, not holidays that are clouded with double messages and neurotic aberrations.

I am sorry if I am putting a damper on the holiday for many of you who so enjoy the merriment that Purim represents. But as I said in the Introduction, this primer, while sometimes light-hearted, is also heavy-handed. The good news is that we non-Orthodox Jews are critical, and sometimes can possess a better grasp of a particular holiday than our Orthodox counterparts, who are wedded to traditions that should long ago have been discarded.

So, instead of derisively hissing at every mention of Haman's name, just say: "Hey Man," let's down a few bloody Marys for the Jewish People.

Passover: We Shall Overcome[1]

We shall overcome, we shall overcome.
we shall overcome someday.
Oh deep in my heart,
I do believe
that we shall overcome someday.

Passover struck a sympathetic chord with me as a youngster because it seemed so terribly relevant — and relevance was "my thing" when I was in my twenties. Indeed, in 1966, when I was interviewed for possible acceptance into the University of Chicago's School of Divinity, I was told by the dean of admissions: "You would fit in here. You look relevant." It was strange that my dismal academic performance in undergraduate school seemed intellectually irrelevant (and apparently unimportant) to my fitness for theological school, compared to the compelling physical relevance of my goatee, long hair and granny glasses.

And so Passover was an appealing holiday, not only because our extended family got together and we ate great food (although by the time we got to the main course, everyone in my household was stuffed with chicken soup and kneidelach,[2] gefilte fish and all manner of Passover treats, unique to the holiday, some that were so hot, like horseradish and that nut dish,[3] which sent steam streaming forth from my navel), but primarily because the theme of Passover was relevant to the social revolution taking place in my America of the early Sixties. Just as we Jews were slaves in Egypt, so too were African-Americans slaves in the United States. We Jews

---

1. That great civil rights song, written by Horton, Hamilton, Carawan and Seeger.
2. A dumpling, made essentially of egg and finely-ground Matzah.
3. Officially referred to as charoset, which is a combination of nuts, apples and cinnamon, which is supposed to symbolize the mortar that was used by the Israelites to build the pyramids while they were slaves in Egypt. Charoset is essentially sweet and is combined with horseradish to remind us that the sweetness of freedom was tasted only after the bitterness of slavery.

had a special mission. Our tradition held that we must become active in the struggle for Black liberation because we were reminded over and over again: "Remember you were strangers (slaves) in Egypt" (*Exodus* 23:9).

The Passover *Haggaddah* recounts the dramatic story of our escape from slavery to freedom. At the outset of the *Seder* one recites: "Let all those who are hungry, enter and eat; and all who are in want, come and celebrate." And then a Jew begins his and her retelling of the story as if it were taking place in the present: "In every generation a person is obligated to regard him- or herself as if he or she personally went out of Egypt." With this sort of up-to-date admonition, how could a Jew in the turbulent Sixties of America not be prompted to act? What a great charge Passover gave to those of us who grew up then.

The message of Passover is still relevant in this new millennium. It has a universal thrust that spans the centuries. Most important of all, because the reading of the *Haggaddah* encourages a round-table discussion, and uses physical symbols to reinforce the theme of liberation, Passover has the possibility of uniting the generations around the important social message of equality and justice.

Oh freedom. Oh freedom. Oh freedom, over me.
And before I'd be a slave, I'd be buried in my grave;
And go home to my Lord and be free.[1]

We are only free when all people are free. "Proclaim freedom throughout the land unto all the inhabitants thereof" (*Leviticus* 25:10). I love Passover. It speaks to me. It makes my religion relevant — yesterday, today and tomorrow.

❖ ❖ ❖

---

1. Traditional civil rights song, sung by Pete Seeger (*We Shall Overcome* album — Carnegie Hall Concert, June 8, 1963) and Joan Baez (*Recently* album).

There are other holidays in the Jewish calendar, such as Tu' B'Shevat (15th of the month of Shevat), known as the Jewish Arbor Day, when it is customary to plant tree saplings in Israel, or Tisha B'Av (9th of the month of Av) a national day of mourning for the destruction of the Second Temple. The greeting for that day is: "Good grief!" And there is Holocaust Memorial Day, Israeli Independence Day, which is preceded by Israel's Memorial Day for Fallen Soldiers. These last three holidays (memorial days are better described as commemorations than holidays) obviously relate to the Jewish state, but it has become customary for Jews around the world to acknowledge these days as well. What is interesting for Americans to note is the juxtaposition of Israel's Memorial Day to Independence Day. (They are not separated by months as are the United States Memorial Day and Independence Day, which for many Americans represent holiday sales more than anything else.) The linking of the two days in the calendar lends a personal and national force to both days. At the close of Memorial Day, we make the transition to celebrating Israel's independence that was made possible by those we memorialized the day before, who gave their lives to guarantee our freedom.

And this is the basic message of all the Jewish holidays as they guide us through the Jewish year: to register our faith and willingness to make sacrifices, to do some serious soul-searching and cleansing, not to hand a victory to the enemies of the Jewish people by letting our Jewishness fall into disuse, to celebrate our triumphs rather than rejoice in our enemies' demise, and finally and most importantly, to guarantee that our freedom will be translated into helping others gain theirs. **The twenty-seventh way to be Jewish is to observe the holidays, thus enabling us to sense the value of living by a Jewish calendar, wherein every month provides us with a theme of social, theological, historical and moral worth.**

YOUR SABBATH
(Henceforth, Your Shabbat)
or:
"Mellow Out"

A thought has blown the market place away.
There is a song in the wind and joy in the trees.
The Sabbath arrives in the world, scattering a song in the silence of the night.
Eternity utters a day.
Where are the words that could compete with such might?

Six days a week we live under the tyranny of space.
On the Sabbath we try to become attuned to the holiness of time.
Six days a week we wrestle with the world.
On the Sabbath we especially care for the seed of eternity planted in the soul.
Six days a week we seek to dominate the world.

On the Sabbath, we try to dominate the self.

To set apart a day in the week;
A day for being with ourselves;
A day on which we stop worshipping the idols of technical civilization;
Is there any institution that holds greater hope for human progress than the
Sabbath?[1]

The idea of setting apart one day a week for rest was a brilliant one on God's part. Of course, God seemed a little stingy with Him/Herself in allowing only one day to kick off His/Her Divine shoes and "chill out," considering the effort that must have gone into creating the world in only six days. But what is significant here is the gradual build-up to this "day of rest," the literal translation of the Hebrew word Shabbat. "With the Sabbath comes a world of rest and repose" (*Tosefta, Sanhedrin*).[2]

The moral of the Creation narrative is that one's weekday has to be sufficiently filled with meaning and activity so as to warrant genuine rest. Now, none of us should have the expectation that our work week will ever be as productive as God's. But the notion of "going-up," of not remaining on a lateral course (see **Way #38 — Your Prayers** and **Way #43 — Your Dreams**), is essential to the understanding of the relationship between weekdays and the Shabbat.

This is outlined in the blessing that a Jew is supposed to recite after every meal. During the weekday, as an introduction to the formal prayer, we say: "By the waters of Babylon, there we sat, and there we wept as we remembered Zion" (contrary to popular belief, these words appear in *Psalm* 137:1, and were not written by Don McLean). As a prelude to the same prayer, on Shabbat we say: "A song of ascent: when the Lord facilitated our return to Zion, it was

---

1. From Abraham Joshua Heschel's book *The Sabbath*.
2. Supplementary Commentary (11th & 12th centuries) on the *Mishnah, Tractate Sanhedrin* that deals with court law.

like a dream. Then were our mouths filled with laughter and our tongues with singing. Those among the nations declared: 'The Lord has done great things...'" (*Psalm* 126:1-2). The Jews did not return from Babylon to their ancestral homeland by sitting around and twiddling their thumbs; they merited their return because they proved themselves worthy of reentry.

After a full and exhausting, and hopefully positive, week, it is crucial to take time out to rest. But, the Shabbat was not institutionalized only to acknowledge the need for some rest and relaxation; the parameters on how to safeguard this day of rest and make it meaningful were also determined by the tradition. As one of the Ten Commandments instructs us: "Remember the Shabbat, and keep it holy" (*Exodus* 20:8). This is where the ritual and the moral commandments intersect, as outlined in **Way #22 — Your Ritual Commandments** and **Way #23 — Your Moral Commandments**. There needs to be present at least a minimal amount of ritual incentives in order to maintain the sanctity (holiness) of the Shabbat, which speaks of peace and tranquility, the moral imperatives necessary to establish a close-knit family unit. We have to make certain that the ritual commandments serve the more spiritual elements of the Shabbat. Otherwise, the Shabbat can turn into an extension of our work week, used only to "mellow out," so much so that eventually we will turn to yellow, then to green and then to waste.

Because American Jews are fortunate in having a two-day weekend, there should be no temptation to spend the Shabbat sleeping late and then watching a football game on TV, because of Sunday — unless, of course, one prefers college football (a Saturday phenomenon) to professional football (a Sunday treat). But to guarantee that the Shabbat does take on a special quality, we are provided with some guidelines, many of which foster family unity and warmth. (I will not include attending services, as that was discussed in **Way #12 — Your Synagogue**.)

There are the rituals that surround the Friday evening dinner: candle lighting (reminding us of the first light of creation), the *kiddush*, which means "sanctification" in Hebrew (the blessing over the wine that reminds us of the sweetness of the day), and the breaking of the bread, sweet *challah*, which is a braided loaf that symbolizes the interconnection between the weekday and the Shabbat. (There is the tradition to sprinkle some salt on the *challah* to further emphasize the contrast between working in the "salt mines" during the week and basking in the sun on Shabbat.) Depending how many customs you would want to observe, you can sing Shabbat songs, study a little bit of *Torah* by discussing the weekly biblical portion, bless your children (as demonstrated in **Way #22 — Your Ritual Commandments**), hold off on phone calls during the meal, and then all watch a video together while your teenage kid runs off somewhere.

One should never plan to diet on Shabbat. The Friday evening meal is followed by another rather substantial family lunch on Saturday, which in turn is followed by a *se'udat shlishit*, a "third meal," albeit a light one. The Shabbat ends with *Havdalah* (separation), which provides a ritual transition from the Shabbat back to the weekday, from the "holy" back to the "profane." *Havdalah* has symbols parallel to those of the Friday night meal: of light (a braided candle), wine and spices (a substitute for the sweet *challah*). At the end of *Havdalah*, the light is extinguished in the wine, and a song of redemption is sung in the dark — not Bob Marley's Reggae hit *Redemption Song*, but the messianic redemption song of Elijah, the prophet. (Although to me, personally, *Redemption Song*, along with Marley's other hit, *Exodus*, may be more compelling.) *Havdalah* brings to a close our Shabbat rest with family (often ignored during the week), which supplies us with the creative energy to start the weekday building process once again. "The Sabbath is a day of rest, of mental scrutiny and of balance. Without it, the workdays are insipid" (Bialik: see **Way #25 — Your**

Internet, footnote 5). But if we build our weekday with an upward flow, then: "The Sabbath will have a flavor of Paradise to it" (*Talmud Brachot* 57b). **The twenty-eighth way to be Jewish is to celebrate the Shabbat, because it is a mini-expression of the cycle of our lives, observed in a quiet family setting, a hint of life everlasting in a world full of "rest and repose."**

YOUR JEWISH EDUCATION

or:

"Study Leads to Action"[1]

> When I think back
> on all the crap I learned in high school,
> it's a wonder I can learn at all.
> And though my lack of education hasn't hurt me none,
> I can see the writing on the wall.[2]

That about sums up the state of affairs of our Jewish education. After all, we live in a computerized age of technology, of virtual reality. And that is what we possess: Virtual education. Certainly, in Jewish terms, we learned virtually nothing, and so we know

---

1. *Talmud Kiddushin* 40b.
2. From Paul Simon's song *Kodachrome*, found on the album: *Simon & Garfunkel — The Concert in the Park*.

virtually nothing, and as a result, we do virtually nothing. That's it. We have become virtual Jews!

Let's examine this thesis. Most of us went to Sunday School, which meant that we were enrolled in some sort of Jewish educational system for approximately four to six hours a week. We were off during the summer months, as well as during all vacations — Jewish and secular. We probably averaged about thirty-six weeks a year, which, multiplied by four hours a week, equals one hundred and forty-four hours a year. If we multiply that number by the ten years that we were enrolled in this highly "intensive" system, we wind up with a grand total of one thousand, four hundred and forty-four hours of Jewish learning, which amounts to that virtually proverbial nothing.

Now, let's add our Hebrew training, which is included only partially in the hours of Jewish learning mentioned in the previous paragraph. We don't begin grappling with the Jewish language until third grade, and finish with it at our Bar or Bat Mitzvah. And, how many of us remember what our *Torah* portion was, let alone are still capable of chanting or reading it?

In short, Bar or Bat Mitzvah ends our Hebrew learning, and Confirmation (a borrowed American Christian term that refers to a religious ceremony in the ninth or tenth grade) ends our formal Jewish learning. While the cognitive side of our Jewish education is terribly weak, the psychological side is extremely strong. It is drummed into our psyche that Jewish education is of secondary or tertiary importance in our life. We are taught at the earliest stages of our intellectual and social development that Jewish education is placed on a shelf, dusted off once or twice a week for a few paltry hours, and then placed back on the shelf. We are taught that, to nurture any sort of Jewish knowledge, we need to invest a minimum amount of time.

As Jews we know: "Excellent is the study of *Torah* together with worldly pursuits" (*Sayings of the Fathers* 2:2). But, we have split the two, having given priority to "worldly pursuits" at the expense of the "study of *Torah.*" We are willing to "schlep" (drag) our kids for tennis, piano and math lessons half way across the world, but "kvetch" (complain) about battling traffic to bring our children to religious school on a Wednesday afternoon. We invest time, energy and emotion in improving our intellectual prowess in our secular lives. But we do not approximate a concomitant investment in and commitment to our Jewish lives.

One does not become knowledgeable in any discipline overnight. We can't just snap our fingers and expect wisdom to arrive at our doorstep. "The beginning of wisdom is this — get wisdom" (*Proverbs* 4:7). If we want to be secure in our Judaism, then we have to know something Jewishly. We don't want to sit at the *Seder* table on Passover and always be chosen as either the "simple son" or the "son who doesn't know what to ask."[1]

We Jews have always had a great thirst for learning. When ghettoized, Jews stressed Jewish education. When we were finally freed of ghetto life, we expanded our "parochial" Jewish learning and pursued general knowledge. We combined Jewish learning and worldly pursuits. The classic paradigmatic example of the successful synthesis of these two worlds was Maimonides — the physician and Jewish scholar. We need not aspire to the heights of Maimonides to achieve such a fusion. We just have to acknowledge the need for a balance between our Jewish learning and secular learning. I would settle even for a seventy-five to twenty-five percent ratio in favor of the secular world.

Like with any endeavor in life, the ultimate way to appreciate what Judaism has to offer is to know something about it. The first way to acquire knowledge is by reading (see **Way #14 — Your**

---

1. In the Passover *Haggadah*, there is a part that talks about four sons: 1) the wise son, 2) the wicked son, 3) the simple son, and 4) the son who does not know how to ask. Tradition holds that they are placed in a descending order of intelligence.

Book Shelf). At the end of this **Way**, you will find a list of primary and secondary source books (not included in **Way #14**) that will aid you considerably in gaining insight into the theology and practices of Judaism.

A second way to increase your Jewish education is by enrolling in a course, either at your local synagogue or at your nearby Jewish community center. Every Jewish community offers lectures on some subject of Jewish interest, not to mention the number of Ulpan (Hebrew) classed conducted. As pointed out in **Way #25 — Your Internet** and in **Way #21 — Your Israel Quotient**, both can help you become more educated, although obviously not in equal measure. And, of course, enrolling a child in a Jewish Day School should be considered, as well as participating in an educational trip to Israel be mandatory.

There is no excuse to reject something because of lack of knowledge. Such an approach to life is not only anti-intellectual but also anti-social. An educated individual has a better chance of interacting with others and influencing those around him or her. "If a person applies his learning correctly, it becomes an elixir to him. If not, then he becomes a hopeless bore" (*Talmud Yoma* 72b). Judaism teaches us about parenting, about work ethics, about aging, about social activism — about all aspects of our lives, which have been partially discussed in previous **Ways** and will be further explored in upcoming **Ways**. Jewish education should be considered the foundation of our lives. **We owe it to ourselves to make Jewish education the twenty-ninth way to be Jewish.**

❖ ❖ ❖

Selected Bibliography: *A Guide to Jewish Religious Practice* (Klein), *Art Scroll Series on the Bible and Holidays* (Art Scroll), *A Torah Commentary* (Plaut), *Back to the Sources* (Holtz), *Code of Jewish Law* (Ganzfried and Goldin), *Comprehensive Jewish Calendar* (Spier), *How* to Run a Traditional Jewish Household (Greenberg), Jewish Literacy (Telushkin), Jewish Liturgy (Idelsohn), Jewish Wisdom (Telushkin), Meditations on the Siddur (Jacobson), Nine Questions People Ask about Judaism (Telushkin), Oxford Annotated Bible (Oxford Press), Popular Halacha (Berman), Marital Relations, Birth Control and Abortion in Jewish Law (Feldman), Reform Responsa Series (Freehof and/or Jacobs), The Book of Jewish Why (Kolatch), The Essential Talmud (Steinsaltz), The Lehmann Haggadah (Lehmann), The Lifetime of a Jew (Strauss), The Mitzvot (Chill), The Torah Anthology (Me'am Lo'ez), The World of Talmud (Adler), Thirteen Principles (Fendel), To Be A Jew (Donin), Understanding the Old Testament (Anderson), The World of Prayer (Munk) and the series of Holiday Anthologies (Goodman).

YOUR GAY AND LESBIAN FRIENDS

or:

"Not that there's Anything Wrong with That!"[1]

This **Way** is not necessarily applicable to the person who is either a homosexual or a lesbian. Indeed, all the **Ways** in this book are relevant to the gay community. Rather, this **Way** is directed primarily at the heterosexual Jew, who may have a difficult time relating to the gay world, not only because of the draconian attitude of the Jewish tradition toward homosexuality, but also as a result of a social discomfort he or she might feel

---

1. A famous line from the *Jerry Seinfeld Show*. A college reporter from New York University suspects that Jerry and his friend George Costanza are gay, and in their denial, they repeatedly say: "We're not gay. Not that there is anything wrong with that!"

because of the perceived norms of society in its dealing with gays and lesbians.

I once attended an interfaith colloquium whose theme dealt with homosexuality, which saw a heated discussion take place on the efficacy of gays and lesbians serving as religious leaders. Being a rabbi, I was called upon to articulate a Jewish approach to the whole matter. Unfortunately, as I stood before the crowd, I found myself at a loss for words, unable to display in a positive light the sanctions in the Jewish tradition against homosexuality. I was simply incapable of uttering the word that the *Torah* ascribes to the act of homosexuality, "abomination" (*Leviticus* 18:22), or mention the resultant punishment that anyone who commits a homosexual act must face: "Whoever shall do any of these abominations, even the souls that do them, will be cut off from their people" (*Leviticus* 18:29). I refused to let my mind even consider the notion of "stoning" someone to death for what were considered aberrations of "normative sexual behavior."

Growing up in a rather protective environment, I knew little about homosexuality. I knew it was "manly" to tease anyone who was the slightest bit effeminate, that police routinely beat homosexuals, that homosexuals were stereotyped in films as incompetents, and that they were the subject of ribald jokes by comedians. It was not until I entered undergraduate school that I began to think differently.

Just prior to the close of the second semester of my sophomore year in college, I discovered that my roommate was a homosexual. He had been acting forlorn and depressed for a few weeks. At that point, he revealed to me that he was gay. Thankfully, I was in such shock that I did not react like others in my dormitory did — with revulsion, scorn, pity and fear. As he disclosed the pain that he had endured in leading a double life, I realized that his pain was not brought on by himself, but by me. Not that I had said anything so terrible prior to his "coming out," but I was certain that over the two years that we shared the same room, I was a party to disparaging remarks about homosexuals.

Recognizing that it mattered little whether I thought homosexuality was a biological phenomenon or psychological disorder — the two points of view (albeit simplistic ones) that dominated the philosophical debate at the time– I knew that the word "abomination" was totally inappropriate for my roommate. Two years later he committed suicide. (One-third of all youth suicides are committed by gay teens.)

No matter how liberal some of us may consider ourselves, we have yet to extend our liberalism sufficiently so that the gay community may feel comfortable in our "straight" world. For Jews, our halachic (legal, referring to Jewish law) restrictions are so extreme on the matter of homosexuality that the gay individual is virtually confined to a sub-human status. Combined with our stress on family, perpetuation of the Jewish People, and our general chauvinism (like that of other peoples), it is little wonder that homosexuals and lesbians find a need to establish their own communities, and for certain their own congregations with their own rabbinical leadership.

For a Jewish homosexual or lesbian to assert his or her Jewishness in a Jewish world that is either halachically hostile or socially demeaning is praiseworthy. Such perseverance deserves inspired leadership. Despite some positive changes in attitudes on the part of the non-Orthodox religious community, basically the religious "establishment" has been inadequate to meet the challenge. So the gay community seeks out one of its own to provide it with the spiritual and religious guidance it needs — because so many of us have contributed to the stigmatization of this particular segment of the Jewish world, declaring it illegitimate.

Orthodoxy's claim that it hates homosexuality, but not the homosexual, is pure and simple nonsense. This sort of warped logic stands in sharp contrast to a legal Jewish system that has always been based on syllogistic reasoning in reaching halachic decisions. Everyone is created in the "image of God." As noted in **Way #18 — Your Social Activism:** "God formed Adam from the dust from all over the world — yellow clay and white sand, black loam and red soil. Therefore the earth can declare to no race or color of man/woman that you do not belong here, that this soil is not your home" (Yalkut Shimoni 1:3).[1] By the simple talmudic formula, *kal v'chomer* (how much the more so), this explanation would apply to gays and lesbians.

There should be no need for separate congregations for gays and lesbians. For a Jew, the universal application of the Divine statement that "all people are created in God's image" must supersede all particular sociological applications, which have been and are prejudicially practiced by us mortals. Therefore, **the thirtieth way to be Jewish is by accepting Jewish gays and lesbians as equal partners within Judaism.** Because they have been so discriminated against, it is essential that we "straight" Jews go out of our way to fulfill the *Mitzvah* of "opening our house and hearts" to them: "Hospitality matters more than greeting the Divine Presence" (*Talmud Shabbat* 127a). Why is this the case? In making everyone welcome, we are acknowledging the Divine Presence in all human beings.

---

1. See **Way #18 — Your Activism**, footnote 2.

WAY #31

YOUR PERSONALITY

or:

Walk, Talk, Smile, Charm, Love[1]

"There are four kinds of character: Easy to provoke and easy to soothe — he loses, not gains; hard to provoke and hard to soothe — he gains, not loses; hard to provoke and easy to soothe — the saintly person; and easy to provoke and hard to soothe — the wicked one" (*Sayings of the Fathers* 5:14). One's general temperament determines a person's personality. Our sources clearly indicate that a calm disposition is "pleasant like a honeycomb, sweet to the soul and healthy for the body" (*Proverbs* 16:24). The message is clear: We Jews need to develop a George Carlin personality of: "Que pasa" (what's happenin').[2]

---

1. From Lloyd Price's Fifties' song, *You've Got Personality.*
2. A Sixties' comedian, who became famous for his routine as "your hippie-dippie weatherman."

We need to be individually "laid back," even as we collectively "chill."

Indeed, should a Jew look back upon his or her history, he or she would discover that the Chinese curse, "may you live in interesting times," is most applicable. In order to survive the tumultuous throes of our long journey from Abraham until the present, we always needed to stay cool. And if one looks to the dominant personalities in Jewish history, while some may have been pushovers (Abraham), some conniving (Jacob), some daring (Moses), some hot-tempered (David), all still possessed a tranquility of spirit that helped guide them through their lives.

Is there any one type of personality to which a Jew should aspire? For certain, the anti-Semites in the world have ascribed specific personality traits to us: stingy, crafty and underhanded. Philo-Semites refer to us as brainy, ambitious and clever. I am certain that some Jews do indeed possess some of these characteristics, but in no way do these appellations define a collective "Jewish" personality. Yet those who would stereotype us, in all likelihood display all those negative attributes aforementioned.

The first place to look for a hint of what should make up our personality is the Bible and the *Prayerbook*, because in both these works of literature we can see Divine attributes. God is wise, compassionate, merciful, long-suffering, slow to anger, forgiving, loving and just. (Negative attributes of God are only exercised in reaction to negative behavior patterns on our part.) Now if these personality traits are good enough for God, then they should be good enough for us.

My parents told me that I was quite shy as a young child. Then, almost overnight, like *Leo the Late Bloomer* (children's book by Robert Kraus), according to my parents: "I came out of the toothpaste tube." When later I remarked that the expression was "coming out of one's shell," they replied: "Once out of the tube, you were such an obnoxious little kid, sadly there was no way we could get you back in! Had it been a shell, sticking you back in it would have been easy — and a delight." I guess shyness is a preferable personality trait to obnoxiousness.

> Cause you've got personality:
> Walk — personality;
> Talk — personality;
> Smile — Personality;
> Charm — Personality;
> Love — Personality,
> Plus you've got a great big heart.

Lloyd Price was right on. Every part of our being reflects who we are: the way we walk, what we say, when we smile and how we love: "When you are sitting in your house and when you walk on the street; when you go to sleep and when you wake up" (*Deuteronomy* 6:7 — part of the *Shema*). There is not a moment in the day that our personality is not exposed.

So, let's see what constitutes a "good personality." There is no end to the emotions that one could choose from to draw the perfect personality. I have chosen to look at those personality traits that have some basis in Jewish sources. Here are but a few. And emulating Maimonides' theory of negative theology, let's move from the negative to the positive (see **Way #9 — Your Car**). Let's find out what our personality should be by deciding first what it should not be, keeping in mind: "The Lord created two desires, one for good (*yeitzar hatov*) and one for evil (*yeitzar hara*)" — (*Talmud Brachot* 61a).[1]

Anger: The Jewish tradition is filled with sources that tell us anger is not an emotion that should dominate one's personality. While modern day psychology indicates that at times it is not good to hold our anger in, our sources say: "The angry individual is no better than the worshipper of idols" (Maimonides, *Dayot* 2). How

---

1. See **Way #19 — Your Sports** and **Way #15 — Your God**.

about these statements: "Be not quick to anger, for anger lodges in the bosom of fools" (*Ecclesiastes* 7:9), "Do not be angry and you will not sin" (*Talmud Berachot* 29b), "If a clever man is angry, his wisdom leaves him" (*Talmud Pesachim* 56b), and "Anger is an angel of destruction" (*Jerusalem Talmud, Ta'anit* 2:1)? Anger does not cut it for a Jew, which is quite surprising because, given the way the world has treated us over the years, we have much to be angry about. It is clearly understood that we must not adopt the personality of those who haunt our worst nightmares, lest we become like them: "All the devils of hell rule an angry man" (*Talmud Nedarim* 22a).

Jealousy: All of us suffer from some form of jealousy. Because jealousy is often such a prominent element in one's personality, we see concern for this trait expressed in the Ten Commandments (previously mentioned in **Way #26 — Your Profession**): "You shall not covet your neighbor's house, you shall not covet your neighbor's wife, nor his man-servant, nor his maid-servant, nor his ox, nor his mule, or anything that is your neighbor's" (*Exodus* 20:14). Like the emotional expression of anger, this tenth commandment is supported by a lengthy list of devastating Jewish sources. "Jealousy rots the bones" (*Proverbs* 14:30), "Jealousy is as cruel as the grave" (*Song of Songs* 8:6), "Jealousy is worse than death" (*Deuteronomy Rabbah*, on 31:1-30).[1] Jealousy is not a personality trait that we would want to embrace, considering that the jealous individual, according to the above commentaries on the tenth commandment is sure to be forced to his or her grave forthwith. If we take these first two emotions together, we are directly admonished: "**Jealousy** and **anger** will shorten your life" (*Ben Sira* 31:24).[2]

Joy (**Being Happy, Contented**): We now move onto the more positive aspects of one's personality. If you are at all like me, then the "smiley" individual, with a ready laugh, and an almost

---

1. Commentary on the *Book of Deuteronomy*.
2. See **Way #13 — Your Leisure Time**, footnote 2.

Pollyannaish view of the world, will drive you up the wall. But to doubt the contentment of another usually reflects some sort of self-dissatisfaction. In our jealousy, we tend to put the "up" person down, as if that would improve how we view ourselves or how others see us. "He who enjoys his labor and is content, avoids intestinal trouble and heartache" (*Yehiel Anav*).[1] How true this is. One's emotional state of being can adversely affect one's physical state of health (see **Way #37 — Your Body**). Therefore, I would rather be the type of person who gives ulcers than gets them! Even our favorite skeptic, the almost archetypal "downer" of a personality, Ecclesiastes, understood that you should "eat your bread with joy and drink your wine with a happy heart" (*Ecclesiastes* 9:7).

Most significant is the comment by Rabbi Nachman of Bratzlav:[2] "Common sense is strengthened through happiness." And the individual with "a pleasant demeanor and a happy disposition has friends" (*A Cedar Box*, Robert Nathan).[3] We are all naturally attracted to the type of person who is happy. He or she can be absolutely infectious: "...receive every person with a cheerful expression" (*Sayings of the Fathers* 1:15).

Patience, Understanding, Sympathy and Humility: Michael Douglas, in the movie *Falling Down*, goes on a murderous rampage because he is caught in traffic. If you have ever traveled the Los Angeles Freeways during rush hour, no doubt you could identify with Douglas. Very few things try our patience more than sitting in our car on the Washington DC Beltway at five-thirty in the afternoon. When we confront irritating gridlock at an intersection, it is amazing to hear the litany of swears that so easily, yet creatively, role off our tongue — often in front of our kids whom we may have just picked up after a soccer practice. But at just such a moment, we

---

1. A synagogue poet and scribe (circa 1250).
2. Hassidic rabbi (1772-1811).
3. Robert Nathan (1894-1982) was a Jewish American poet and novelist.

should realize that "powerlessness has nothing better than patience" (*Mivhar HaPeninim*, Ibn Gabirol).[1]

Patience leads to two of the most important personality additives: sympathy and understanding. These characteristics can lead to other endearing traits. The *Book of Proverbs* is a veritable well-spring of psychological information that can help fashion a positive personality. "Good understanding gives grace" (*Proverbs* 13:15) and "With all your getting, get understanding" (*Proverbs* 4:7). The first blessing in the *Prayerbook* in which one asks for something for him or herself is called: "A prayer for understanding" (*Daily Siddur — Prayerbook*), which is recited as part of the Eighteen Benedictions. "Understanding leads to self-control, which leads to righteousness, which leads to courage; and there is nothing more profitable than these" (*Apocrypha: Wisdom of Solomon* 4:1).[2] Add to these four elements a sympathetic bent to an individual and we have almost achieved perfection. After all, sympathy comes from the heart. It tunes the heart to catch the music of love. And what can anyone of us want out of life more than "to love" and "to be loved."

A person who is patient, understanding and sympathetic is one who is obviously humble. And of all the human attributes that are lauded in Judaism, this is probably the most important. Not only are we Jews told: "The humble will inherit the land" (*Psalm* 37:11), but this is also one of the most widely quoted sources, which found its way into the New Testament (*Matthew* 5:5). Not to dwell too long on this last trait, suffice it to cite two famous talmudic entreaties to support the view that humility should be the paramount element of one's personality: "Love humility and

---

1. Solomon Ibn Gabirol — Spanish poet (1021-1058).
2. Apocryphal book belonging to the "wisdom" literature, which includes late biblical books (*Proverbs*, *Job*, *Ecclesiastes*, etc.) that contain practical aphorisms pertaining to the upright life.

prolong your life" (*Talmud Derech Eretz* 7b)[1] and "Even if you are otherwise perfect, without humility, you fail" (*Kallah Rabbati* 3).[2]

Now we could add other characteristics, such as altruism, compassion, sensitivity, empathy, humor, intelligence and modesty. Yet all of these are derivatives of the positive personality traits mentioned above. **The thirty-first way to be Jewish is to cultivate the human emotions of contentment, patience, understanding, sympathy and humility** (all virtues of the *yeitzar hatov*). Placed against anger and/or jealousy (all qualities of the *yeitzar hara*), the former will lead to a quiet strength of character, an easy calm — the "chill factor." You will shine when you "walk, talk, smile and love: cause you've got personality, plus you've got a great big heart." With such a personality, not only will you like yourself, but others will too. "A happy heart makes a cheerful countenance" (*Proverbs* 15:13).

---

1. A lesser tractate appended to the *Babylonian Talmud*. "Derech Ertez" means literally "way of the land," but it is used colloquially to mean "use your common sense" and "show respect."
2. Another minor tractate in the *Babylonian Talmud*.

YOUR ENVIRONMENT

or:

The Little White Cloud that Cried²

Let's face it: we have made a mess of God's Creation. With all the technological advancements since the creation of the world, from the moment that human beings inhabited the earth until this very moment in time, we have royally screwed up the environment. With global warming, the slow disappearance of rain forests, radio-active nuclear waste, oil spills, the pollution of our rivers, lakes, land and skies, is it any wonder that our clouds, one of God's works of Creation, should be crying?

At the very beginning of the world's recorded history, after the

---

1. The numerical value of the letters forming the word "heart" in Hebrew (*lev*) is 32. Indeed, a healthy heart is often dependent on a healthy environment (particularly one that is smoke-, exhaust- and smog-free).
2. A popular song in the Fifties, written and sung by Johnny Ray (1951).

creation of the heavens and the earth, the waters, the forests, the grass, all forms of animal life, we read in our biblical text: "God blessed them [man and woman] and said to them, be fruitful and multiply, fill the earth and master it; and rule the fish of the sea, the birds of the sky, and all living things that creep on earth. See, I give you every seed-bearing plant that is upon the earth, and every tree that has seed-bearing fruit... (Genesis 1:28-29).

An awesome responsibility was placed on us human beings. We are Divinely commanded to look after our world. The natural beauty of the universe is described as Paradise: "And God planted a Garden of Eden in the East, and placed there the man whom he had formed" (Genesis 2:8). Some would pervert the notion that to become "masters" of God's Creation provides us with justification to exploit the environment, leading us to explain away the spoliation of natural resources. This is a distortion.

The Bible and those who interpret its fine print prohibit such exploitation. Judaism insists that we have an obligation not only to conserve the world of nature, but also to enhance it, because God's intentions were clear: to make us co-partners in the work of Creation. All animal life and all growing and life-giving things have rights in the cosmos that we must consider, even as we strive to ensure our own survival. The war against the spoliation of nature and the pollution of the environment is therefore the command of the hour and the call of the ages.[1]

Therefore, it makes perfect sense that the formal prayers of a Jew begin in the morning with the recitation of the Shema and its surrounding blessings. There are two prayers that precede the Shema and one that follows it (two in the evening prayers). The first blessing, both in the morning and in the evening, concentrates exclusively on matters of nature. In short, the first priority of a Jew, as he or she addresses God in the morning, is to give thanks for the

---

1. Robert Gordis, Congress Bi-Weekly, 38:5 (April, 1971).

miracle of Creation and the on-going wonders of nature. Paradise is an ideal that we should strive to achieve every day. This first prayer includes a definitive entreaty: "God renews every day, always, the works of Creation" (*Siddur* — morning prayer). In short, the world is created anew each day with us. And while the *Prayerbook* tells us that the whole earth is "God's possession," it also tells us that we have been handed the responsibility for taking care of this Divine inheritance.

Should we all join the "Green" movement? Probably yes. But not all of us are going to chain ourselves to the gates at Seabrook Nuclear Power Plant in New Hampshire or stand in the freezing cold in Davos, Switzerland, to demonstrate against the ecological abuses of the industrial nations gathered there for some environmental summit. But we can protest the expropriation of protected forests for commercial development, the construction of nuclear power plants for weapons of destruction, the domestication of rain forests.

Also, in our private lives, we must become ecologically determined: No more colored toilet paper because of the polluting dye; no more keeping the water running while washing dishes (shower in twos); no more throwing away bottles, papers or plastic except in recycling bins; no more putting out cigarette butts in the sand so that the tide sweeps them up for turtles to swallow and eventually die, making them one in a long list of endangered species; no more fox-hunts, deer shooting, bird-dogging.

Did we ever try to get along with one car, using public transportation whenever possible? For certain that third car for our teenage child is unnecessary. What about ceasing to use our cell phones, whose energetic waves clog up the atmosphere? As gross as it sounds, why not recycle our leftovers, making them into compost, planting a compost outpost in our backyard?

I know there are conflicts. What do new parents do regarding diapers? Should they use the throw-away kind (*Pampers* or *Huggies*) or use the old cloth kind? Both alternatives pose a minor threat to the environment. It is the waste of paper products versus the spilling of a soapy liquid into our water. Probably the use of cloth diapers would be less damaging to the environment. Yes, it requires more work, and may demand a clothespin on the nose as well as on the line, but to paraphrase Astronaut Neil Armstrong's immortal words: "One step for our surroundings, a giant leap for our environment!"

Preserving the environment and becoming ecologically sensitive demands an effort on our part. We have to think about future generations, and what we will bequeath to them. Technological and scientific advancement need not be attained at the expense of environmental sensitivity. The two are not mutually contradictory. They can and must be harmonized.

> I went walking down by the river,
> Feeling very sad inside,
> When all at once I saw in the sky
> The little white cloud that cried.
>
> He told me he was very lonesome
> And no one care if he lived or died,
> And said sometimes the thunder and lightning
> Make all the little clouds hide.
>
> He said: "Have faith in all kinds of weather,
> For the sun will always shine.
> Do your best and always remember
> The dark clouds pass with time."
>
> He asked if I'd tell all my world,
> Just how hard those clouds try.
> That's how I know I'll always remember
> The little white cloud that sat right down and cried.

I wonder how God felt when forced to expel Adam and Eve from

Paradise because of their abuses. I suspect God felt very lonely and disappointed. A Divine world was on its way to being defiled. Is a sudden burst of rain no more than the tears of a heavenly sadness, transmitted to the world through little white clouds that cry?

Unlike the hopeful words of our song, in our world today, the sun does not always shine. It is clouded over with bellowing smoke from oil refineries, smog, nuclear debris. Our environment is out of kilter. The balance of the heavens and the earth has been altered by our excesses, carelessness, selfishness, expediency and immediacy. In order to survive, Johnny Ray's Fifties' song must give way to one of the theme songs of the Sixties:

> When the moon is in the seventh house
> And Jupiter aligns with Mars,
> Then peace will guide the planets,
> And love will steer the stars.
> This is the dawning of the Age of Aquarius.[1]

The thirty-second way to be Jewish is to embrace a genuine love and appreciation for Creation, so that environmental peace will descend upon our world. Once we are committed to this Jewish value — to harmonize our actions with the rhythm of the heavens — then can we can sing the closing stanza to the above song:

> Let the sunshine in!

---

1. The song *Aquarius/Let the Sunshine in* from the Sixties' musical *Hair*.

WAY #33

YOUR FOOD

or:

You are what you Eat

"There can be no joy without food and drink" (*Talmud Mo'ed Katan* 20a). "Only in meat is there joy" (*Talmud Pesachim* 109a). "Meat is the prince of all foods" (Yiddish expression). "The best of milk dishes is a slice of beef" (Shalom Aleichem). Now, this is my type of Judaism. Too bad that we are forewarned against taking advantage of these pithy talmudic instructions: "The drunkard and the glutton shall come to poverty (*Proverbs* 23:21). Well, it was good while it lasted. I guess we will have to forget about "eating and drinking, for tomorrow you may die" (*Isaiah* 22:13).

All these above quotes point out that food is central to Jewish life. The notion of what one should eat, how one should eat, when one should eat and where one should eat, occupies virtually volumes of Jewish literature. For a Jew: "You are what you eat."

A Jewish student at a university in Boston, approached his Hillel rabbi, confessing that he had "sinned."

Student: Rabbi, I ate a pork sandwich on Yom Kippur.

Rabbi: What happened to you? Don't you know that it is forbidden to eat on Yom Kippur?

Student: I know. It slipped my mind.

Rabbi: Don't you know that pork is not *kosher*?

Student: I know. I didn't remember.

Rabbi: Then why did you do it?

Student: I forgot that I was Jewish!

There are many ways to remember that we are Jewish, but according to Judaism, one of the most compelling ways is to watch what we eat. Like our language, our prayers, our dress, food links us to our Jewish past and to Jews around the world.

There was God on the top of Mount Sinai dictating to Moses, who, like a good stenographer, was taking down every word.

God: Do not boil a kid in its mother's milk (*Exodus* 23:19).

Moses: Wait a minute. Does that mean we must have two sets of dishes?

God: Moses. Do not boil a kid in its mother's milk (*Exodus* 34:26).

Moses: Hold on. Does that mean I have to wait six hours before I have a glass of milk after I just devoured a T-bone?

God: One last time, Moses. Do not boil a kid in its mother's milk (*Deuteronomy* 14:21).

Moses: I don't get it. Does that mean I can't eat a cheeseburger?

God: Okay Moses. Have it your way!

One of the greatest misconceptions within Judaism is that *kashrut* — dietary laws — was instituted for health reasons. The primary reason that a Jew is commanded to keep *kosher* is based on the biblical verse: "For I am the Lord your God. Therefore, sanctify yourself and be holy, for I am holy...I am the Lord your God who brought you 'up' out of the land of Egypt to be your God. You shall therefore be holy" (*Leviticus* 11:44-45). Like so many aspects of Jewish life, the concept of *kashrut* is introduced as a way to elevate the Jew, to bring him or her "up" in his or her everyday life to "holiness." Holiness in Hebrew means to set oneself apart. Therefore, a Jew is commanded not to walk into the restaurant, "Cheeseburger in Paradise," in Lahaina, Maui. However, we are instructed: "Eat well with your teeth and you will feel it in your toes" (*Talmud Shabbat* 152a). Indeed, Maimonides maintained that the keeping of the dietary laws "train us to master our appetites; to accustom us to restrain our desires; and not to consider the pleasure of eating and drinking the end of man's existence" (*Guide for the Perplexed*, 3:35). Beyond this definition, the early rabbis, in interpreting the biblical dictates relating to *kashrut*, believed that the secret of Jewish survival was this maintenance of separatism.

Most of the dietary laws are set forth in *Leviticus*. They were maintained and expanded throughout the generations, often taking on added meanings because of the sociological turmoil of a particular time-frame in which the Jews lived. It was reasoned that if Jews had a separate code for eating, then they would be prevented from dining with their non-Jewish neighbors, and from socializing with them, thus reducing the chances of intermarriage, thereby helping to guarantee the survival of the Jewish People. This view is perhaps best illustrated by the story of a sixth grade student in a Sunday School class. When asked about interdating, the student responded: "I could never go out with a Moslem because Moslems don't eat pork!"

Today, such reasoning may seem far-fetched, even racist. But given the sad reality that Jewish life is undergoing massive assimilation, a Jew does need to ask him- or herself, what are the minimum standards of Jewish practice required to hold onto one's

Judaism? Since eating is the most basic element of one's daily survival, attention to what one eats becomes important. Indeed, many argue that, according to Judaism, vegetarianism is the highest form of *kashrut* because the eating of fruit and vegetables is the first reference to food consumption in the Bible.

Admittedly, this **Way** cannot accommodate an explanation of all the laws surrounding *kashrut*. They are too numerable and particular to do them justice in such a brief entry. While there are hygienic and humanitarian reasons[1] that would justify maintaining the laws surrounding *kashrut*, this **Way** intended to illustrate that the basic motivation for keeping some aspects of *kashrut* is so that a Jew does not forget that he or she is Jewish. Simply put, maintaining aspects of *kashrut* makes one aware of one's Jewishness. (All the prayers that surround the Jewish meal add to a notion of sanctity: that is, we should not take anything for granted, particularly the food that we consume. We should be grateful for the "fruits of our labor.")

"A physician restricts the diet of only those patients who he expects will recover. So God prescribed the dietary laws for those who have hope of a future life. Others may eat anything" (*Leviticus Rabbah*, 13:2).[2] **The thirty-third way to be Jewish is by maintaining a respect for *kashrut*, and incorporating some, if not all, the rules governing a *kosher* home into one' life.** By doing so, one has a decent chance of holding on to his or her Judaism, and contributing to the perpetuation of the Jewish People, guaranteeing a future life for Judaism.

1. A hygienic reason for keeping *kosher* can be found in the biblical verse: "Eat neither fat nor blood" (*Leviticus* 3:17, 7:23). A humanitarian reason for keeping *kosher* is that a Jew is commanded to slaughter an animal humanely — to cause as little pain as possible. How prescient of the on-going spread of animal diseases (mad-cow and foot and mouth): "If slaughter-houses were placed under the supervision of a Jewish butcher, disease would be less prevalent, and the average duration of life would be increased" (*Israel Among the Nations*, Leroy-Beaulieum 1985, p. 159, and *Races of Europe*, Ripley, 1899, p. 384).
2. Midrashic commentary on the *Book of Leviticus*.

YOUR SEX LIFE[1]

or:

"Love is the Answer, but while you're Waiting for the Answer, Sex Raises Some Pretty Good Questions"[2]

"When love was strong, we could have made our bed on a sword's blade; now when it has become weak, a bed of sixty cubits is not large enough for us" (*Talmud Sanhedrin* 7a). In Judaism, to engage in a sexual act — of any kind — without a concomitant commitment to love is unacceptable, as is any sexual

---

1. David M. Feldman's book, *Marital Relations, Birth Control and Abortion in Jewish Law* (Schocken Books, 1974) is one of the finest sources on Judaism's attitude toward matters of sex.
2. As stated by Woody Allen.

involvement before or outside of marriage. No doubt the latter part of the previous sentence poses a moral challenge to those of us of the Sixties generation, who were schooled on a credo of "free love" and "sexual liberation." (I suggest that the reader not be entirely discouraged, because if we combine the "love" and the "sex" from these two banner headlines, we may be able to make some sense out of Judaism's "dos and don'ts" as they impact on our sex life.)

Yes, the message is crystal clear: Love and Sex go hand in hand, not "hand in gland," as President Bill Clinton proffered in his famous statement: "I did not have sexual relations with that woman," which really meant that he refrained from sexual intercourse with Ms. Monica Lewinsky, yet did engage in other forms of sexual dallying. Despite his semantic gymnastics, condemnation for his behavior should have been promulgated for numerous reasons: from his abuse of the delicate relationship between love and any physical act that should be an expression of that love, to the abuse of his power and position. Indeed, sex in the absence of love can lead to abuse: "Wherever you find sexual license, you may expect to find abuse" (*Genesis Rabbah* 36:5).[1]

Now what would an entry about love and sex in a book be, if it were to omit Sigmund Freud? Indeed, since Freud was a Jew, it would seem almost blasphemous not to make mention of him (see **Way #43 — Your Dreams**). But, suffice it for this **Way**, to quote Pete Seeger's song about Freud that was written in 1956, the one hundredth anniversary of his birth.

Oh, Doctor Freud, oh, Dr. Freud,
How we wish you had been differently employed.
For this set of circumstances
Sure enhances the finances
Of the followers of Dr. Sigmund Freud.

He forgot about sclerosis,

---

1. Midrashic commentary on the *Book of Genesis*.

But invented the psychosis,
Plus a hundred ways that sex could be enjoyed.
He adopted as his credo:
"Down repression, up libido!"
That was the start of Doctor Sigmund Freud.[1]

While not completely contradicting Freud's theory, which would hold that totally freeing oneself from any sexual inhibitions is a solution for a repressed individual, according to Judaism, this is not necessarily the best recipe to achieve psychological equilibrium in one's life. And so Freud may not be as relevant as one might think when a Jew considers matters of sexual activity.

However, not to disregard the father of modern psychoanalysis entirely, it should be noted that Judaism is more in keeping with the progressive attitude toward sex that is, in part, reflective of Freud's thinking, because, unlike many religions, Judaism is not "prudish" when it comes to matters of sex. Asceticism and self-denial are features of Stoicism, of Christianity, and even more so of Hinduism; the religious life of Christianity to this very day is characterized by elements of monasticism, reclusion and austerity.[2] Such an attitude is alien to Judaism. "One might say, inasmuch as jealousy, passion, love and honor may bring about a man's downfall, I will therefore remove myself to the other extreme. I will refrain from meat and wine or marriage or a pleasant home or attractive garments. This is an evil way and is forbidden. He who follows these practices is a sinner" (*Yad Chazakah, Hilchot Dayot* 3:1, Maimonides). To deny oneself the pleasures of the flesh, which were part of Creation, is considered an act of defiance of the Divine. "Man will have to render an account to God for all the good things his eyes beheld, but which he refused to enjoy" (Commentary by Rav, founder of the leading academies of talmudic learning; *Kiddushin* 2:65). Unlike

---

1. Lyrics by David Lazar (1956).
2. David M. Feldman, op. cit., p. 81.

some other monotheistic religions, "at no time was sexual asceticism accorded the dignity of a religious value, and the mystics make no exception."[1]

It is important to point out that the act of love-making between a husband and wife is discussed in Jewish sources (see **Way #39 — Your Marriage**). Most significant is the statement: "A man is required to give joy to his wife in the matter of *Mitzvah*...even during pregnancy when procreation is not involved..." (see *Talmud Eruvin* 100b). This is all based on the biblical verse in which a husband is commanded: "to thrill his wife" (*Deuteronomy* 24:5). Therefore, marriage must be considered the supreme opportunity to express one's love through the act of sexual communion. While it may be considered that intercourse's highest goal is to procreate, it is clear that the very act itself must also involve pleasure. (The first commandment in the Bible is to "be fruitful and multiply" — see alternative usage of this commandment in **Way #4 — Your Language**). In Judaism, there is not a hint of guilt or the possibility of "the stain of sin" attached to love-making that is emotionally legitimate. Even if either partner in a marriage is incapable of procreation, there is no limitation placed upon the couple's physical engagement.

While there are restrictions in Jewish law on the woman's privilege of denying marital relations to her husband — she is termed "rebellious" if she refuses relations...without valid reason and can thereby forfeit her divorce settlement (see *Talmud Ketubot* 63a) — the burden and primary concern of the law is with her husband. The difference is illustrated by one of those unlikely but highly instructive talmudic provisions: "If a man took a vow to deny his wife the pleasure of marital intercourse, his vow is automatically null and void; he cannot vow against what the *Torah* requires of him" (*Talmud N'darim* 81b). Indeed, the tradition does not allow for

---

1. *Major Trends in Jewish Mysticism*, Gershom Scholem (Schocken Books, 1965 — originally published in 1941), p. 106.

exaggerated intervals, as a time limit is imposed: one to two weeks (with no age limit attached). It should also be noted that a woman can initiate love-making, and upon that initiation, a man should satisfy her, even kissing her wherever he pleases.[1]

Judaism does not shy away from fine-tuning the act of love-making. The *Shulchan Aruch* is literally filled with sections that deal with matters of sex, as are many other sacred Jewish texts (see footnote 5, **Way #25 — Your Internet**). (There is no need for a Jew to enroll in "sexual enhancement" courses or to read "How to Improve Your Sex Life" books.) Throughout all the descriptions of how, when, where and why one should engage in sexual activity, there is one constant theme: love and sex should never be confused or compromised.

So, what does Judaism say about premarital sex or about love-making between two people of the same sex? As for the latter, I refer you back to **Way #30 — Your Gay and Lesbian Friends**. Regarding premarital sex, the Bible does not hide the open, non-marital relationships of such dominant individuals as Abraham or David. However, the weight of Jewish law is such that pre-marital cohabitation is essentially forbidden. Now this is particularly problematic for our generation, because, as aforementioned, the Sixties ushered in the "sexual revolution." If we did not engage in premarital sex then, (though it is hard to believe that this was not the case), for certain our children do now; although I suspect that we are far more conservative when it comes to our own children's sexual promiscuity than we were regarding ours when we were their age. Rabbi Zalman Schacter speaks of a "sliding scale" in various "neo-halachic" practices. For certain, in this day and age, it would be difficult to argue for an all or nothing policy — celibacy or marriage — primarily because all of the pious pronouncement mentioned until now would simply be ignored. But a sliding scale

1. David M. Feldman, op. cit., p. 89.

has its risks. Therefore, the only way out of some of Judaism's sexual prohibitions is to extrapolate from the tradition's basic guidelines, as those articulated above, which prevent one from reducing sexual coupling to a frivolous or expedient activity.

The syllogism here is that true pleasure cannot be attained when sex is devoid of love, for ultimately "love is the fount of pleasure" (*Sefer HaMiddot*),[1] not the sexual act in and of itself. For a Jew, there can be no such concept as: "Love them and leave them," or "a one night stand." A Jew must not indulge in "casual sex." This is true not only in theory, but also in practicality, for rarely, if ever, do two people find agreement in such a disrespectful attitude toward sex (not to mention the possibility of contracting some sexually transmitted disease). One of the parties involved is bound to be hurt, thus diminishing the sexual act, and demeaning the human dignity and worth of the other. Therefore, **the thirty-fourth way to be Jewish is to make certain that sex and love are harmonized, because "the act of sexual union must be holy and pure..." (*Iggeret HaKodesh*, Nachmanides, 13c).**[2]

---

1. Book of morals, Germany, 15th century.
2. Moses Ben Nachman, also known as the Ramban (1194-1270). He was a Spanish communal leader, talmudist, kabbalist and biblical commentator. As rabbi of Gerona, he was regarded as the spiritual leader of Spanish Jewry.

WAY #35

YOUR AGING

or:

"How Terribly Strange to be Seventy"[1]

"Anyone can get old. All you have to do is live long enough" (Groucho Marx). The part of life we live as elders is a gift. Very few species live as long beyond the reproductive years as humans do. Perhaps we have this relatively long life span because elders serve such important roles in human society — as repositories of wisdom, guardians of history and family memories, and backup care-givers for the young. The feeling of joy that comes from filling these roles — the joy of grandchildren, the joy of allowing others to benefit from our experience — is built into the design of human life.[2]

---

1. From Simon & Garfunkel's song *Old Friends* from their album *Bookends* (1967).
2. From the Introduction to *When Someone You Love has Alzheimer's*, by Earl A. Grollman (Beacon Press, 1996).

Although the aging process is emotionally, mentally and physically difficult, achieving a status of "elder" can usher in years of great contentment and unsurpassed joy. According to the tradition, Abraham was one-hundred-and-nine years old and his wife Sarah was a whopping ninety-nine when they became parents. The biblical motif of this story is to teach that, even when we arrive at old age, it is possible to find new life and a renewed sense of inner strength.

❖ ❖ ❖

Today, we are deeply aware that a very unfortunate stigma has been applied to the process of aging. Added to the new discriminatory "isms," like sexism, racism and anti-Semitism, we now have "ageism." We have experienced a radical shift in attitude concerning the process of aging. In 18th century America, the authority of the elderly was very high. For example, in New England town meetings, the seats of highest honor went to the oldest rather than the wealthiest. People were rarely forced to retire to make way for the young. Ninety percent of all colonial ministers and magistrates remained in office until their later years. Two hundred years ago, age was so highly respected that people tried to make themselves look older than they actually were.

In the 19th century a change in attitude began to take place, when a person like Henry David Thoreau could say: "I have yet to hear the first syllable of value or even earnest advice from my seniors. They have told me nothing, and probably cannot teach me anything." This reminds me of our sloganeering: "Don't trust anyone over thirty!" Indeed, today, aging is viewed as a social problem, which is intensified by a youth culture where instead of aging gracefully, the old try to emulate the young. Often we are embarrassed by the ways of the old: their forgetfulness, their repetitiveness, their reminiscences, their clumsiness. We often make the elderly feel self-conscious, tentative, unsure, thus reducing their self-worth. While in his nineties, my father would joke: "If you can't remember something, just forget it." However, old age can usher in all forms of dementia, the most pronounced being Alzheimer's, which robs the once central figure in our lives of the joy of occupying center stage in his or her "golden age". Indeed, a deteriorating mind can be more devastating than physical limitations. (See **Way #42 — Your Parents** for a fuller discussion on mental and physical deterioration in our later years, and the painful decision of committing elderly parents to home care or homes for the aged.)

A patronizing attitude towards our parents contradicts the very basic tenets of Judaism. A Jew needs to look no further than the Bible to understand the respect and care for the elderly that is demanded of us. We are duly commanded to: "Rise before the aged and show deference to the old" (*Leviticus* 19:32). The Psalmist tells us: "Abandon me not when I grow old" (*Psalm* 71:9). And finally we learn of the stages of the aging process: "At five years old, one is fit for *Scriptures*, at ten for *Mishna*, at thirteen to fulfill the commandments, at fifteen to study *Talmud*, at eighteen for wedlock, at twenty for a calling, at thirty for office, at forty for discernment, at fifty for counsel, at sixty to be an elder, at seventy for white hairs, at eighty for vigor, at ninety for a bowed back...and at one hundred, you are as one who has died and left this world" (*Sayings of the Fathers* 5:25).

This is a clear indication that the later years can be one of the most creative periods in an individual's life. The great classical cellist, Pablo Casals, was living proof of the Jewish aging prescription's validity, as he was still performing in his late eighties. When he ascended the conductor's podium, at first glance his appearance would cause apprehension. He seemed barely mobile. His face was drawn. He even trembled a bit. But then there was a sudden transition. As he began to lead the orchestra, baton in full swing, he underwent an amazing transformation. He was suddenly vibrant and full of life. His body swayed with strength and vigor. His face assumed a radiant glow, as he conducted a Bach concerto with grace and beauty.

❖   ❖   ❖

Yet getting old is no easy task. Often, we are unaware of our own aging process, unless ill health strikes us as we advance in age. As Bernard Baruch said: "To me, old age is always fifteen years older than I am." During the Jewish High Holidays, we wish each other the traditional greeting: "May you be inscribed in the Book of Life for a New Year of health and happiness." What might help us get a more balanced view of the human condition would be if we also received our actuarial tables from the insurance company, which would tell us that our life expectancy has just been reduced from the last New Year to the present one by a whole year. Why not reverse our method of counting birthdays? When one is twenty, a person should not say "I'm twenty years old," but rather "I have sixty-five more years to go!" At fifty, one should say there are thirty-five more years to go, and so on. When celebrating birthdays, instead of adding up the years, make a countdown.

This is a sobering view of life, but does support the Jewish dictum that a "Jew should repent the day before he dies" (*Sayings of the Fathers* 2:10). How does an individual know when will be the day before he or she dies? The person does not know; therefore he or she should seek repentance everyday of his or her life. Such an aging process can eliminate the possibility of looking back on one's life with regrets.

A hundred-year-old woman, Nadine Slair, of Louisville, Kentucky, was asked the question: "How would you live your life if you could do it all over again?" Her answer was simple, yet telling: "I'd dare to make more mistakes. I'd relax. I would limber up. I would take fewer things seriously. I would take more chances. I would take more trips. I would climb more mountains and swim more rivers. I would eat more ice cream and less beans. I would, perhaps, have more actual troubles, but I'd have fewer imaginary ones. I would start barefoot earlier in the spring and stay that way later in the fall. I would go to more dances. I would ride more merry-go-rounds. I would pick more daisies. I've been one of those persons who never goes anywhere without a thermometer, a hot water bottle, a raincoat and a parachute. If I had to do it all over again, I would travel lighter."

It would be most helpful if we adopted Albert Einstein's view of the world: "I never think of the future. It comes soon enough." Few things in life are more painful, yet more challenging, than being the last one to survive among one's friends. "It will come soon enough." Nadine Slair's retrospective view of her life points to a time in our own lives when we will have to call ourselves to witness. If we are of sound mind, how we live out our later years can be an indication of how we lived our entire life, and how we would want to be remembered.

Old friends, Old friends,
Sat on their park bench like bookends.
A newspaper blown through the grass
Falls on the round toes on the high shoes
Of the old friends.

Old friends, winter companions,
The old men —
Lost in their overcoats, waiting for the sunset.
The sounds of the city, sifting through trees,
Settle like dust on the shoulders
Of the old friends.

Can you imagine us years from today,
Sharing a park bench quietly?
How terribly strange to be seventy.

Old friends,
Memory brushed the same years,
Silently sharing the same fear...

At seventy, memories brush our years, and we consider the legacy we will leave behind. And as we approach our twilight years, confronting our mortality, what can comfort us most, and what can gain us a measure of immortality, is if we know that the values we have transmitted over the years have been positive ones. Examining the Jewish way of aging, we find a unique and moving inspiration for articulating these values: Ethical Wills.

According to the Jewish tradition, community leaders, parents and grandparents left to their posterity neither material goods nor valuables, but values. These wills dealt with principles, not property. For example, in his ethical will, Shalom Aleichem left to his children the example of his Jewish commitment: "Live together in peace, bear not hatred for each other, help one another in bad times and pity the poor." The humorist, Sam Levenson, in an ethical will to his grandchildren noted that his unpaid debts were his greatest assets. He wrote to his grandchildren:

"Everything I own, I owe. I leave you not everything I never had, but everything I had in my lifetime — a good family, respect for learning, compassion for my fellowman and some four letter words for all occasions, like: 'help, give, care, feel and love.'"

❖ ❖ ❖

If we we are not mentally or physically incapacitated in our old age, our final years can remain a time for "helping, giving, caring, feeling and loving." This also applies to our attitude to those who are "always fifteen years older than I am." We must help them, give to them, care for them, feel for them and love them. We can learn this from our elders: "From my elders (teachers), I became wiser" (*Psalm* 119:99).

Also, in our later years, we must be prepared to receive help from our loved ones. Pride should not overwhelm our need for support due to increasing physical and/or mental disabilities. Indeed, such help can forge stronger relations between the old and the young, often between parent and child (see **Way #42 — Your Parents**). But, as aforementioned, any help that we offer the elderly must be given with absolute sensitivity. We must let our seniors grow old gracefully.

> Time it was, and what a time it was,
> It was…
> A time of innocence, a time of confidences.
> Long ago…it must be…
> I have a photograph.
> Preserve your memories;
> They're all that's left you.[1]

"With age comes wisdom, and in length of days, understanding" (*Job* 12:12). In old age, wisdom and understanding can lead to a delightful new innocence and surprising new confidences, to a time of continued creativity and accomplishments. But this will only be the case if we accept that **the thirty-fifth way to be Jewish is to reach our later years with a photograph of memories that leaves only a few snapshots of regrets, but multiple pictures of values and principles**. A Jew who can tell him- or herself that this is the measure of his or her life will reach old age with the greatest gift of all — contentment: "Happy is the man who has not followed the counsel of the wicked…rather the teaching of the Lord is his delight…He will be like a tree planted beside streams of water, that yields its fruit in season, whose foliage never fades, and whatever it produces thrives" (*Psalm* 1:1-3). For a Jew: "Gray hair is a crown of glory, which is attained by ways of righteousness" (*Proverbs* 16:31).

---

1. Theme song from the Simon & Garfunkel *Bookends* album.

YOUR HOLOCAUST AWARENESS[2]

or:

Jewish Identity-Building —

Positive or Negative?

In **Way #18 — Your Social Activism,** I put forth the thesis that Jews are generally engaged in issues of social conscience for religious, practical and historical reasons. Religiously, Jewish sacred literature demands Jews to be aware of the needs of others. From the Ten Commandments to the dictates of the prophets to the maxims of the *Sayings of the Fathers,* Jews are expected to be

1. The number thirty-six refers to the "thirty-six" righteous men (*lamed vav tzaddikim* in Hebrew), who according to Jewish tradition (*Talmud Sanhedrin* 97b), remain anonymous in every generation and by whose merit the world is saved from destruction. The idea of these "hidden saints" was propagated by the Kabbalah and has become a popular theme in Jewish folklore.
2. See **Way #14 — Your Book Shelf** for a bibliography on the Holocaust.

involved in *tikkun olam* — repairing the world. Practically, our suffering at the hands of oppressors throughout too much of our lifetime should make us keenly aware of any pain caused to others because of persecution and prejudice. Historically, we were born as a people on the anvil of enslavement in ancient Egypt and liberated to set a new world order based on the prophetic vision of social justice and equality (see **Way #18 — Your Social Activism**).

We Jews have felt that we should be committed to the idea of universal decency and harmony, which was nurtured by our particular experiences as Jews. This attitude motivated many of us to be active during the Sixties. But beyond our theological, pragmatic and historical motivation for social engagement, we leaned on the soul-searching experience of the Holocaust as the major incentive for our activism. However, along the way, we took this most tragic event in Jewish history, and perhaps in all human history, and universalized it to such an extent that any claim that we were the prime victims of Nazism became lost. For example, during the dark days of Sheriff Bull Conner and Governor Lester Maddox who routinely persecuted Blacks (African-Americans), as Whites we accepted the thesis that we (they) were as guilty as the Nazis in our (their) persecution of Blacks.

This universal application of the lessons of the Holocaust was best played out in our protests against the Vietnam War. The American government was committing genocide against the Vietnamese. When we joined the "Moratorium against the War" in Washington in 1969, stuffing flowers into the guns of National Guardsmen and "levitating" the Pentagon, we chanted Nazi insults at our soldiers with a vitriolic force that matched the bigoted epithets we hurled upon Governor George Wallace, and the fascist perorations we attributed to Mayor Richard Daley's Chicago police at the 1968 Democratic National Convention.

As I look back on that period of my life, I am amazed to recall how Jewish activists, which included the most marginal and illiterate of Jews, like Abie Hoffman and Jerry Rubin, started out with a perfectly logical formula and misapplied it, so that it became a ridiculous piece of mischievous nonsense. Things equal to the same thing are not equal to each other. Even though the Jews and the Nazis are all members of the human race, they are not interchangeable. American soldiers, Southern Whites, Jewish landlords, Robert MacNamara were (and are) not the natural descendants of German National-Socialism. Palestinians are not the new Jews, and the Israelis the modern Nazis — no matter how justified some may feel in charging Israelis with injustices committed against Palestinians. (Another abuse of the Holocaust was former President George Bush's comparison of Saddam Hussein to Hitler during the Persian Gulf War. Hussein's invasion into Kuwait may have been illegal, and even brutal, but by no stretch of the imagination did it equal Hitler's and Germany's bestiality.)

To be sure, the Holocaust should sensitize Jews to the suffering of others, but it cannot be applied to such a universal extent that the atrocities the Germans committed against us Jews become diminished in the process. A Jew must never accept such comparative drivel in order to make some lame social comment about universal guilt and responsibility. Sadly, the advent of the Holocaust has a unique place in the annals of Jewish history, as we were Hitler's primary victims. Others should not rob us of this fact. For certain, we should not.

So, what are the lessons we can learn from the Holocaust? First and foremost, we must be ever watchful that we do not persecute others. It is we, not others, who should call ourselves to task in order to guarantee the freedom of others. For the Jewish state, it means building a society that lacks even the slightest hint of repression or discrimination. Even with the present realities that Israel faces, those in the Jewish state must always hold up as their ideal the aspiration to be a "light unto the nations," not only because of our ancient history, but also because of our recent tortuous reality.

We must fine-tune this lesson by questioning any psychological manifestations of our personality that would hint at even the slightest inclination towards indifference or apathy or disinterest or denial. Such characteristics can cripple one's sensitivity to the needs of those less fortunate. Without cheapening the Holocaust by measuring every injustice by the monstrous scope of that tragedy, we must not turn a blind eye to the ills of society that swirl around us.

Outside the "Hall of Remembrance" at Yad VaShem, the Israeli memorial to the Holocaust, stands a statue: "The Silent Cry." During the Holocaust, not only did much of the world remain silent, but even many Jews of the free world did not speak out. After all, by 1933, when Hitler assumed the position of chancellor, *Mein Kampf*, his magnus opus which essentially defined the "Final Solution" (a euphemism for the slaughter of the Jews), had entered its twenty-fifth edition.[1] What he intended to do to the Jews once he attained total power was no secret. The near-annihilation of European Jewry must prompt us to not remain silent when any form of anti-Semitism rears its ugly head. Whether anti-Semitism comes in the wake of a Neo-Nazi demonstration in Skokie, Illinois, or an Arab attack on Jews because of the on-going conflict between Israel and the Palestinian Authority, we Jews must speak out and stand up against it.

Rarely in history has a single event elicited such diverse reactions, as has the wanton slaughter of six million Jews. The murder of the Six Million cannot be wholly explained for in terms of either passion or madness, or of overwhelming and irresistible

---

1. The Final Solution was officially adopted at the Wannsee Conference in Berlin (January 20, 1942). Under the leadership of Reinhard Heydrich, the Nazis announced what they called the "Final Solution" for the "Jewish problem," a euphemism for the mass extermination of the Jews of Europe.

social forces. Therefore, it is of prime importance to remember the Holocaust, never letting it fade from our consciousness. It is an obligation we have to the survivor generation, which soon will no longer be among us to recount that terrible time. We should view this as an obligation, which provides us with a second lesson.

The capacity to assume the burden of memory is not always practical. Sometimes recollection arouses feelings of guilt, brings on nightmares and induces depression. While the moral function of remembering cuts across the different worlds of art, knowledge, reason and history, it must always be compatible with basic truths. Whatever conclusions a Jew ultimately chooses to draw from the Holocaust, the one basic lesson that must endure is the act of remembering.

This remembrance must not find its expression exclusively in grief over the loss of the Six Million. Tears only shed at Auschwitz for the Six Million would miss the enduring point of a visit to what was "Jewish Europe" (see **Way #3 — Your Trips Abroad**). Not only was Jewish life lost, but also a thousand-year-old Jewish culture that was so rich and vibrant was snuffed out, with barely a trace of its glory remaining. We owe the victims this recognition. To mourn them is essentially to honor them through the reinstitution of a similarly rich Jewish culture.

Sadly, it would be too easy for a Jew to fashion his or her Jewish identity in negative terms. Such identity building, particularly based on the Holocaust, promotes feelings of resentment, which can lead to self-indulgence, intolerance and even vengeance. Since Jewish life has always been maintained by an eternal faith in renewal, and in a hope that sustained us for two thousand years of Diaspora existence, culminating in the establishment of the modern state of Israel, any negativism would be contrary to the continued perpetuity of the Jewish People.

This leads to another lesson to be derived from the Holocaust: not to give up hope. A conversation with Holocaust survivors is destined to give us faith in the future. Their resilience shames those of us who fret over the most minor issues. And so it becomes incumbent upon us to probe the memories of those Holocaust survivors, to hear their story, to share it with others, so that such events may never recur. We should not just leave it to the professionals, the Steven Spielbergs of this world, to set up a Holocaust video library. We need to hear the stories first-hand — for ourselves.

More so, another lesson would be for us to thwart the would-be Holocaust deniers, of whom there are too many floating around — from pseudo-intellectuals like David Irving to rabid anti-Semites like Ekrema Sabri, the chief Mufti of Jerusalem, appointed by the Palestinian Authority. Once the last survivors have left us, these people, along with others like them, will continue to assert their preposterous claim that the Holocaust never happened, or did not assume the proportions that we know to be factually accurate. The death of the Holocaust generation will sadly heighten any sense of credibility that they might garner by virtue of the fact that no longer will there be witnesses to expose their lies.

Then there is the very personal lesson that one can take from the Holocaust. A sixteen-year-old boy returned from a visit to Poland with his class. As he and his classmates began to process their visit to Auschwitz and other Nazi death camps, he said: "When I was ten years old, my father died. But I still have my mother and my brothers, and my nieces and nephews, and grandparents." Appreciation for what we have is clearly one of the most important and significant lessons of the Holocaust.

And of course, the ultimate lesson is for us to maintain our Judaism, so that their deaths will never be in vain. A natural Holocaust brought on by assimilation would be too painful to bear. To achieve culturally what Hitler could not achieve physically would be the ultimate irony of Jewish history. Jewish theologian, Emil Fackenheim, himself a Holocaust survivor, has added an "eleventh commandment:" "Thou shalt not let Hitler get a posthumous victory."

The thirty-sixth way to be Jewish is to hold on to the memory of the Holocaust, not as a negative incentive to maintain our Judaism, but rather as one of the most powerful and compelling Jewish historical motivations to preserve Jewish life. It is incumbent upon every one of us to sanctify those who died in the Holocaust through acts of positive Jewish identity: increased Jewish learning, consistent involvement in social causes, active engagement with Jewish practices and traditions, wider identification with Israel in the hope that it will realize its ancient calling to be a "light unto the nations," strength to combat prejudice, particularly anti-Semitism, and a continual commitment to raise our children in an enlightened Jewish environment, so that the Jewish People will live.

WAY #37

YOUR BODY (YOUR HEALTH)

or:

I Got Life[1]

```
I got my hair,
            I got my head,
                        I got my brain,
I got my mouth,                         I got my ears,
            I got my teeth,                         I got my eyes,
                        I got my tongue,                         I got my nose,
I got my heart,                         I got my chin,
            I got my soul,                         I got my neck,
                        I got my back,                         I got my tits,
I got my fingers,                         I got my ass,
            I got my legs,                         I got my arms,
                        I got my feet,                         I got my laugh,
I got my guts,                         I got my toes,
            I got my muscle,                         I got my liver,
                        I got life,                         I got my blood.
```

---

1. Song from the musical *Hair* (1968).

The popular musical, *Hair*, was, in many ways, a celebration of the body. It was the first time a Broadway show was so explicit, not only in its language, but also in its public exposal of the human body. Basically, the play said that one should be proud of his or her body, not afraid to show it off, and to share it with others (see **Way #34 — Your Sex Life**).

Maimonides, who, in addition to being a great theologian, was also a physician, wrote: "Perfection of the body has precedence over the perfection of the soul" (from his *Letters of Morality*). As such, a Jew is instructed to look after his or her body. This is not to say that body-building should be the main occupation of the Jew. Yet, keeping in shape is certainly a worthy Jewish mission. Although admittedly, when I asked my doctor about the value of jogging, he replied: "I suppose it is good for you, but did you ever see a person smile while they were jogging?"

What is interesting to note is that, like the actors in *Hair*, both Adam and Eve, the very first human beings — even if in an allegorical sense — paraded naked around the Garden of Eden; their bodies beautifully sculpted like the rest of their being — "in the image of God." While we cannot ascribe any anthropomorphic features to God, the notion of perfection is attached to the Creator. And so it can be assumed, at least in human terms, that Adam and Eve must have been one physically good-lookin' couple — to be emulated by those who came after them.

In the *Prayerbook*, one of the first blessings has to do with our being thankful for the fact that we have orifices. If this were not the case, then our lives would be quite abbreviated.[1] This blessing is immediately followed by a slew of supplications that culminate in

---

1. "Blessed are You, Lord our God, Ruler of the Universe, who in wisdom formed the human being, creating channels and passages innumerable. In Your sublime wisdom, You know that should they be torn or obstructed, we could not survive and stand before You. Blessed are You, Lord, who heals all flesh and works miracles" (from first prayers in morning service).

our thanking God, who "gives strength to the weary." In short: "Is not the body the soul's house? Then why should we not take care of the house so that it fall not into ruins" (Philo, *The Worse Attacks the Better*, 10)?[1]

If you have ever been in one of those "all you can eat" Chinese restaurants in Florida, or "country buffet kitchens" in California, or any Burger King, Kentucky Fried Chicken, Taco Bell throughout the US (and the world), you will notice a predominance of overly endowed human beings. The amount of grease that one person can consume in these places is unlimited. I am certain that the reason those people who stuff themselves with a daily diet of a Big Mac, French Fries, a fried chicken nugget and "Diet Coke," cannot keep their pants up is because they would "slide" off of them. If "the human body has three kings: brain, heart and liver" (*Midrash HaNe'elim*, ed. ch.1, p. 12b), it would be best to guard them, and not to eat them! (In Israel, the "mixed grill," which includes brain, heart and liver as a specialty, undermines the physical stamina of Israel's army.)

So what do we say to those cumbersome individuals who abuse their bodies, refusing to regard it "as an instrument of the soul to carry out all its works" (*Tehiyat HaMaitim*, Maimonides)? Well, Maimonides provides encouragement to those who feel they are incapable of subduing their desires and who are convinced that they lack the discipline to gain control of their physical excesses. In so doing, he definitively states that a sound body is essential to the cultivation of the Divine within each and every one of us: "A good and sound body, which does not disturb the equilibrium in man, is a Divine gift...but it is not impossible to conquer a bad constitution by training" (*Guide to the Perplexed* 3:8). Yes, there is hope for us to complete the Jane Fonda Workout Video. Maimonides elaborates on this theme: "When the body is healthy and sound, one walks in

---

1. Alexandrian philosopher (20 BCE — 50 BCE).

the ways of the Lord, it being impossible to understand or know anything of the knowledge of the Creator when one is sick; therefore it is obligatory upon man to avoid things which are detrimental to the body, and acclimate himself to things that heal and fortify" (*Mishnah Torah, Hilchot Dayot* 4:1).

None of these Jewish sources argue that one can protect him- or herself against certain illnesses and diseases, but the command is quite clear: whenever possible one should look after his or her body, treating it as a gift from God. Preventive medicines therefore become a necessity within Judaism, provided they have a chance to ward off disease, both physical and emotional; however one must be cautioned against addictive drugs. Any abuse of the body that is induced by harmful drugs, such as cocaine, ecstasy, and even stronger substances, are strictly forbidden within Judaism. The hallowed notion of "cleanliness is next to Godliness" (*Talmud Avodah Zara* 20b) contradicts the "dirtying" of one's body with these foreign and harmful products. The Betty Ford Drug Rehabilitation Clinic should not be on the list of one of the places of Jewish interest.

And then there are those whose concern for their body is so exaggerated that "looks" mean everything. It is here where real physical damage to one's body can result. I refer to those (primarily young girls) who are unduly impressed by the *Victoria Secret* catalogue or by the *Sports Illustrated* swimsuit edition. The young women who appear in these magazines would make Twiggy look well endowed. Fashion channels and MTV, not to mention the popular show *Friends* with its three undernourished female stars, have turned "skinny" into an ideal, spurring on the physical and psychological phenomenon of anorexia nervosa or bulimia nervosa. More than the family constellation, society's norms play an often devastating effect in this area. Such care for one's body must not turn into an obsessive illness. (One might add here that the advertisement industry is basically exploitative and demeaning when it comes to the "selling" of women's bodies — the presentation always being some toothpick looking girl successfully enticing her man!) This would also relate to those whose concentration on body-building at the gym turns them into pagan worshippers in the spirit of the ancient Greeks, whereby Adonis and Venus become their new gods.

It is fairly obvious that emotional stress can affect the body: "Three things sap one's strength — worry, travel and sin" (*Talmud Gittin* 70a). But no one should believe that illegal drugs can solve one's emotional difficulties, just as no one should believe that cosmetic changes in one's body can be a salve for one's worries. They cannot serve as substitutes for a proper diet (see **Way #33 — Your Food**) and a daily regimen of exercise. Both of these disciplines can alter the emotional well-being of an individual for the better. But even here, balance is advised. One can overdo a good thing: "Too much sitting aggravates hemorrhoids; too much standing injures the heart; too much walking hurts the eyes. Hence, divide your time among the three" (*Talmud Ketubot* 111b).

Ultimately, ill health, due to lack of caring for the body, diminishes our Divine worth. A story is told of Hillel.[1] "When he finished a lesson with his pupils, he accompanied them from the house of study. They said to him: 'Master, where are you going?' He replied: 'To perform a religious duty.' 'Which religious duty,' they asked? He answered: 'If somebody is appointed to scrape and clean the statues of the king that decorate the theaters and circuses, is monetarily rewarded for the work, and furthermore fraternizes with the noble class, how much more so should I, who am created in the Divine image and likeness, take care of my body'" (*Leviticus Rabbah* 34:3).

The thirty-seventh way to be Jewish is to cherish and treat

1. 1st century rabbinic authority, who became the president of the Sanhedrin (Council of Jewish Sages). Many of the statements in *Saying of the Fathers* are attributed to him.

one's body as if it were a precious stone: so its worth increases with time, even though age will eventually subdue it. Jews are expected to treat their bodies with the reverence that being created in the "image of God" would demand. After all: "There is no wealth, like health" (*Apocrypha*, Ben Sira, 30:16). Preventive medicine, a proper diet, exercise, emotional stability all contribute to a healthy body. To return to our philosopher/doctor, Maimonides: "The well-being of the soul can be obtained only after that of the body has been secured" (*Guide to the Perplexed*, 3:27). And in Judaism, while the body withers and fades with time, the soul is eternal.

So let's look after our: "hair, head, brain, ears, eyes, nose, mouth, teeth, tongue, chin, neck, tits, heart, back, ass, arms, fingers, legs, feet, toes, liver, blood, guts, muscles...and soul." Remember: "I got life," so let's guard it with all our Divine might.

YOUR PRAYERS

or:

I Pray, therefore I am

It is said that there are no atheists in foxholes. I know this to be true. During the Lebanon War of 1982, I was with my Israeli army unit just above the Beirut-Damascus Highway, when a hail of Syrian missiles rained down on our outpost. Quickly, we dashed for the bunkers that we had dug around our encampment. Suddenly, I heard a devout non-believer next to me involuntarily "praying his guts out." Of course, as soon as he noticed me observing him, he regained his composure. Trying to make light of his sudden religious awakening, which obviously embarrassed him (like me he had moved to Israel from the United States), I said: "Maybe we should reevaluate our Zionist commitment!"

Meyer Levin, in his book *The Harvest*, describes a scene where the deeply religious patriarch of a large and dispersed family gathers his entire clan together in his house at the end of World War I. His children, all having been raised in Ottoman Palestine, had each adopted a different life-style; one became a businessman, another an Orthodox scholar, and yet another a socialist, who helped to found the Kibbutz Movement. His socialist (and non-believing) son had been conscripted into the Turkish army to fight the British. In his attempt to escape, he was captured and sent to a prison in Damascus. It had been assumed that he was killed by the Turkish forces. As the family celebrated its reunion after years of dislocation because of the war, the father walks out to the field, deeply saddened that his first-born is not there. Suddenly, he sees his son approach from the distance. The two men fall into each other's arms. Neither can find the words to express the high emotion of the moment, until simultaneously and intuitively they recite together, despite the theological worlds that separate them, the traditional prayer for a safe journey.

In Elie Wiesel's book *Legends of our Time*, his first story, "Kaddish for my Father," tells of the virtual impossibility for him to recite the *kaddish*, the mourner's prayer, because the words are a singular statement of unabashed praise for God. Given all that he witnessed during the Holocaust, he considers the words insulting, too painful to utter. But his need to speak overwhelms him, and so he finds that he must recite these expressions of adulation, not to praise God, but to blame God, to mete out a measure of guilt to the Almighty. Wiesel is unable to remain silent, as his prayer rises to the heavens.

To pray is difficult. It is challenging. It is not entertainment. It is a discipline, like music, running or meditation. It is like playing jazz. The more you pray, the richer and more varied your prayer becomes. Musicians improvise on a set of musical themes. They can play together in harmony one moment, and in the next, they can each play at their own rhythm and/or at their own volume.

The synagogue supplies the band, while the *Siddur* provides the notes.[1]

I will not relate to prayer in terms of the synagogue, as that was discussed in **Way #12 — Your Synagogue**. In addition, the notion of the importance of the *minyan* has been referred to in a number of **Ways**. As for the *Siddur,* one should know that it contains a collection of spiritual yearnings, which have lived on through thousands of years of religious piety, embedded with a richness of Jewish literature and historical narratives.

Yet one should always try to reach a proper balance between the "pray-er" and the prayer, and between the "pray-er" and other "pray-ers."[2] But here too the *Siddur* is not the focal point of this **Way**. Nor does the choreography of prayer occupy any role in this **Way**. Standing erect, shuffling back and forth, bowing, or wrapping oneself in religious garb are all elements that surround the act of prayer; but for the purposes of this **Way**, I would like to focus on the human need for prayer, which, like the jazz artist, often finds its expression in spontaneity and improvisation. Of interest to most Jews is the *kavannah* of worship (intention of prayer) rather than the *keva* of worship (fixed prayer, as recorded in the *Siddur*).

In the fight against evil, according to the Jewish tradition, a Jew relies upon three weapons, which occupy a central place in the High Holiday liturgy: "Repentance, prayer and charity can avert the evil decree." Of these three, prayer, once the strongest in the arsenal of Judaism, has become the weakest. Prayer used to be the answer to every problem, but today it is the problem itself. Is prayer obsolete? Are we really missing anything important in our spiritual and moral development if we do not pray? Is there any value to prayer for the modern Jew? Is prayer an exercise in futility?

---

1. From the Introduction by Rabbi Levi Weiman-Kelman to the *Siddur, Service of the Heart.*
2. *Ibid.*

Part of the reason we feel that prayer does not speak to us is because whenever we attempt to pray, particularly from a prayer book or within the confines of a formal service, we are left with a feeling that it is as dry as dust, that what we are experiencing is a tedious mumbling of words. What should we expect? Perhaps to follow in the footsteps of Mel Brooks' "Two Thousand Year Old Man," and run up to a tree, sniff its bark and jump in the air singing *Sweet Sue*? Some of us expect such an instant rush. But was it ever claimed that religious feeling could come easily like water from a faucet? After all, what worthwhile intellectual or spiritual goal can be reached without an investment of time and energy? Can we really expect to acquire wisdom at short range?

Such an attitude reminds one of an actual legal case about a student who graduated from university, and later sued the institution. He argued that, after having earned his liberal arts degree, contrary to the statement in the school's catalogue that a liberal education would lead a student to wisdom, he was certain he had not become wise. Spiritual sensitivity is no less difficult to develop than a logical mind — or wisdom. It takes a lifetime to develop. In everything that we do, steadfastness and intimacy is the prerequisite for proficiency. Such is the case with prayer, too. It is hard work to pray. So, what are the advantages of working at praying?

Prayer serves as a means to preserve memory. Karl Marx gave atheists one of their strongest arguments: "Religion is the opium of the masses. It is an escape, a way of forgetting reality." I wonder which religion he had in mind. Jews always prayed, not to forget, but to remember. The last words of Moses before his death describe one of the prime objectives of worship: "Remember the days of old, consider the years of past generations" (*Deuteronomy* 32:7).

We Jews are a people of memory. Every ritual, every occasion is tied up with a recollection of an event of joy of sorrow. Our holidays are our collective memory: bitter herbs on Passover to remind us of our ancestors' enslavement in ancient Egypt. To forget this would mean the loss of what should be the most tender spot in the Jewish heart — a sympathy for the downtrodden, a passion for freedom. The Chanuka *menorah* speaks of the courage and self-sacrifice of enduring generations of Jews. The Shabbat candles revive the mystery of Creation. And when we stand up to say the *kaddish*, how we remember those we loved, our childhood.

The Baal Shem Tov[1] said: "Remembrance is the root of redemption." A profound thought if one bears in mind the utter helplessness of the amnesia victim. A person without a memory turns into a lifeless individual. Failing to remember the past, we are doomed to repeat it. There is no culture, no progress, no redemption from the evils of yesterday if we do not remember. Another name for the High Holidays is the "Days of Remembrance." A section of the prayers is called "Remembrances." And more specifically, there is one particular part called *Yizkor* ("Let one remember"). It is at the *Yizkor* service that one recalls those who have died. These prayers become deeply imprinted within us, all very private thoughts. At that time we remember those who used to sit next to us, the familiar face of a mother or a father, the closeness or rivalries of a brother or a sister, the affection of, or arguments with, a friend. Sometimes our recollections mingle with feelings of remorse and guilt, things left undone or unsaid, haunting memories that may even shame us.

Are there any memories without some regrets? Inevitably the hour of prayer turns into an inventory of conscience. So prayer not only serves as a key to memory, but also as a door to promote self-judgment and self-improvement.

---

1. Israel Ben Eliezer (1700-1760) who founded the Hasidic Movement (an eastern European religious ecstatic movement — Hasid means "pious one"). Authentic biographical material of his life is scant, but it is believed that he was orphaned as a child, spending considerable time alone in the woods, meditating in solitude in his Russian village of Podolia. He was considered a miracle worker.

There is a parable of a sensitive young architect, who, at the sight of an ugly structure, would suffer physical pain verging on apoplexy. One day he took a walk in his neighborhood and saw a new house. Its ugliness nearly made him faint. He was so afraid that he might see the house again, that he took the only sure way of avoiding the sight of it: he moved into it himself. Then the house became so familiar to him that he never really saw it again, and lived happily ever after. Often this can be the case with any one of us. We become so adjusted to who we are that we come to accept ourselves uncritically. So, of all the benefits of prayer, perhaps this is the most significant. After all, the confessional element is never absent form worship. Prayer offers us the opportunity to examine ourselves.

I would maintain that true worship is not a petition to God, but rather a sermon to ourselves. The ultimate aim of prayer is the purification, enlightenment and uplifting of our inner self. So where is God in this whole process? If we use prayer only as means to address issues of remembrance, loneliness, alienation, guilt, self-examination, or fear, then it could very well be that God is not part of the worship process. However, when we consider the wonders in our life, when we are thankful or hopeful or thoughtful or awe-struck, we naturally tend to believe in a Force or Being greater than ourselves (see **Way #15 — Your God**). And so, knowingly or unknowingly, wittingly or unwittingly, for a Jew, God is the Source that prompts prayer. "When you pray, know before whom you stand" (*Talmud Berachot* 28b). It is before God that we stand, as "our prayers become a window to heaven" (Baal Shem Tov) — but not only. Prayer is also a "gateway to our own heart" (*Talmud Ta'anit* 2a).

The thirty-eighth way to be Jewish is to incorporate prayer into our lives. Prayer should not be a problem, it should be an opportunity. It can give voice to our most important memories; it can lead to profound self-assessment; it can provide the emotional outlet to express our greatest fears and hopes. During prayer we can lose ourselves, as "we remove our hearts from all worldly concerns" (Nachmanides, Letter to his son Nachman, circa 1268). Prayer is basically a conversation with ourselves through God, by which we aspire to lift ourselves to a world of perfection.

YOUR MARRIAGE

or:

"Love and Marriage, It's an Institute you can't Disparage"[1]

"**M**arriage is a wonderful institution, but who wants to live in an institution" (Groucho Marx)? The idea (and ideal) of marriage is indeed one of the most important institutions in Jewish life: "God creates new worlds constantly. In what way? By causing marriages to take place" (*Zohar* I:89a).[2] Marriage is a basic *Mitzvah* in Judaism, which is affirmed by all the codes of Jewish law. At the very beginning of humankind, the notion of marriage is introduced.

1. From one of Frank Sinatra's famous songs, *Love and Marriage*, written by Sammy Cahn and Jimmy Van Heusen (1965).
2. The *Zohar* is a book of kabbalistic teachings believed to date in part from the 2nd century.

"And the Lord God said: It is not good for man to be alone, I will make a fitting helper for him" (*Genesis* 2:18), and "Hence a man leaves his mother and father and clings to his wife..." (*Genesis* 2:24).

The sixth blessing of the seven recited at a Jewish wedding ceremony makes reference to the joy of the Garden of Eden, of Paradise. It reminds one of the gallant saying by Goethe: "A wife is a gift bestowed upon man to reconcile him for the loss of Paradise." At its best, marriage is Paradise, the idealization of life, a unity of spirit — the only realizable utopia.

What are the requirements for such a marriage to embrace these lofty concepts? They are a mystery. No generalizations or easy formulas are possible. There are no duplicates in marriage. Each is a unique relationship. The Kabbala expounds on the theory of the mystics: that before releasing a soul for life on earth, the Creator splits it in two, and when these two parts find one another in life, their encounter is true love, and their union fulfills the biblical saying: "...and they shall become one flesh" (*Genesis* 2:24).

Despite all this biblical "man" talk, there should be no misunderstanding; marriage should be an equal venture, even though certain religious roles within traditional Judaism tend to favor the male. Indeed, the traditional wedding ceremony itself has elements of pure chauvinism. And of course, Jews are influenced by the norms of the society in which they live, and sadly those norms too often bypass the concept of equality within the species. But if we look to the actual source of the above quoted kabbalistic statement, we will find that equality is a sacred concept within marriage: "When a soul is sent down from Heaven, it is a combined male and female soul. The male part enters the male child and the female part enters the female child. If they are worthy, God causes them to reunite in marriage. This is true and equal mating" (*Zohar*, III:149b). There is no room for misinterpretation here.

Marriage in Judaism is supposed to provide the opportunity for procreation, although any hint of this cannot be culled from the aforementioned verses in *Genesis* 2:18-24. There is no inclusion of reproduction, as procreation is mentioned in another context, in another narrative account of the creation of man and woman. What is important to us is that when the bearing of children is commanded, it reinforces the idea of equality in a marriage. "And God created man in His image, in the image of God, He created him: **male and female**" (*Genesis* 1:27). Immediately following this equal creation, the first commandment in the Bible appears: "God blessed them and said to them, be fruitful and multiply, fill the earth and master it..." (*Genesis* 1:28). Notice that God's directive is given to the two of them equally. And so, without an equal partner in life, a person is not complete.[1]

But the sole purpose of marriage is not just to provide kids; after all, there are those couples who are unable to have children. First and foremost, marriage fulfills the Godly suggestion that "it is not good for a human being to be alone." Companionship and completion are two essential elements in any marriage. "Rabbi Tanhum ben Hanilai[2] said: 'Whoever is not married abides without joy, without blessing, without good. Without joy' — as it is written: 'And you shall rejoice, you and your household' (*Deuteronomy* 14:26); 'Without blessing' — as it is written: 'To cause blessing to rest in your house' (*Ezekiel* 44:30); 'Without good' — as it is written: 'It is not good for man to be alone'" (*Genesis* 2:18).[3]

So, now that we have established that marriage is a good thing, and you've gotten married: What next? "You sleep in separate rooms, you have dinner apart, you take separate vacations. You're doing everything you can to keep your marriage together" (Roger

---

1. *Genesis Rabbah* 17:2 — "Without a wife, a man is incomplete."
2. A Palestinian rabbinic teacher in the 3rd century.
3. See *Talmud Yevamot* 63a. In *Talmud Yevamot* 63b, it is written: "The one who remains unmarried impairs the Divine image."

Dangerfield). Marriage is a constant. You are basically committed to live together for your entire lives, during the grand times and the hard times. Therefore: "Never go to bed mad. Stay up and fight" (Phyllis Diller)!

But how does one deal with arguments, disagreements, unpleasantries, knowing that they are unavoidable? So many aspects of a life together can arouse conflicts: the raising of children, the choice of home and/or career, relatives (particularly the "in-laws," although this conflict is highly exaggerated). Even the most mundane matters can leave a marriage teetering on edge: which TV show to watch, when to activate the air-conditioner, what movie to see. And, how many couples have almost ended their marriage over "refurbishment," the bane of all marital bliss: a new bathroom, a new bedroom, and most challenging of all — a new kitchen! Jewish literature is understanding of this reality: "There is no marriage wherein there is no quarreling" (*Talmud Shabbat* 130b).

If a couple cannot find a way to reconcile their differences, then they might have to consider divorce, because their original choice in a partner was probably wrong: "Two who quarrel constantly should not marry one another (*Talmud Kiddushin* 71b). But running to a divorce lawyer every time one differs with his or her spouse is not advisable. In a world of "instant gratification," we need to disavow ourselves of the common notion that if we don't like something, or if a particular matter is a bit difficult, we can simply "switch channels." If we don't like our car, we exchange it. If we are dissatisfied with our work, we seek another job. If we are unhappy with our home, we move. Therefore, if our spouse gives us grief, we can trade him or her in.

Marriage is not easy. Happiness in marriage is not a guaranteed gift, but it is a creative opportunity. Marriage is an obligation, not an experiment. The marriage contract stipulates that one is to work through matters of contention. In order to struggle constructively with conflicts, a marriage must be based on mutual respect and mutual obligation; hence, we return to the absolute necessity of maintaining a marriage that is predicated on absolute equality, which is the ultimate guarantor for a successful union. How does one demonstrate respect for the other? By seeing him- or herself as being obligated to always be sensitive to the needs of the other — and, above all, to be honest. Complete openness with the other is an absolute requirement. One should never be embarrassed for the other, or in front of the other. Such is the meaning of the words: "The two of them were naked, the man and his wife (Adam and Eve), yet they felt no shame" (*Genesis* 2:25).

Great is the marriage where a husband and wife have found each other to love and trust unconditionally. Better is the marriage where each one considers the other the most important person in his or her eyes. Divine is the one who, in the presence of the other, can be him- or herself without pretense or fear, as George Eliot put it so well:

> Oh, the comfort, the inexpressible comfort of feeling safe with a person, having neither to weigh thoughts nor measure words, but to pour them all out, just as they are, chaff and grain together, knowing that a faithful hand will take and sift them, keep what is worth keeping, and then, with a breath of kindness, blow the rest away.

"A matron once asked Rabbi Jose ben Halafta: 'What has your God been doing since He finished making the world?' 'He has been matching couples in marriage,' came the reply" (*Genesis Rabbah* 68:4). The act of marriage is considered a heavenly act. In the consciousness of sharing a life with someone else, in that sense of constancy resides the sanctity, the beauty of marriage, the essence of matrimonial love, which helps to endure pain more easily, to enjoy happiness doubly, to nurture our best instincts; all the while giving rise to the fullest and finest development of our personalities, both separate and together. **For these reasons alone, the** thirty-ninth way to be Jewish is to be married: to cultivate that marriage through all the emotional and physical ups and downs and highs and lows, so as to ultimately help each other be worthy of the other: "If a husband and wife are worthy, then the Divine Presence will abide with them…" (*Talmud Sota* 17a).

YOUR SPIRITUALITY[1]

or:

"Turn On, Tune In, Drop Out"[2]

It was during my junior year in high school (circa 1961) when I was invited to Timothy Leary's home to experiment with a relatively new "non-addictive" mind-altering drug: LSD. I was told that I would have a spiritual high. Since I was then at an age and stage in my life, that whenever my parents asked me to do something, I would respond (always in an annoyed tone (see **Way #42 — Your Parents**): "Alright, I'll do it — when the spirit moves me," I was more than ready to dabble in some sort of spiritual experimentation. I was not the least bit concerned about drugs.

1. Suggested reading is *Zohar, the Book of Splendor: Basic Readings from the Kabbalah*, edited by Gershom Scholem (Schocken Books, 1978 — Tenth Printing).
2. Said by Timothy Leary (1920-1996), the LSD guru of the Sixties, who authored *The Psychedelic Experience*.

Despite the meteoric rise of marijuana use at the time, having grown up in a home with a father who smoked three packs of cigarettes a day, I had an aversion to smoke. (As a result I am certain I was saved from ending up in a methadone clinic.) Indeed, one dose of LSD sent me to the bathroom vomiting, leaving not only my physical guts on the floor, but also my spiritual insides.

A concept of "the spiritual" was already introduced in the very first verses of the Bible: "In the beginning God created the heaven and the earth. And the earth was unformed and void, with darkness over the surface of the deep, and the spirit of God swept over the face of the waters" (*Genesis* 1:1-2). Ever since that time, humankind has been trying to figure out what is "spirit," who possesses it or who is possessed by it. A byproduct of this search also includes the "soul" of our being. What is the difference between believing in "spirits" and feeling spiritual? Can Judaism abide a séance where one tries to raise the spirit of the dead or converse with a deceased's spirit? I remember once conducting a *Havdala* service in the presence of our fifteen-year old Greek-Catholic baby-sitter. With the lights off, a twisted candle burning, incense being passed around and sweet wine being drunk, I was certain that she must have thought we were communing with Jewish ghosts or angels. (Indeed, within the *Prayerbook*, there is a section called "angelology.")

The Bible is full of references to the "Spirit of God" being within each of us: "I will pour out My Spirit upon all flesh" (*Joel* 3:1), "I will put My Spirit in you, and you shall live" (*Ezekiel* 37:14), or "My Spirit abides among you; fear not" (*Haggai* 2:5). Most convincing is that which is written in the *Apocrypha:*[1] "The Creator planted His sweet Spirit in all, and made It a guide for all mortals" (1:5). That being the case, all we have to do is cultivate that Spirit, or as the Bible would have it, the Divine within us. But that's not so easy. The

---

1. Body of Jewish literature written in later Second Temple times, and for some subsequent decades; most of the works originated in Palestine.

question is: How? Well, to answer this, let's hope "the spirit moves me," otherwise this will be a very short **Way**.

Recently, there has been an attempt within Judaism, particularly among the Reform and Conservative Movements, to introduce "spirituality" into the life of a Jew, primarily to offset what is perceived as a somewhat overly cerebral religious approach to Jewish life. There is little question that those of us who grew up in the Sixties and who are now approaching the last quarter-of-a-century of our days here on earth, have developed a renewed need to find meaning in our lives. Ever impatient, we want to return to the "spiritual" high of those days. (Of course, in retrospect we tend to romanticize our youth.) It is as if we want to become "flower children" all over again, floating slightly above ground. We are all too willing to be participants in a spiritual renewal. But the expectation that we can walk into a religious service and dance with angels is naïve at best, certainly for any sustainable period of time. Yet, there are exceptions where we see sudden "religious conversions," or what is known in Judaism as *chozrei b'tshuva*, those who are penitent and return to their Jewish religious roots.

As outlined in **Way #38 — Your Prayers**, steadfastness and intimacy are the prerequisites for proficiency. Spiritual and intellectual fulfillment take a lifetime to develop; it cannot be gained at a moment's notice, prompted by a sudden urge to unveil the purpose of one's life. A jump-started emotional outpouring of religious ecstasy will eventually evaporate if there is not some sort of intellectual basis for spiritual expression. Therefore, without the requisite background, and because it often lacks Jewish depth, the current attempt to introduce "spirituality" into Jewish life smacks of Christian evangelical pre-dominance. Sitting in a circle, clasping your neighbor's hand, eyes tightly shut, talking of the power of God to "heal," seem to create an identification more with those who attend a Protestant revivalist tent meeting than with other Jews.

This form of religious syncretism, while understandable, is not necessary as an approach to Jewish spirituality.

Judaism has a long history of spiritual influence, which gained prominence through the *Zohar* and the kabbalists. Today, spirituality is most closely identified with Hasidism, the popular religio-social movement with strong pietist and mystical roots. Hasidism finds its expression in *Psalms*: "Raise a shout for the Lord, all the earth; worship the Lord in gladness — come into God's Presence with shouts of joy" (100:1-2). It stresses prayerful devotion over exclusive study and talmudic expertise. What is important to note here is: While "prayers of the heart" are emphasized over intellectual immersion, they are not at the expense of it. Jewishly, a Hasid is the bearer of a vast knowledge of Jewish laws and practices. Thus, the Hasid, fortified by a strong familiarity with Judaism, is free to indulge in ecstatic prayer, cheerful optimism, communion with God, personal redemption, humility and love of his or her "brothers and sisters." (The egalitarian appellation here is the author's, as Hasidism generally refers to men). For a Jew, there should be no need to seek his or her spiritual self in Eastern religions or Christian cults. We need to know that Judaism has within it a spiritual dimension.

At its core, Hasidic philosophy displays many original elements in its application. Central doctrines are: God's living presence fills the universe (immanence) and is everywhere (omnipresence); that there is a relation between the lower, terrestrial world and the upper, celestial one, and the communication between them is possible on the spiritual plane; that true Jewish life demands an outpouring of heart and soul in the performance of *Mitzvot*, which must be filled with spontaneity and enthusiasm, not in a lifeless, mechanical fashion; and, most important, the ordinary person needs a spiritual guide or mentor. As indicated in the previous paragraph, that guide need not be the Dalai Lama or the late Jerry Garcia.

So, how does one attain a semblance of spirituality in his or her life? First, one has to study. A basic knowledge of the daily prayers is essential for spiritual growth: "Who prays without knowing what he prays, does not pray" (Maimon Ben Joseph, *Letters of Consolation*). Second, one has to work at it. Meditation, yoga, lying alone and, as Maimonides urged: "Abstracting oneself from all worldly matters" — all contribute to a sense of trusting oneself to get in tune with oneself. For one to let spirituality into his or her life, one has to be completely focused in prayer and thought: "If a man can concentrate, let him pray; not otherwise" (*Talmud Berachot* 30b). Third, hone in on a particular issue in your life — be it troubling, sad, curious, joyful, melancholy, suspenseful, unsettling or inspiring — and let your mind run with your thoughts: "Prayer needs attuning of the mind" (*Jerusalem Talmud Berachot* 4:1). Fourth, visualize a matter of great concern, and approach it anew each time you pray: "Do not let your prayer become perfunctory" (*Sayings of the Fathers* 2:13). Indeed, the Hasidic Rabbi Nachman of Bratzlav (1772-1811) suggested: "It would be better for every man to pray when he feels inspired, to pray his own prayer and in a language familiar to him." Fifth, if the synagogue setting is not your "spiritual thing," then make certain that you find a place that is: "A man needs no fixed places to say his prayers, no synagogues; among the trees of the forest, everywhere one can pray" (Baal Shem Tov). Sixth, seek out a teacher, a mentor, a guide: "...provide yourself with a teacher and get yourself a friend..." (*Sayings of the Fathers* 1:6). In other words: "provide yourself with a teacher," from whom you can learn, and "get yourself a friend," with whom you can review that which you have learned.

But just as one's spiritual quest can only be fulfilled if there is some prior knowledge, so too is it an absolute necessity that one's belief in God is tested, if not definitive. That is: one's faith in a Higher Being must be assumed, even though one cannot necessarily define all the parameters of one's belief.

The fortieth way to be Jewish is to "let the spirit move you." There are so many times in our lives, especially as we grow older, when we need to believe in something beyond ourselves: beyond rationality, philosophy, logic and science — and to call upon that something to give us a spiritual lift. Each of us is "created in the image of God," which means, by simple logical deduction, as stated at the outset of this **Way**, that there is a portion of God within each of us, whose designated name in Judaism is "spirit." So when you are all alone at night, conjure up all your deepest thoughts — both fears and hopes — and: "Commune with your own heart (spirit) upon your bed, and be still...and trust in the Lord" (*Psalm* 4:5-6). If you do this, the "spirit will move you."

YOUR FRIENDS

or:

"Love your Friend as you Love yourself"[1]

There were three compelling songs of the Sixties, still popular today, that accurately summarized the great need for a friend: 1) Carol King's song, *You've Got a Friend,* which essentially defines the positive elements of friendship; 2) *Easy to be Hard,* from the musical *Hair,* which characterizes the need for consistency in any relationship; and 3) Simon & Garfunkel's *Old Friends,* which addresses the need for close friends to combat the loneliness of old age (see **Way #35 — Your Aging**). Each one of these ballads had a profound effect on my generation, as they guided us through our teenage and college years.

But as attractive as these songs are, none of them defines the

---

1. From *Leviticus* 19:18.

basic essentiality of friendship as well as those prescribed in Jewish sources. So, to parallel our modern day folk-prophets, here are three quotes from the Jewish tradition that encapsulate the power of friendship: 1) "How inherently good and thoroughly pleasant for friends to dwell together" (*Psalm* 133:1); 2) "Who finds a faithful friend, finds a treasure" (*Ben Sira* 6:13); and 3) "Friendship fans love" (*B'chayai* — Yosef Ibn Pakuda).[1] And let's add a fourth for good measure — one that captures the beauty of having a friend: "Friendship is a human being's greatest gift" (*Shirat Yisrael*, Moshe Ibn Ezra).

But with all of these "pie-in-the-sky" proclamations, friendship requires hard work. It is like a bank account, you cannot take more from it than you put in. We must never take friendship for granted, nor exchange friends for social expediency. Ben Sira, in his *Wisdom Literature*, seems to understand this point better than most: "Who casts a stone at a bird will frighten it away, and who abuses a friend will estrange his affection: (22:23). Indeed, the notion of working hard to make and keep friends is such a lofty ideal within Judaism, that we regard the essence of a hero as "he who turns his enemy into a friend" (*Avot de Rabbi Natan* 23).[2] So if a Jew is commanded to turn his very foe into a social partner, then how much more important is it to nurture and cherish a friend who begins as one.

Carol King, Simon & Garfunkel, and *Hair* may speak to us, but their contemporary wisdom is not all that original, for it is given force by a Jewish tradition that has maintained that wisdom for thousands of years. But since religious syncretism is very much a part of Jewish historical development, especially in the area of music, there is no reason not to relate to the words of their songs from a Jewish perspective. So, let's juxtapose these songs with Jewish sources, as if we were building a traditional commentary

---

1. Spanish religious philosopher (1050-1120).
2. Tannaitic and amoraic sayings, collected during the gaonic period (7th-11th centuries).

around them. Please note that I have set up the commentaries on these songs in the manner of a page of *Talmud*, with the text in the middle and the interpretations surrounding it. The only difference is that, if this were exactly like the *Talmud*, the entire page would be written in Hebrew (and Aramaic).[1] But such a venture would require one to fully adopt **Way #4 — Your Language**, and since the likelihood of that having happened in the short time that it takes to read this book, I thought it best to stick to English.

30a Tractate: Friends

When you're down and troubled: "A friend will prove himself in time of trouble" (*Shirat Yisrael*, Moshe Ibn Ezra, 12c). ***When you're down and and troubled***: "A faithful friend is a powerful defense" (*Ben Sira* 6:14). ***You just call out my name***: "It is better to be with company than to be alone" (*Talmud Yevamot* 118b). ***To brighten up even the darkest night***: "A person who has friends, will naturally show himself to be friendly" (*Proverbs* 18:24). ***You've got a friend***: "Better one old friend than ten new ones" (Bialik). ***You've got a friend***: "Let the honor of your friend be dear to you as your own..." (*Sayings of the Fathers* 2:10) ***You've got a friend***: "Love your friend as you love yourself" (*Leviticus* 19:18) — that is, you should regard your friend in the same way that you regard yourself; or, treat him as you would have others treat you.

When you're down and troubled, and you need a helping hand, and nothing is goin' right. Close your eyes and think of me, and soon I will be there – to brighten up even the darkest night. You just call out my name, and you know wherever I am, I'll come running to see you again. Winter, spring, summer or fall, all you have to do is call, and I'll be there. You've got a friend.

Helping hand: "A faithful friend is the medicine of life" (*Ben Sira* 6:18). ***Helping hand***: "When you wish to befriend someone, befriend a person whom you will extol, and he will extol you in return; and whom if you will honor, will honor you in return; and whom, when you need his help, will help you; and when you are wroth, will bear with you" (*Mivhar Hapeninim* – Book of Proverbs attributed to Shlmo Ibn Gavriel, Spanish poet and philosopher, 1021-1056).

---

1. Early Semitic language closely related to Hebrew. Small sections of the Bible (*Ezra* and *Daniel*) are written in Aramaic, as are sections of the *Talmud*, both the *Babylonian* and the *Jerusalem*.

The message here is clear: friendship is a twenty-four hour a day investment. A true friend is one who is ready to drop everything at a moment's notice in order to help out. According to most Jewish commentators, the famous saying, "love your friend as you love yourself," is meant for us to step into our friend's shoes. It is likened to the Passover entreaty: "In every generation, each person should see him or herself as if he or she personally went out of Egypt." Empathy is the ultimate emotional tool to build a solid, deep, trusting and lasting friendship.

30b Tractate: Friends

How can people be so heartless: "He sins who despises his friend" (*Proverbs* 14:21). *How can people be so cruel*: "Even my bosom friend in whom I trusted, who ate of my bread, has lifted his heel against me" (*Psalm* 41:10). *How can they ignore their friends*: "He who belittles a friend lacks a heart" (*Proverbs* 11:12). *Do you care about a bleeding crowd, how about a needing friend*: "When you pay your friend the respect he deserves and he fails to honor you as you merit, it is better that you give him up" (*Mivhar Hapeninim*). *Do you care about the bleeding crowd, how about a needing friend*: "Every friend says 'I like you,' but there are only a few friends who merit the name friend" (*Ben Sira* 37:1). *I need a friend*: "It is not good for man to be alone" (*Genesis* 2:18). *I need a friend*: "A friendless person is like a right hand without a left" (*Mivhar Hapeninim*).

How can people be so heartless? How can people be so cruel? Easy to be hard, easy to be cold. How can people have no feelings? How can they ignore their friends? Especially people who care about strangers, who care about social injustice. Do you care about a bleeding crowd, how about a needing friend? I need a friend.

Easy to be hard: "Never weary of making friends" (Asher ben Yechiel, c. 1320). *Easy to be hard*: "Bring all people into friendship with you" (*Apocrypha Aristeas* 228). *How can people have no feelings*: "Be on guard against your friends" (*Ben Sira* 6:13) *How can people have no feelings*: There are friends who present their own hurt; but there is a friend who sticks closer than a brother" (*Proverbs* 18:24).

Judaism holds a special place for the "stranger in our midst" (see **Way #18 — Your Social Activism**). *Tikkun olam* (repairing the world), a theme that is emphasized in the writings of the prophets, has its roots in those moral commandments that insist on our active participation in social causes (see **Way #23 — Your Moral Mitzvot**). However, a friend must never be sacrificed for a "cause." Indeed, in order to guarantee a continued commitment to a particular idea, one must first be certain that one has been able to sustain a relationship. But when a friendship goes sour, it is "easy to be hard," to close oneself off in self-defense. However, Judaism would urge one not to lose hope. There is no room for cynicism in the pursuit of friendship. It is not enough to love humanity, one must love human beings as well.

Now, where do Jewish friends fit into this **Way**? It should be eminently clear that if one wishes to raise a Jewish family, it is advisable to marry another Jew. While there are exceptions to this rule, they remain exceptions. So, acquiring Jewish friends is the best guarantee that one has of eventually linking up with another Jew for life. Throughout the life cycle of a Jew, there are numerous events that have Jewish religious significance. Birth, Bar/Bat Mitzvah, marriage have rich Jewish rituals and customs. There is a real joy in sharing these events with friends who have an under-standing of them and have experienced them as well. But as we ease into the last song, *Old Friends* — or the final tractate of our mock page of *Talmud* — we should consider the comfort we can derive from a friend who shares the same customs and practices. As we grow older and we see our friends die one-by-one, we receive solace in the religious rituals that surround each death. They provide a familiarity that strengthens us as we face our own impending demise (see **Way #46 — Your Death**).

31a Tractate: Old Friends

Old friends: "Forsake not an old friend... (*Ben Sira* 9:10). **Old friends**: "Friendship: one heart in two bodies" (*Sefer Shashuim*, Zabara, ch. 7).[1] **Waiting for the sunset**: "Lovely and pleasant in their lives, even in their death they were not divided" (*II Samuel* 1:23). **How terribly strange to be seventy**: "Your true friend is the one who knows your faults and yet will always love you" (Popular). **How terribly strange to be seventy**: "Old friends and old wine do not lose their flavor" (Yiddish saying). **Silently sharing the same fears**: "Where you die, will I die too, and there be buried. May the Lord do so to me and more besides if even death part me from you (*Ruth* 1:17). **Silently sharing the same fears**: "A scholar, told that his friend had died, exclaimed — 'the whetstone of my wits is broken'" (*Shirat Yisrael*, Moshe ben Ezra). **Silently sharing the same fears**: "I am, you see, so old that I do not know how soon I may die" (*Genesis* 27:2).[2]

Old friends, winter companions, the old men.... waiting for the sunset.... sitting through trees, settles like dust, on the shoulders of the old friends. Can you imagine us years from today, sharing a park bench quietly? How terribly strange to be seventy. Memory brushes the same years. Silently sharing the same fear...

Winter companions: "False friends, like birds, migrate in cold weather" (Yiddish saying). **Winter companions**: "The older, the colder" (Ladino saying).[3] **Can you imagine us years from today**: Abandon me not when I grow old" (*Psalm* 71:9). **Can you imagine us years from today**: What a man does in his youth affects his old age" (*Talmud Shabbat* 152a).

Those old friends sitting on that park bench strike us as being true friends, not convenient ones: "Who makes friends too easily (indiscriminately) will lose them as soon" (*Shevat Yehuda*, Rabbi Shlomo Ibn Verga).[4] In order to avoid facile relationships, a friendship must be based on mutual respect and trust — and unconditional love. "A wise man was asked: 'Whom would you love more, your brother or your friend?' He answered: 'I will not love my brother until he becomes my friend'" (*Mivhar Hapeninim*). Such was the

---

1. Joseph Zabara: Hebrew satirist, poet, physician from Barcelona (13th century).
2. Isaac's words to his son Esau.
3. Ladino is a Judeo-Spanish dialect spoken by Jews of Spanish origin (Sephardim).
4. Solomon Ibn Verga was a 15th century Spanish physician and historian.

relationship between the tragic/heroic biblical figures of David and Jonathan. And herein lies the plea for Jewish friends, in addition to other friends. The power and attraction of David and Jonathan's relationship, and their ability to sustain it, was that they shared a commonality of Jewish experiences that solidified their friendship over time — despite competing loyalties and a hostile environment. Their "memories brushed the same years."

None of us lives in a vacuum. Friendships have a better chance of meeting the test of time when they are measured against a shared past that goes beyond just two people. "Love that depends on a certain thing, if that be no more, then the love dies with it...What love does not depend on a certain thing, yet endures? This is the love of David and Jonathan" (*Saying of the Fathers* 5:19). True friendship has a better chance to endure if it is rooted in a common history, which is based on cultural, religious and moral compatibility. Friends are friends for life when their life experiences encompass more than just their own private intimacies.

To place this **Way** into a dramatic setting, the Jewish tradition is extreme when putting forth friendship as an essential aspect of one's life: "Either companionship or death" (*Talmud Ta'anit* 23b). **That being the case, the forty-first way to be Jewish better be: "...to get yourself a friend"** (*Sayings of the Fathers* 1:6).

YOUR PARENTS

or:

"Honor your Father and your Mother"[1]

"A Jewish man with parents alive is a fifteen-year-old boy, and will remain a fifteen-year-old boy till they die" (Philip Roth). In this vein, one is reminded of the sixty-five-year-old architect who invited his ninety-year-old mother to join him and some of his friends at the symphony. At the end of the performance, as the son was helping his mother with her coat, she turned to him: "Son, perhaps you have to go to the bathroom before we leave!" This anecdote is indicative of much of the tension that exists between parent and child, bringing to mind the following scene.

---

1. *Exodus* 20:12.

(Two psychiatrists bumped into each other on the street):

First Psychiatrist: How are you? You look a bit troubled.

Second Psychiatrist: I am. I did something terrible. I committed a real Freudian slip.

First: Tell me about it.

Second: I can't. It's too embarrassing. It was a real whopper of a Freudian slip.

First: You'll feel better if you tell me.

Second: Alright. I went to my parents' house for dinner, and did I make a Freudian slip. I wanted to tell my mother to pass the salt, but instead I heard myself saying: "You bitch. You ruined my life!"

No matter how exasperated we can get with our parents (see **Way #48 — Your Kids**, to see how frustrated parents can get with their children), the fifth commandment of the tried and true Ten Commandments says it all: "Honor your father and your mother, that your days may be long upon the land, which the Lord, your God, has given you" (*Exodus* 20:12). It is significant that the previous four commandments are between human beings and God and that the very first commandment wherein we are commanded to relate to others, speaks about our relationship with our parents, thus giving this Divine dictate the highest priority of all human relations.

This commandment appears elsewhere in the Bible, but in a slightly different context: "You shall fear, every person, his mother and his father" (*Leviticus* 19:3, see *Talmud Kiddushim* 30b-31a). In this paraphrase of the Ten Commandments, the commandment to respect your parents comes before observance of the Sabbath and the warning against believing in false idols. Indeed, support for this view is found in the *Jerusalem Talmud*: "To honor parents is more important even than to honor God" (*Pe'ah* 1:1). This is probably the case, because while we are never sure of our relationship with God, we know all too well the intricacies of our relationship with our parents. And, the *Talmud* assumes that if the relationship between parent and child is good and trusting, then force is given to the words: "The honor due to parents is like the honor due to God" (*Mechilta* to *Exodus* 20:12).[1]

Even when a parent and child have a shared identity of ideals, standards, basic commitments and values, this does not guarantee smooth sailing. Comedian (and rabbi) Bob Alper tells of the time when he called his friend. The friend's five-year-old daughter answered the phone, and, upon hearing Bob's request to speak to her father, responded: "My Daddy is the greatest Daddy in the world. He is fantastic. He is just wonderful. I love my Daddy." When the friend finally got on the line after this litany of praise, Alper said: "Fred, enjoy them while they're still stupid!" Only a few years later would our pre-pubescent children, particularly our daughters, insist that we stay in our cars when picking them up after an extra-curricular activity. Or if it were our turn to car pool, we were always forewarned not to do anything that would embarrass them, which always served as a clarion call to say: "Hi guys, I have been warned not do anything embarrassing...Did you hear the joke about...?"

Then come the teenage and college years. I will not dwell on the delicacy of the parent and child wrestling matches during the years of the latter's adolescence, as that will be dealt with in **Way #48 — Your Kids** (although admittedly **Way #48** will delve into the subject of adolescent behavior only in a passing manner, as this entire subject matter is literally "way" beyond the scope of this book). Suffice it to say that during the high school and university period of our lives, virtually everything our parents did got on our nerves. And of course, we responded to their obvious foolishness in a highly sophisticated manner, with the exasperated sigh that included a roll of the eyes, and with a new-found sarcasm: "Yeh,

---

1. The *Mechilta* is a midrashic commentary on *Exodus*.

right Dad" — thus dismissing the possibility that their experience and age could play any role whatsoever when it came to understanding anything in the world. All the while, their ability to pay for our tuition, room and board was never treated with disdain, but also rarely with appreciation.

The love affair that exists between parent and child during the very early years in their respective lives undergoes, with growth and time, bumps and grinds that are often painful. Given the fact that many of us are products of the "permissive" era, we may have taken liberties with our parents that, in the name of honesty, were terribly hurtful. This is not to say that there are not peeks of genuine communication and love along the way. But, would that our tolerance levels for our parents equal their tolerance level for us! Yet, somehow the urgings of our sources escape us: "Hear, my son, the instruction of your father, and forsake not the teaching of your mother" (*Proverbs* 1:8). Add to this the mishnaic statement: "These are the things whose fruits a person enjoys in this world while the capital is laid up for him in the world to come: honoring one's father and mother" (*Pe'ah* 1:1). And if, as quoted above, "the honor due to parents is like the honor due to God" and "to honor parents is more important even than to honor God," then the relationship between child and parent all boils down to a matter of respect. Naturally this is based on the assumption that most of us look back on our lives and recognize that our relationship with our folks was basically a positive one. (As can be surmised, this **Way** does not touch upon those relationships where the parents are truly abusive.)

And then there is the world of the unknown. Events that may have affected the manner in which our parents raised us rarely receive a sympathetic hearing until we mature sufficiently to recognize that we are not the center of the universe. My parents' first-born child, a daughter, was killed in a street-car crash at the age of twelve. It was not until almost five years later, when I was born, that my mother had a nervous breakdown and had to be hospitalized for almost a year-and-a-half. Since there were no pictures of my sister around the house, or any remembrances that indicated that she ever lived, it was not until my teenage years that I even knew of her existence; and then, I learned about it from my aunts and uncles. (I was told that my grandmother on my mother's side was a very superstitious person, who had convinced my mother to remove anything from the house that would remind her of my sister, lest the pain of her loss overcome my mother, which eventually was the case anyway.) Parents often keep things from us in order to protect us. Only much later, when my father was old (my mother suffered from dementia for the last ten years of her life), did he speak to me about his (their) pain.

The emotional breakdown of one's wife, coupled with the tragic death of one's daughter, would incapacitate most of us. As noted in **Way #27 — Your Holidays,** in the discussion of the near sacrifice of Isaac by his father Abraham, there is nothing more painful than the loss of a child. My parents knew and felt that pain when they lost their twelve-year-old daughter. How much they lived in the shadow of that tragedy or how it affected their parenting, I will never know. What I do know is that, while there may be no greater pain than the loss of a child, at the moment of my parents' death, the loss I felt was just as great and painful. In their death, I gained a fuller appreciation of them as parents, and I only wished that the developing respect for them that I acquired when I was in my forties had been a reality when I was younger. We all love our parents, but we should not make a distinction between love and respect. They must go hand in hand. "Respect is not the root from which love grows, but the elm on which it creeps up and brings forth that love into a precious blossom" (Ernst Toller, German Jewish dramatist, 1893-1939).

But if respect is the Jewish order of the day, then we have to show that respect not only with love, but primarily with deeds. In Judaism, one is judged by his or her actions: "Say little and do much" (*Sayings of the Fathers* 1:15). One of the basic acts that can demonstrate respect for a parent is to seek a father or mother's advice. As much as we would like to believe that it is our friends to whom we should turn, ultimately we know, that in addition to seeking help from them, we must approach our parents, as they will advise us with a total commitment to suggesting only that which will help us. (Often, despite their total belief in us, they can be remarkably objective.) "Rely not on the counsel of your peers to overrule the guidance of your parents" (Yehuda Ibn Tibbon).

But since this book is written for my generation, the true test of the relationship between our parents and us is now. We watch as they grow older, and in too many cases the aging process can be devastating. It is at this time that we are called upon to disprove that piercing Yiddish proverb: "One parent can take care of ten children, but ten children cannot take care of one parent." Can we adjust to their aging process with the required sensitivity and attention, rather than with a sense of embarrassment and a feeling of being inconvenienced? How do we deal with the deterioration of our parents' mental and/or physical health in such a way that we are neither overcome by our sad new reality nor belittling of them in their sad new reality? At what point do we take away their independence? Should we? Do we have the right to?

Moving a parent to home care or to a home for the aged is one of the most difficult and delicate emotional transitions in the life of a parent and a child. Of course, many important questions must be asked: Should we place our aging mother and/or father in Golden Village or Century Park or Heavenly Acres or whatever other euphemistic name for a nursing home exists in our community? Need it be a Jewish home? Is our motivation selfish? Is it the best thing for our parents? Why do so many of us feel compelled to convince our parents to move into a home, even against their will? Do we not owe them the respect not only to listen to them, but also to hear them?

The Jewish tradition has always been to keep the family unit together. In today's nuclear family, with one child on one Coast and the other on the opposite, family unity has become an oxymoron. Why can we not have our parents move in with us? But what if they are resistant to the idea of living with us? They most likely would not be, if, throughout our mutual lives, we had sown the type of relationship whereby such an inevitability was not only warmly accepted by both parent and child, but also looked upon with great anticipation of forging an even closer relationship. (Admittedly, if both sets of parents entered into this stage of their life at the same time, it would become quite crowded in one's house, but since the possibility of this happening is very remote, a child need not be scared off.) Most of us can afford to hire the requisite home care. And if we cannot, then we are instructed: "Whether you have money or not, you should respect your father and mother — even if you have to go begging from door to door" (*Jerusalem Talmud Pe'ah* 1:1). So, why can we not consider altering our lifestyle to suit their needs? Are we so invested in our own lives, that when our parents need us the most, we cannot find time for them? It would be best for us to heed the words of our wise friend Ben Sira: "Remember your father and mother when you sit in council among the mighty" (23:4).

None of the above underestimates the complications in caring for parents who become physically infirm or mentally incapacitated. I am writing mostly in the form of questions because there are no clear-cut answers. Indeed, there are many cases where full-time in-house nursing care with hospital accessibility is best for a parent. But too often, parents are placed in some sort of a home before it is really necessary. Yet there are some parents who may seek the comfort of others that a nursing home can provide. If so, it is incumbent upon us to make certain that our visits, and those of our children, are constant and frequent.

"Dear to God is the honoring of a father and mother. For the

Bible employs the same expression about honoring, revering or cursing parents, as about honoring, revering or cursing God. The rewards attached to them are equivalent. It is logical that father, mother and God should thus be joined, for they are, so to speak, partners in bringing the child into life and rearing him" (*Mechilta* on *Exodus* 29:12). Perhaps then, only when we have children of our own, can we truly appreciate our parents' dedication and devotion. Hopefully, with that appreciation will come an understanding on our part that, at that crucial time when they confront **their death**, they truly need us as much as we needed them at **our birth**. A bi-weekly visit to the "home" leaves a parent alone to face a lonely and sad end. We are not alone at birth. So too must we not be alone at death. After all: "He who does not sustain his parents testifies to his own illegitimacy" (*Eliyahu Rabba* 26).[1]

For all the years of our lives, our parents were the care-givers. It is time for us to now become the care-takers. Maimonides cautions us: "If you do not respect your parents, then your children will not respect you" (*Guide to the Perplexed* 4:18). In other words: "What goes around, comes around." **The forty-second way to be Jewish is to acknowledge the Jewish truism: "A child is compelled to support his or her parents" (*Jerusalem Talmud, Nedarim* 9:1) — not out of any sense of guilt, but rather out of a passionate commitment to that inseparable duo of love and respect.**

---

1. Commentary by Elijah Ben Benjamin Wolf Shapiro (1660-1712) on the *Levush*, a commentary written by Modecai Jaffe (1535-1612).

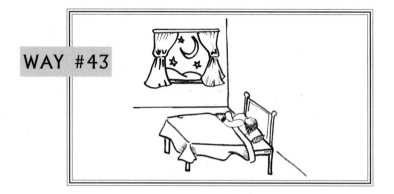

YOUR DREAMS

or:

I'll See you in my Dreams[1]

I was fast asleep, and for some reason — in my dream — I was hanging a picture above my head, holding it with my right hand. Suddenly — in real life — the alarm clock went off on the right side of my bed. So — in my dream — I took the picture in my left hand so as to free up my right hand to shut off the alarm clock — in real life. Unfortunately, I was unable to resume the hanging of the picture, as that alarm clock meant I had to drag myself out of bed and go to work. So, like other things in my life, my dream went unfulfilled.

Okay, back to Freud, as interpreted by Pete Seeger (**see Way #34 — Your Sex Life**):

---

1. Song made popular by Jimmy Durante from his album *As Time Goes By: The Best of Jimmy Durante*, written by Isham Jones and Gus Kahn.

Oh, Doctor Freud, oh, Doctor Freud,
How we wish you had been differently employed.
For this set of circumstances
Sure enhances the finances
Of the followers of Doctor Sigmund Freud.

He analyzed the dreams
Of the teens and libertines,
And with ego and with Id he deftly toyed.
Instead of toting bed-pans,
He bore analytic dead-pans,
Those ambitious Doctors Adler, Jung and Freud.

There is nothing like a good dream. I particularly like day-dreams. Since I walk virtually every day to work, my mind takes me on the most wonderful fanciful excursions. The best thing is that the only person to interrupt my flights of fantasy is myself. As for the nighttime, at my age, sadly my dreams often get flushed away. This is even sadder than imaginable, because according to Jewish tradition: "Every dream has a particle of prophesy in it" (*Talmud Berachot* 57b). Certainly that was the case with Martin Luther King Jr.'s famous "I have a Dream" speech in Washington DC (1963). Indeed the significance of one's dreams is deemed so important in one's life that a good part of the last tractate of *Berachot* in the *Talmud* deals with the effects of dreams upon an individual.

Well before Freud came on the scene, we Jews were big dreamers. Indeed, if Freud had been alive during the time of our ancestor Jacob, the latter would have been his prime patient. Of course, Jacob's son Joseph, known as the "dreamer," would have given Freud stiff competition as an interpreter of our night-life mind-games. Basically, Jacob had two major, and universally well-known, dreams that are recorded in the Bible: 1) the ladder, and 2) the wrestling match with the angel. Both these dreams have inspired artists of all kinds. The most instructive lesson to be garnered from Jacob's dreams is that they pose a problem that needs to be solved: "There is no dream that needs not to be resolved" (*Sifre*).[1]

Jacob's first dream comes after he had stolen the blessing that was supposed to be bestowed upon Esau as the first-born through a deceptive ruse, whereby he pretended to be Esau, thus taking advantage of his father Isaac who was nearly blind at the end of his life. Recognizing the fact that Esau would not be too pleased, Jacob flees, and on his way takes a break at a rest stop outside Haran. "He had a dream; a ladder was set on the ground and its top reached to the sky. And angels of God were going up and down on it. And the Lord was standing beside it..." (*Genesis* 28:12-13).

The second dream builds upon the first. Jacob, after years of serving his uncle Laban as little more than a slave (see *Genesis* 29:1 — 31:54), takes his family and his possessions and heads out on his own. At some point along the way, he realizes that he must confront his brother Esau. Still fearful of Esau's response, he places his family at a safe distance, and goes off on his own to hopefully reconcile with his brother. He stops for a nap, and as he dozes off, he dreams that an angel wrestles with him through the night. Now if you and I were gamblers, chances are we would give one hundred-to-one odds in favor of a Divine angel whipping little mortal Jacob. But like Muhammad Ali's upset of George Foreman in the "Rumble in the Jungle," Jacob gets the angel in a half-nelson, but instead of screaming "uncle," he gives Jacob a new name — Israel (see **Way #1 — Your Name**): "Said the angel, your name shall no longer be Jacob, but Israel, for you have striven with beings Divine and human, and have prevailed" (*Genesis* 32:25-29). As written in **Way #23 — Your Moral Mitzvot**, Rashi states that the name Jacob is based on the word "deceit," while the name Israel is based on the word "legitimacy."

---

1. Commentary on *Book of Numbers*.

So here is a classic example of Erich Fromm's insightful prescription: "Dreams are like a microscope through which we look at the hidden occurrences in our soul" (*The Forgotten Language*). For Jacob this was certainly the case. Never having overcome his sense of guilt for having stolen, through deceit, not only the blessing from his brother, but also, through cunning, the birthright (*Genesis* 25:27-34), Jacob first climbs a "stairway (ladder) to heaven" to gain some sort of purification, and then symbolically struggles with his conscience; and so he moves from a youthful wily stage in his life (as Jacob) to a mature responsible one (as Israel).[1]

Viennese psychiatrist, Victor Frankl, in his book, *The Unconscious God*, developed a theory, which recognizes the possibility of God having access to us through our conscience. He wrote: "Conscience would be ineffective if it is only me speaking to myself. Conscience is experienced as a dialogue, and not as a monologue." Anyone, who, like Jacob, has experienced "pangs of conscience," knows the tension of conflict, with the ego contesting and resisting the pull of a commanding sense of "what I ought to do" with, in fact, "what I actually do." There is an "I" within me that wants the opposite of another "I" within me; the two cannot be identical. For Jacob, his dreams not only resolve these two contesting "Is," but eventually harmonize them: "Who sees well in his dreams will see peace" (*Talmud Berachot* 56b).

That there could be any Divine aspect to our dreams, as Frankl hints, whereby God is our conscience, tugging at our thoughts, is rarely considered. While we acknowledge that we may have dreamed most of the night, more often than not we cannot remember our dreams. And those we do remember we can often identify with something that was on our mind during the day. However, our usual reaction to our nocturnal fantasies is: "I had the

---

1. Again one should refer to **Way #23 — Your Moral Mitzvot**.

weirdest dream last night. Where did it come from?" And we leave it at that.

Yet, in Judaism, this sort of dismissal of what was happening in our imaginary world would be mistaken, for "a dream reflects the dreamer's hopes" (*Talmud Berachot* 55b). The song *Last Night I had the Strangest Dream* (Ed McCurdy), made famous by The Weavers, expresses the hopes of one who dreams of peace. So many love songs of our era reflected the hope of unrequited love being redeemed: *Dream a Little Dream of Me* (The Mamas and Papas), *All I have to do is Dream* (Everly Brothers), *Little Dreamer — Dream On* (Perry Como), *All I do is Dream of You* (Dean Martin), *The Impossible Dream* (*Man from La Mancha*) and *I'll see you in my Dreams* (Jimmy Durante), along with many more.

With full understanding that what follows falls under the category of a sweeping generalization (not to mention it sounding like our parents, who disapproved of our "rock n' roll to psychedelic" music), today's generation — a generation that, for the most part, "has it all" (particularly if one happens to be Jewish) — seems more grounded in the real world than we were at their age. Sadly, too many of their songs are not filled with dreams, but rather with harsh realities that find their expression in "rap" music, which is often mean-spirited, as evidenced by rap star Eminem, whose popularity is derived from lyrics of hate, prejudice and violence.

Our children's dreams, unlike ours, seem far more practical, sometimes cynical (although in many ways there was much more about which to be cynical when we were young), and often parochial (which is a euphemism for selfish). And if "a dream reflects the dreamer's thoughts" (*Talmud Berachot* 55b), then our dream should be to hold on to those dreams of the Sixties, which were prophetic ones: to build a world based on social justice and equality.

The Jewish message is clear: dreams are not idle reflections, but a window on our thoughts. Some of us sleep peacefully through our dreams, while others toss and turn all night because of them. Dreams can express our innermost fears and our most deep-felt held hopes. "Dreams are real" (*Ecclesiastes Rabbah*).[1] Our adventures in sleep are an amalgamation of dream and reality, as reflected in the opening confession of this **Way**. Therefore, no dream should be left unattended. If we recognize that our dreams, be they blissful or troubling, are some sort of Godly intervention, or in Frankl's terms, a Divine spark within us, tweaking our conscience (as was the case with our Jewish ancestors, Jacob and his son Joseph), then we should want to understand them. Otherwise we might become frustrated. "A dream not interpreted is like a letter not read" (*Talmud Berachot* 55a). A dream understood can help us ascend a ladder to emotional tranquility, psychological stability and moral improvement. **The forty-third way to be Jewish is take our dreams seriously.**

---

1. Midrashic commentary on *Ecclesiastes*.

YOUR LIFE CYCLE EVENTS

or:

Let the Good Times Roll[1]

Throughout the life of a Jew, there are a number of religious events that warrant a genuine celebration. From birth to marriage, Jewish ceremonies are marked with solemnity and ecstasy. The challenge here is neither to exaggerate the solemn aspects of the particular life cycle event nor to underplay them. As for the celebratory aspects of the occasion, the challenge is almost exclusively to not overdo them. For example, too often at a Bar Mitzvah, we tend to emphasize the "bar" and not the "*Mitzvah!*"

Judaism looks upon religious ceremonies as a means to strengthen our religious/ethical sentiments. When such ceremonies do not fulfill this primary purpose, they essentially turn

---

1. A song first made popular by Jerry Lee Lewis. It has gone through many revisions, most recently by B.B. King, written by Sam Theard and Fleecie Moore.

into a social affair, providing perhaps a convenient excuse to get together for a joyous occasion, yet ignoring the basic reason for the celebration. Jewish ceremonies link us to previous generations and unify Jews who are spread across the four corners of the world. Most importantly, all Jewish ceremonies are inclusive, with family participation occupying a central role. Such is the case with the three ceremonies discussed in this **Way**: Brit/Brita, Bar/Bat Mitzvah, wedding.

The first life cycle ceremony is the "Brit" (circumcision) or "Brita" (parallel event for the birth of a girl, also known as a "Simchat Bat" — The Joy of a Daughter). The Brit/Brita symbolizes the entrance of a child into the traditional Jewish covenant with God, and thus with the Jewish People. It is based on the biblical verses in *Genesis*: "Such will be the covenant between Me and you and your offspring to follow, which you shall keep — every male among you shall be circumcised. You will circumcise the flesh of your foreskin, and that will be the sign of the covenant between Me and you. And throughout the generations, every male among you will be circumcised at the age of eight days..." (17:10-12).

The Brit is the third of the three covenantal signs between God and us. The Sabbath is the first sign: "The Israelite people shall keep the Sabbath, observing the Sabbath throughout the ages as a covenant for all time; it shall be a sign for all time between Me and the people of Israel" (*Exodus* 31:16-17). The second sign is the rainbow which came to symbolize the renewal of humankind after the flood: "...This is a sign that I set for the covenant between Me and you, and every living creature with you, for all ages to come...When I bring clouds over the earth, and the bow appears in the clouds, I will remember My covenant between Me and you and every living creature among all flesh, so that the waters shall never again become a flood to destroy all flesh." (*Genesis* 9:12-15).

Now admittedly, after chopping off our kid's foreskin, a party with a six-course meal may not be particularly appetizing. Perhaps that is why it is easier to host a nice feast after a Brita. Some claim that the Brit has African tribal origins or real health values, others relate it to blood rituals, castration acts or initiation rites.[1] Whatever the case, Judaism sees the practice as a significant milestone in the life of a family. To have a doctor perform a Brit in the confines of a hospital robs us of an emotional identification with the generations of our people. The Brit/Brita also provides drama as the child's name is announced for the first time in a public gathering (see **Way #1 — Your Name**).

A Brit/Brita is one of the most profoundly moving experiences for a mother and father. Most importantly, it employs elements that are inclusive, making it into a real family affair that sensitively relates to the emotional whirlwind surrounding the birth of a child; for example, what is the role of the grandparents who may feel a sense of fulfillment, but finality, of closeness, but separation. The religious ceremony itself is not all that complicated, but like other **Ways** in this book that relate to ritual, this **Way** does not include a discussion or a full explanation of the particulars of the Brit or Brita ceremony (or the other ceremonies that are included in this **Way**).

There is something to be said for naming a child in a synagogue, but for the most part such a "coming-out" party for a newborn is pretty stilted. So it is usually best to have some sort of gathering in one's home or in another place that provides for an informal setting. Because of the nature of the Brit/Brita ceremony, there is little chance that the follow-up celebration will be exaggerated. The miracle of birth, which is an affirmation of Creation, while being cause for an outburst of high exuberance, and therefore some sort of party, is also cause for reflection and contemplation; thus, it does not lend itself to a dinner-dance.

Not so with the Bar/Bat Mitzvah, the next rite of passage in Jewish life. It is often here where celebration overwhelms

1. See the *Second Jewish Catalog* by Sharon and Michael Strassfeld (Jewish Publication Society of America, 1976).

ceremony, where the social aspect of this life cycle event dwarfs the religious side of it.[1] What is interesting to note is that the Bar/Bat Mitzvah is not biblically based. While there are some mishnaic and talmudic references to the age of thirteen for a boy and twelve for a girl, the actual ritual dates to the 13th and 14th century. In the *Talmud* it is mentioned that a boy of thirteen and a girl of twelve must already fast for a full day on Yom Kippur (*Ketubot* 50a). The most definitive statement that the age of thirteen is considered the point at which someone can become a responsible member of the Jewish community is: "At age thirteen one becomes subject to the commandments" (*Sayings of the Fathers* 5:21).

The elements of the Bar/Bat Mitzvah are relatively simple, but sometimes painfully challenging for the kid. He or she is expected to learn to chant a number of verses from the weekly portion in the *Torah* Scroll, the *Haftara* (the prophetic commentary on the *Torah* portion) and to give a sermon. While the rabbi or tutor does his or her best to make the whole process interesting, most of our kids, confronting a particular *Torah* reading for the first time, often out of context, and sometimes on matters so esoteric as to be incomprehensible, do not understand what is going on. And so they commit their part to memory, uttering words that have little meaning in their lives. But the very fact that they stand up in front of so many people and get through the ceremony should be counted as an admirable achievement, and thus worthy of celebration.

The word *Mitzvah* means commandment, but colloquially it is understood as a "good deed." Therefore, meaning can be added to the Bar/Bat Mitzvah event if the child is charged with performing good deeds, leading up to and culminating in the ceremony itself. Being a big brother or sister to a disadvantaged child, adopting an elderly person at a nearby nursing home, or giving a tenth of his or her cash gifts to the needy (see **Way #17 — Your Money**) are some

---

1. See Philip Roth's description of a Bar Mitzvah party in his book *Goodbye Columbus*.

of the ways to satisfy the *Mitzvah* aspect of a Bar/Bat Mitzvah. Parents should be intimately involved in the process, not primarily concentrating on the event itself.

So, how do we celebrate? Many are the Bar/Bat Mitzvah parties that we all have attended, some we may even have hosted, where we should have been genuinely embarrassed by the excessiveness of the event. I was invited to one at the Pierre Hotel in New York City on a Shabbat afternoon. It was a black tie event and featured a twelve-piece orchestra with a lounge singer. The kids were in a separate room with their own live rock band. The Bat Mitzvah girl was chauffeured from the synagogue to the hotel in a stretch-limo. I doubt seriously if the Italian kabbalist poet Moses Haim Luzzatto (1707-1746) would have approved: "A ceremony is not adequately discharged unless it is performed with beauty and dignity." Swinging away to Jerry Lee Lewis' *Let the Good Times Roll* cannot be readily considered as a vehicle to spiritual heights. There has to be a balance between the seriousness of a child being ushered into the Jewish community, and the type of community we want him or her to be a part of. Exaggeration leads to exaggeration. Modesty encourages sensitivity — and that is what the Bar/Bat Mitzvah is all about — becoming part of the Jewish community, sensitive to its needs, responsible for its perpetuation by assuming the role of a newly enfranchised Jew in the ritual and moral sphere of Jewish life (see **Ways #22 and #23 — Your Ritual Mitzvot and Your Moral Mitzvot**).

"Marriage is something special. I guess you have to deserve it" (Clifford Odets, *Golden Boy*). Now we're talking. A marriage is the time to "let the good times roll," because here is a celebration of love at it best: "A man is happy insofar as he loves, a man loves insofar as he is happy. After all, there can be lunacy without love, but is there any great love without lunacy?" (Yochanan Twersky).[1]

---

1. Hebrew writer (1900-1967).

Clearly, there is no provision for "showers" or bachelor parties within Judaism, because the mandate to let loose at a marriage seems to be endemic to a Jewish wedding.

We all are familiar with the famous wedding scene in *Fiddler on the Roof*, where, after the solemn and moving candlelit ceremony, the townspeople of Anatevka celebrate with abandon, despite the ever-present fear of a pogrom striking them at a moment's notice. This need for dancing as an outlet for expressing our joy at the union of a couple (see **Way #39 — Your Marriage**) found its way into that Jewish sentimental favorite, sung by Al Jolson: "Oh, how we danced on the night we were wed, we vowed our true love, though a word wasn't said" (from *The Anniversary Song*, written by Jolson and Saul Chaplain).

Of course, even with a rich tradition that calls for ecstatic celebration, we can go overboard. For some, to spend forty to fifty thousand dollars on a wedding seems like chicken feed, unless one feels a need to take out a second mortgage in order to satisfy some warped sense of social pressure to give our kids "the best." Should this happen, then the ceremony becomes diminished, and what one remembers is boogieing to Bill Haley's *Rock Around the Clock*, or dancing cheek-to-cheek to Elvis' *Have I Told you Lately that I Love You*.

The forty-fourth way to be Jewish is not to turn our life cycle events into a ceremonial absurdity, a ragged garb which neither sanctifies the event nor adorns it. Rather it is to strike a balance: between solemnity and gaiety, between traditional practices and artistic innovations, between ritual reverence and carefree celebration, between Jewish continuity and creative persistence, between family cohesiveness and community elasticity, between covenantal responsibility and personal happiness.

YOUR RELATIVES

or:

A "Theory of Relativity"

My Aunt Sophie was off the wall. My Uncle Sol was a total nut. My older cousin was an emotional basket case. My father supported one of my mother's brothers-in-law. My grandmother's sisters were dye-in-the-wool communists who eventually immigrated to America from Russia because Palestine, their first choice, was going to become a socialist state! (Once in the United States, they all became capitalists.) It seemed that everyone "argued his and her way to happiness." And I, as a youngster, thoroughly enjoyed observing this Neil Simon tragi-comedy (or was it theater of the absurd?).

Mine was a huge family. My mother was one of five children, my father one of six. The extended family included my great-aunts and uncles, and therefore dozens of second cousins and third cousins and cousins removed once (and some I would have liked to remove). All lived in the Boston area. Some even lived with us: my grandmother on my mother's side after my grandfather died, and off and on, a first cousin whose own parents were always on the verge of divorce. And not infrequently, I would be shipped off to an elderly aunt and uncle when my parents went on vacation. But the best was when both sides of the family got together. Talk about discordant harmony: "The Jewish family at the table speaks with one voice — it is the voice of everyone talking at once" (*Musings of a Jewish Social Worker*, Ben Smoke, circa 2001). Our family was "divided by a common identity." Given the heated political debates, you would never know that they were all Roosevelt Democrats.

Growing up in my family during the Fifties and Sixties was a real challenge, because the ideological outlook of my relatives was based on that oft-repeated, yet still brilliant historical perspective: "Is it good for the Jews?" As a result, uncles and aunts who often were at each other's throats would suddenly unite when they felt threatened by the *goyim*. Who cared if a clan mentality developed out of negative motivation? When push came to shove (which sometimes was the case), we were one big happy "it's your family." I loved it. And to this day, nostalgia overwhelms me when I think of that time in my life. I only pray that my children will experience the same harmonious chaos that enveloped me.

In Barry Levenson's emotionally powerful film, *Avalon*, a family gathers together every year for Thanksgiving. On one occasion, one of the uncles arrives late, and the rest of the family decides to begin the meal, symbolized by the carving of the turkey. When the late uncle finally walks in, he is offended that the festive meal has begun without him, and, in a moment of rage, goes on a tirade how his brother and his sons, upon acquiring a little wealth, moved to the suburbs and "broke up the family." And then, the final blow: "You cut the turkey without me!" In other words: "You may just as well have stabbed the knife into my heart."

"A little hurt from a kin is worse than a big hurt from a stranger" (*Zohar* — *Genesis* 151b). Once there was a popular bumper sticker: "Don't get mad, get even." When it comes to relatives, often we are filled with grudges and resentments. Contrary to popular wishful thinking, there is no such thing as "sweet revenge." Vengeance is a terrible taskmaster.[1] It is amazing how many of us spend precious hours harboring grudges and nursing old resentments. It may be said that time is "the great healer," but yesterday slights are not easily forgotten. In order to overcome resentments, we do not need more time, but more insight, more understanding, more forgiveness and most importantly, more objectivity: "No man can examine the leprosy of his own relatives" (*Sifre, Numbers* 105).[2]

When facing family disputes, a Jew must be guided by the principle of *sh'lom bayit* — peace within in one's home. Many personal preferences, including the maintaining of many halachic *Mitzvot*, can be set aside for the sake of *sh'lom bayit*.

I'll never forget how upset I was when one of my closest college friends got married. He did not invite his grandfather on his father's side to the wedding because he had a complete falling out with him ten years earlier, and they had not spoken since, even though they both knew how disruptive this dispute was within the family constellation. I asked my friend, whose grandfather I had met when we were in university together, if I could speak to him about his marriage. His reply: "Whatever — it will be a waste of time."

I called the grandfather who listened in silence and thanked me for the information. The wedding was held in a small chapel with

---

1. So all-encompassing in Judaism is the demand not to seek vengeance that the Reform Movement chooses as its *Torah* reading for the Afternoon Service of Yom Kippur this passage from *Leviticus*: "You shall not hate your brother (or sister) in your heart, rather you must reason with your kin, so that you do not incur guilt on their account. But you must not seek vengeance, nor bear a grudge against your kin..." (19:17-18).

2. *Sifre* is a midrashic commentary on *Book of Numbers*, the fourth book of the *Torah*.

many friends, but only a handful of relatives, as the rift between grandson and grandfather affected and divided the entire family. After the documents were signed, the bride and groom stepped under the *chuppah* (wedding canopy), and at that very moment, a door to the chapel opened and an elderly man entered: the groom's grandfather. My friend turned around, stared for a long few seconds, and literally fainted on the spot. He soon came to, was married, and, after kissing his bride, embraced his grandfather in a tearful reconciliation. How often have we heard the story of a reunion taking place only upon the deathbed of a family member? So many years are wasted because we prefer maintaining rather than diffusing our resentments, whose longevity finds its strength in some sort of pride, which is a highly overrated personality trait, especially when misplaced.

One is reminded of the Hassidic master who said: "I take a lesson from my tailor. Whenever I order a new suit, he doesn't cut it according to the previous pattern, but, each time takes a fresh measure of my size" (*The Hassidic Masters*, Martin Buber).[1] In shaping our attitudes toward our relatives, we need to take a fresh measure of an aunt, an uncle, a cousin, a grandfather, and not judge him or her by previous patterns of behavior. This is the significance of the powerful drama that occurs in *Genesis* when Abraham's first son, Ishmael, born of his handmaiden, Hagar, is forced to leave his home with his mother because his behavior is so intolerable, and because he is such a negative influence upon his half-brother, Isaac, born of Abraham's wife, Sarah. Soon mother and child wander in the wilderness, and, having run out of food and water, Hagar, tears streaming down her cheeks, lays down her whimpering child in the shade of one of the desert's shrubs, and prays for help. Then: "God heard the voice of the lad where he is" (*Genesis* 21:17). The rabbinic commentators focus on the words "where he is." Ishmael may have

---

1. Famous Jewish philosopher (1878-1965).

previously been a troublemaker who brought expulsion upon himself, but God, looking upon his misery at a different moment in time, "where he is," and seeing him a hopeless child, responds and provides him water to survive. The point is clear. We should always judge another person not where he <u>was</u>, but where he <u>is</u>. We should always give our family members (as well as our friends) a second look and be ready to change our mind in light of the new situation, whatever it may be.

How sad to see grownup siblings and relatives perpetuate childhood rivalries and feuds, which may have been real enough in the past, but now live on only in memory! How tragic it is when we carry into maturity our youthful resentments of parental control or mishandling long after our aging parent has lost the power and desire to run our lives (see **Way #42 — Your Parents**). We must avoid becoming emotionally locked into a certain perception or judgment of a relative by an event or personality trait, which we may have found repulsive years ago; or by actions that hurt us deeply in the past. Meanwhile, time has passed. We have changed, and hopefully they have. "When we discredit our family, we discredit ourselves" (*Numbers Rabbah* 21).

It is not easy to navigate the peculiarities of one's family. There is little question that one's flexibility is constantly put to the test. Everyone vies for a position of influence and preference. Competition can be fierce. We may cringe when we get one of those "Schvitz Blitz" letters ("schvitz" in Yiddish means to brag exaggeratedly) from a relative, where every little event in his or her family is included as a testimony to their brilliance, success and creativity — especially when you know that cousin Joanie may have achieved Dean's List status last semester, but presently she is about to stand trial for peddling marijuana on her campus, after having been arrested for disorderly conduct when caught returning from an overnight with a married professor. Now this does not mean that: "If one in a family is a tax collector or a robber, they are all tax collectors or robbers, for they shield the sinner" (*Talmud Shavuot* 39a). But it does mean that we have to be long-suffering, knowing that braggadocian claims by one relative may just be a sad cover-up for some dysfunctional familial infrastructure, and that one of our "clan" members is in need of attention and understanding from the rest of the clan.

"Happiness is having a large, loving, caring, close-knit family... in another city" (George Burns). In today's reality, when one's immediate family is spread all over the United States, and in some cases the globe, interaction with one's relatives plays little role in a person's life. When this occurs, something is clearly missing. To interact with relatives only at family occasions, either happy or sad, excludes the possibility of having them join us along the way to the commemoration of the milestones in our life.

Universally, we speak of the "family of man (and woman)" or the "family of nations." Generically, we Jews speak of the "people of Israel." Particularly, we speak of the *minyan*, the community of which we are directly a part, and so we are instructed: "Do not separate yourself from the community" (*Sayings of the Fathers* 2:4). This stands in contrast to the words of that great Jewish philosopher, Groucho Marx, who once said: "I don't care to belong to any club that would have me as a member." Well, there is one thing we cannot change, and that is our relatives, including our relatives-in-law: "Honor your father-in-law and mother-in-law, because henceforth they are your parents" (*Apocrypha* 10:12). So much for all the Jewish mother-in-law jokes. We are members of our family, for "better and for worse."

And so, **the forty-fifth way to be Jewish is to embrace our family, recognizing that in a world that has become more impersonal, where alienation is an increasing reality, the comfort and support of our relatives, despite the differences both large and small, can sustain us in times of joy and sadness.** "A clan and a family resemble a heap of stones: one stone removed and the whole shatters" (*Genesis Rabbah* 100). This precept has its historical antecedent in the return of the Jewish People to its ancestral homeland after two thousand years of dispersion. The survival of the Jewish People was based on this concept of family unity: "Without family life, no nation can be made" (A.D. Gordon).[1] Without a positive "theory of relatives," no family can be maintained.

---

1. Labor Zionist philosopher (1856-1922), whose teachings included the "religion of labor," which profoundly influenced early Zionist thinking.

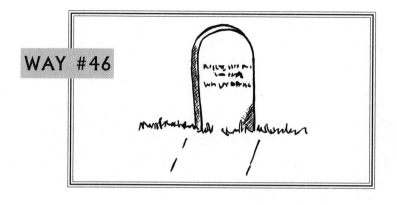

YOUR DEATH

or:

................?

"It's not that I'm afraid to die. I just don't want to be there when it happens" *(Woody Allen).*

"Do not be afraid to die, it is your destiny" *(Apocrypha,* Ben Sira 41:12).

"Human beings do not live forever. We live less than the time it takes to blink an eye if we measure our lives against eternity. So it may be asked, what value is there to a human life? There is so much pain in the world. What does it mean to have to suffer so much if our lives are nothing more than the blink of an eye? A blink of an eye in itself is nothing. But the eye that blinks, *that* is something. A span of life is nothing, but the man who lives that span, *he* is something. He can fill that tiny span with meaning, so its quality is immeasurable though its quantity may be insignificant. A man must fill his life with meaning. A life filled with meaning is worthy of rest" (*The Chosen*, Chaim Potok, Simon and Schuster, 1967).

Mel Brooks' Two Thousand Year Old Man has this to say about death: "You know how you can avoid the Angel of Death? Before you go to sleep at night, eat a pound-and-a-half of garlic. When the Angel of Death comes over to you and taps you on the shoulder, you say: 'Whhhhhooo is it?' You heard of the kiss of death. Well, he's not gonna kiss you. You're full of garlic."

Yes, we all want to avoid death, but there is no escape: "What person can live and never behold death" (*Psalm* 89:49)? And the eternal questions that plague us are: How do we prepare for death? Can we? Are we even capable of doing so? Are we ever ready for death? Upon celebrating his one-hundredth birthday, George Burns (1896-1996) quipped: "I can't die now — I'm booked." Elie Wiesel tells the Hassidic tale of a 19th century tourist from the United States who visited a famous Polish rabbi, the Hafetz Chayim. He was astonished to see that the rabbi's home was only a simple room filled with books. The only furniture was a table and a bench.

Tourist: Rabbi, where is your furniture?
Rabbi: Where is yours?
Tourist: Mine? But I'm only a visitor here.
Rabbi: So am I.

Simply put, it is impossible to be "booked" for life. We are all guests of existence. When we die, everyone else's story goes on, but we are not there to discover how it turns out. Our lives stop in the middle. They do not reach a conclusion, they simply stop. The middle of the story is where all our stories end. As a rabbi, rarely does a day go by that I do not think about death, as I am constantly involved in memorial services, funerals and counseling the bereaved. Naturally, I think of my own demise. I am not an especially morbid individual, but apart from undertakers, doctors and nurses, clergy probably deal most with death. And death comes in so many unpredictable ways.

It is possible to become preoccupied with one's own mortality. But thankfully, we are fortified with a reservoir of resiliency. If we actually thought about death with any regularity, we could be driven crazy. There are moments in my life when I am so filled with contentment, when my love for my family is so overflowing, that I can't imagine ever letting go. I want life to stand still. I suddenly become panicky. How will my children survive my death? What will happen to them? Inevitably, contemplation of our own death brings to the fore our concern for the effects of our demise on those whom we love most. Yet if some messenger were to come to us with the offer that death should be overthrown as postulated in the popular film, *Cocoon*, but with one inseparable condition that birth should also cease; if the existing generation were given the chance to live forever, but on the clear understanding that never again would there be a child, a youth, or first love, never again new persons with new hopes, new ideas, new achievements; ourselves for always and never any others — could the answer be in doubt?[1]

Our life, at its best, is an endless effort for a goal we never attain. Death finally terminates our struggle, and like children falling asleep over their toys, we relinquish our grasp on our earthly possessions.[2] On the other hand, we can be in denial, so enraptured by our own existence that the thought of our death is unreal. After all, when we are alive, it is extremely difficult to imagine things happening without our being present to experience them. While this may seem a typical example of youthful exuberance, it also

---

1. Excerpted from the Reform Movement's *Gates of Repentance* — Memorial Service.
2. *Ibid.*

afflicts those of us older souls who are overwhelmed with the wonder of ourselves. As a result, we forget the words of playwright Arthur Miller: "Immortality is like trying to carve your initials in a block of ice in the middle of July!"How a person faces his or her death is an indication of how one has approached his or her life. Just as this book serves as a "Jewish way of life," so too is there a "Jewish way of death." Perhaps the two best books to understand Jewish concepts of death and the accompanying Jewish rituals that surround death are Maurice Lamm's *The Jewish Way in Death and Mourning* and Leon Wieseltier's *Kaddish*. Also Earl Grollman's many books dealing with issues of death as they relate to surviving family members should be considered mandatory reading. Suffice it to say that Judaism has within it practices, customs and laws that speak sensitively of Judaism's concern for the dignity of the individual, be he or she the person whom death will strike or those who are affected by someone else's death.

We are granted the gift of life although we did nothing to deserve it. We must be grateful for the allotted time granted us, and thus must use that time-span between birth (over which we had no control) and death (about which we have no choice), and use it wisely. Time waits for no one. It could be said that God created time so that everything would not happen at once. Indeed, if we lived forever, we could constantly postpone everything. However, given the finitude of time, we cannot. We must do something. As we accept life, we must also accept mortality as part of the bargain. And so death becomes as much a part of life as birth; and we live in the interval between two eternities. We are obliged to render something of meaning out of that finite piece of eternity, as Potok urges, or as otherwise phrased: "The day of death is concealed that man may build and plant" (*Talmud Kedoshim* 38b).

Judaism has two conflicting views of what happens after death. In the biblical rendition, one returns to the dust from which one was created: "He that goes down to the grave shall come up no more" (*Job* 7:9). Upon the destruction of the Second Temple, when prayer replaced sacrifice as a form of worship, a rabbinic concept of the "world to come" was introduced, based on the messianic notion of the redemption of the "Dry Bones" from *Ezekiel* 37:1-14. While Judaism may be vague regarding any sort of ultimate physical renewal, whichever belief one clings to, the prevailing view in Judaism is: "The dust returns to the earth as it was, and the spirit returns to God who gave it" (*Ecclesiastes* 12:7). Spirit can be best defined in Jewish terms as a Divine spark implanted in all of us at birth, that antithetical moment to death: "The Creator planted His sweet spirit in all, and made it a guide to all mortals" (*Apocrypha* 1:5). Indeed, many of the prophets speak of the "spirit of God" abiding within us. And thus, while we may physically be absorbed into the earth, our spirit, remains — and it is the spirit of an individual that constitutes our memories of him or her, adding an everlasting dimension to one's being.

And so, in Judaism the concentration is on those of us who remain behind: "Weep for the mourners and not for the dead, for he is gone to his rest and we are left to lament" (*Talmud Moed Katan* 25b). Every Jewish observance regarding death is geared towards helping us confront this new reality of physical absence: from the tearing of the garments, to assisting in throwing dirt upon the open grave, to reciting the mourner's prayer, to sitting *shiva*,[1] to commemorating the *shloshim*,[2] to dedicating the tombstone, to ending the formal mourning period on the first anniversary of the death. We are also not left to mourn alone, as the mandatory *minyan*

---

1. *Shiva* literally means seven, the number of days for "intensive" mourning that begins with the burial. The period of time has biblical origins (Joseph mourned seven days following the passing of his father, Jacob). After the Revelation at Sinai, Moses established seven days of mourning by special decree.
2. *Shloshim* literally means thirty, and constitutes the full mourning for all relatives other than father or mother. Mourning for those bereaved of their parents terminates at the end of twelve Hebrew months.

extends the circle of comforters that we so desperately need at our time of loss.

Perhaps the most frightening element of death is waiting for it, knowing that we have been stricken by a fatal disease, and it is only a matter of time till darkness will envelop us. Would it be better if we could choose the moment of our death and the method of it, the manner by which we die? Of course. But how would we go about doing so? (Euthanasia, while essentially forbidden in Judaism, may undergo a reevaluation. In Israel, where virtually all life cycle events are controlled by Orthodoxy, Israel's Supreme Court recently ruled, not as a precedent, but in one specific case, that the life support systems for the particular individual whose case was brought before the Court could be shut down.) There is sufficient proof that how we live our life physically and emotionally can affect the length of our days. Yet, still there is no chance for survival when our time on earth comes to an end. Perhaps the most important thing for us is to "set our house in order" (II *Kings* 20:1).

We must realize, while we are still among the vibrant living — and are able — that we must set our affairs in order. Thus we are free not only to concentrate on preparing ourselves for the inevitable, but most significantly on helping our loved ones cope with their eventual loss, all the while freeing them as well from tidying up our affairs. If we can look back on our life with the satisfaction that what we will leave behind are sweet memories and positive examples, then death becomes easier to embrace, so that we can be as: "One who dies in perfect harmony, wholly at ease and secure..." (*Job* 21:23).

Judaism is a religious expression that embraces all of life — and death — as a part of that process. Just as we have numerous rituals that lead us through moments of joy, so too do we have an amplitude of customs that guide us through moments of sadness.

For all the questions that arise at the moment of death — of our own and that of others — Judaism, through its rich tradition, attempts to provide answers: from the most mundane, such as cemetery etiquette, to the most existential, such as the reason that we might be fated to die earlier than a normal life expectancy or to die by tragedy. Lamm's, Wieseltier's and Grollman's books help familiarize the Jew with all the practices that are so comforting to us in this most trying hour of our life.[1]

What can ultimately make death easier to face? If you have been loved, and have loved in return, death is easier because you know that you will be remembered by those who loved you. Love ushers us into a peaceful and eternal repose.

Death is the crisis of our life, but it is not our enemy, rather it is a friend. "For each one of us the moment comes when the great nurse, death, takes man, the child, by the hand and quietly says: 'It is time to go home. Night is coming. It is your bedtime, child of earth. Come, you're tired. Lie down at last in the quiet nursery of nature and sleep. Sleep well. The day is gone. Stars shine in the canopy of eternity'" (*Peace of Mind*, Joshua Loth Liebman[2]). Cognizant that there is a Jewish way that helps us to deal psychologically, theologically, ritually and humanly with our mortality, **the forty-sixth way to be Jewish is to consider death as our friend, for death reminds us that our years are limited, which makes them so precious.** But as dear as is our life, we must always be prepared to let it go at a moment's notice. "The day of death is when two worlds meet with a kiss: the world going out, and the future world we left (through our children) that continues on" (*Jerusalem Talmud Yevamot* 15:2). As noted in **Way #35 — Your Aging**, we live on through the memories we create, and so our life is guaranteed — immortalized — after we depart this world.

---

1. One of the most important books to help one comprehend the different stages in confronting death is *On Death and Dying* by Elizabeth Kubler-Ross. Also Harold Kushner's *When Bad Things Happen to Good People* is recommended.
2. American rabbi (1907-1948).

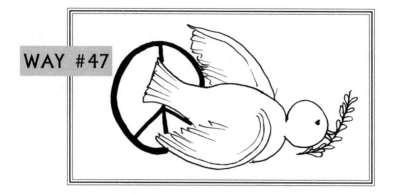

YOUR PEACE

or:

Give Peace a Chance[1]

We Jews were the first genuine hippies. If one looks to the *Prayerbook*, which is that guidebook that catalogues our beliefs, one will notice that the formal service begins with the *Shema* and its surrounding blessings, and its prevailing theme is one of love. The service reaches its climax prior to the reading of the *Torah* on Mondays and Thursdays,[2] and Saturdays, with a declaration of peace. In short, we were running around preaching "peace" and "love" during the original Sixties (60 CE).

The highest goal of the Jewish People is to live in peace. Since

---

1. John Lennon's famous anthem., which can be found on the 1998 release: *The Lennon Legend — The Very Best of John Lennon.*

2. In addition to the Sabbath, the weekly *Torah* portion was read on Mondays and Thursdays, because these were market days when many people were in the city and could hear the *Torah* reading.

the Jewish exile from ancient Palestine two thousand years ago, Jews faced Jerusalem and prayed for peace three times a day. The words that close our daily blessing after every meal are: "God will give strength unto His (Her) people and bless His (Her) people with peace." Most significant is the last sentence of the mourner's lament, said by those who may have lost someone in war: "God who makes peace in the heavens will grant peace to all of us and to all of Israel." And finally the famous priestly benediction, with which God commanded Moses to instruct Aaron to bless the Israelites, is recited today, not only during the daily worship service, but also at special occasions, such as at the naming of a child or at the uniting of a bride and groom at the wedding ceremony. It has peace as its central message: "May the Lord bless you and guard you. May the Lord light up your face and be gracious to you. May the Lord lift up a Divine Countenance to you and grant you peace" (*Numbers* 6:24-26).[1] Peace is the spiritual yearning of the Jewish People.

Tragically, Israel has yet to be crowned with peace. The modern state of Israel, while having forged a peace accord with Egypt, the historical enemy of the Jewish People, as well as with Jordan, still has been plagued by an on-going struggle. Without discussing the particulars of the Israeli-Palestinian conflict and assessing blame for the current morass (see **Way #21 — Your Israel Quotient**), Israel's desire for peace has yet to be granted. Admittedly, as a religious Jew living in Israel, I am continually baffled that the one segment of the population, which seems most militant when it comes to reaching any accommodation with the Palestinians, is the Orthodox community. One would think that since religious Jews so often "pray for peace," the power of this spiritual supplication before God would find them at the forefront of Israel's peace movement. But what has happened is that religion and nationalism have been fused, resulting in a chauvinistic theology in which the

---

1. For an alternative usage and translation of the Priestly Benediction, see **Way #22 — Your Ritual Mitzvot.**

national ego has been projected on to God, and Divine blessing is seen to be bestowed upon one community above the other. This is a recipe for an explosion. And yet we are told: "Seek peace and pursue it" (*Psalm* 34:15), which essentially means that we should set peace as our goal, and pursue it unfailingly. The ultimate fulfillment of Zionism is to see Israel live in peace with its neighbors. And Jews around the world should be committed to this goal.

Yet while we are moved by such dictates as: "The blessing of the Holy One is peace" (*Talmud Megilla* 18a) and "The world is established in peace" (*Zohar, Leviticus* 10b), we cannot bring about peace if we are not fortified with internal peace: "Peace, like charity, begins at home" (Yitzhak Ben Tzvi).[1] Indeed, we are formally commanded to: "Seek peace in your own place so as to pursue it in others" (*Jerusalem Talmud Pe'ah* 10:1).[2] It is no accident that both the traditional and colloquial greeting among Jews is *shalom aleichem*, peace be with you. Indeed, the word *shalom* (peace) in modern Hebrew means both "hello" and "goodbye," which echoes the celebrated Jewish expression: "May you come in peace and may you go in peace." Peace is to embrace us at all times.

I would refer the reader back to **Way #41 — Your Friends**, to the song *Easy to be Hard* from *Hair*, whose thesis is that caring about the abstract concepts of social injustice and peace cannot come at the expense of ignoring a friend in concrete need. One must first make *sh'lom bayit* — peace at home (see **Way #45 — Your Relatives**). Indeed for a peaceful home, Judaism permits all sorts of ritual compromises, almost likened to the postponement of even Shabbat observances for *pikuach nefesh* (the saving of a life). Indeed, Jewish responsibility operates on a concentric set of circles — to care for: 1) yourself, 2) your family, 3) your immediate community, 4) your people, and 5) the world at large. We move from the

---

1. Israel's second president (1884-1963). This was part of his inaugural address to the Knesset, December 10, 1952.
2. This is a commentary on *Psalm* 34:15 quoted in the previous paragraph.

particular to the universal; and so we are forewarned by Martin Buber: "You can only find peace elsewhere if you first find it in yourself" (*The Way of Man: According to the Teaching of Hassidism*).

Given the hustle and bustle of our daily lives, it is no easy task to find peace within ourselves, and maintain it. A peaceful disposition is difficult to attain. That is why the notion of Shabbat is so crucial for us (see **Way #28 — Your Sabbath**). How do we Jews greet each other on Shabbat? With a simple, but powerful incentive: *shabbat shalom*, let this Shabbat be a Shabbat of peace. God rested on the seventh day of Creation. The Creation was completed and the world was at peace.

But peace is based on basic foundations. If "upon three things the world is upheld: judgment, truth <u>and</u> peace" (*Sayings of the Fathers* 1:18), then "world peace is possible only through the application of the familial laws of morality and righteousness..." (Nachman Syrkin).[1] Therefore, our homes must be a sanctuary of moral decency, and our relationships with others must be a haven of righteous dignity. We must have peace within our walls so that there is prosperity in our palaces (see *Psalm* 122:7). **And so, the forty-seventh way to be Jewish is to pursue the theoretical enticements of world peace, even as we solidify the practical elements of domestic tranquility.** We must guarantee: "Peace, peace to him who is far off and to him who is near" (*Isaiah* 57:19).

---

1. Yiddish author (1868-1924).

YOUR KIDS

or:

"Insanity is Hereditary — You can get it from your Kids!"[1]

There is the story of a man who had just finished laying concrete for a new driveway. After a few hours, he saw some children running over the newly poured cement leaving their footprints, prompting him to yell out: "I like kids in the abstract, not in the concrete!" Judaism is a youth-oriented religion. Not only is the reading of the *Haggaddah*, which recounts the story of the Exodus where we Jews became a people, geared toward children, as is the entire Passover *Seder*, but also the *Shema* commands us to teach our tradition and history to our children, because: "Children constitute

---

1. Comment by humorist Sam Levenson.

our eternity, they are our best surety, better than patriarchs and prophets..." (I.L. Peretz).[1]

All of us would agree that it is extremely difficult to raise children. But have you ever noticed that a baby does not begin to walk until he or she is tall enough to reach a parent's hand? From the moment of birth, our children are dependent upon us, and until the moment of our death, we are dependent upon them. Therefore, it is incumbent upon a parent to: "Train a child in the way he should go, and when he is old he will not depart from you" (*Proverbs* 22:6). Much easier said than done!

Listen to the protagonist's narration in Anne Tylers's *Ladder of Years*: "And Delia's baby, her sweet, winsome Carroll, had been replaced by this rude adolescent, flinching from his mother's hugs and criticizing her clothes and rolling his eyes disgustedly at every word she uttered. Like now for instance. Determined to start afresh, she perked all her features upward and asked: 'Any calls while I was gone?' And he said: 'Why should I answer the *grown-ups*' line?' Not bothering to add a question mark. *Because the grown-ups buy the celery for your favorite mint pea soup*, she could have told him, but years of dealing with teenagers had turned her into a pacifist...'"

As one who lives in Israel, I can say that we may be the most fortunate of parents. At the age of eighteen, most Israeli kids are inducted into the army. Despite all the anxiety that military service causes both parent and child, there is little that is more satisfying to hear than that our bratty teenage children, who have had nothing but insouciant disdain for all that we are and do, are now being ordered to do fifty push-ups and clean the latrine because they talked back to their commanding officer. There is Divine retribution.

There is a tradition during the Bar/Bat Mitzvah ceremony

---

1. Isaac Lieb Peretz (1852-1915) was one of the greatest Yiddish novelists, poets and critics.

whereby the *Torah* is passed from generation to generation, from grandparents to parents to children. The idea is to convey that the positive values that spring forth from our history and tradition have met the test of time and can insure that our children, should they follow the precepts of the *Torah*, will turn into decent human beings. Of course, there is an expectation that we, as parents, are well versed in the ethical teachings of our religion. Yet the manner in which we overindulge our children with things rather than noble purposes seems to reinforce a view that we are not particularly moored in the moral commandments of Judaism.

Today, our kids are being handed too many values that are anxiety-provoking and loneliness-inducing, thereby producing a lack of commitment to the worth and welfare of others. The media engulfing us reflect society's values as seen on MTV or AXN channels. These values often replace those we intuitively know to be enduring and worthwhile (see **Way #50 — Your Instincts**).

Everybody loves a winner, and we judge others in these terms — he's a loser or she's a winner. We should not fool ourselves into thinking that these attitudes have no effect or make no impression. There is the story of the father who took his son to a movie in which the significance of the story was unclear to the boy. The child asked his father which character was the hero. The father related how he pulled his child close to him and whispered: "You are my hero." The boy then looked at him in embarrassment and said: "No Dad, to be a hero you have to be a winner." This attitude is constantly reinforced in our children. Their training is a barometer of our times. Too often we place too high a premium on winning, on achievement, on success (see **Way #20 — Your Heroes**).

I once counseled a teenage girl who was always being compared to her older brothers. One went to Princeton and the other to Stanford. Her parents would constantly urge her to do better in school, after all, they added, not only did her brothers go to top universities, but they had also won numbers of scholastics prizes.

Yet, as much as she tried, she was simply not a great student. In tears, she turned to me and said: "I am not good in academics, but I am a good person. Aren't there any prizes for being nice?" We are told quite pointedly: "Never favor one child over the other. Because of a scrap of silk of little worth Joseph's brother's envied him mortally" (*Talmud Shabbat* 10b).

Noted child psychiatrist Aaron Stern reported: "At the beginning of my career, when I was associated with the child development center at Yale, people came from all over the country to have their children evaluated. If, at the end of a rather elaborate evaluation we could say to the parents, 'you have a nice normal average child,' they were delighted and left happily. If, today, I say to parents at the end of an evaluation, 'you have a nice normal average child,' they leave depressed." We want our children to excel, and if they do not, then we feel they may grow up to be "failures." With a glance or an expression, we make our dissatisfaction known; and we utter the most dangerous words: "Why can't you be like...?"

This constant pressure to "succeed" is reflected in the pre-schools springing up all over the country, which actually have screening tests for toddlers, and that in order to insure placement at the "right" pre-school that leads to the "right" elementary school and thereafter to the "right" prep school and then to the "right" college, we hire tutors for toddlers to start them on their escalating drive toward upper mobility. One of the first gifts my one-week-old granddaughter received was infant flash cards! The tyranny of achievement chases our children from Little League to Ivy League.

Now one must keep in mind, as described in Anne Tyler's account above, that teenagers can be absolutely exasperating, causing one mother to remark: "Being a mother is very educational. Now I know why ferrets eat their young." One of the reasons that I allow my kids to have parties in our home is to remind me that there are children more awful than mine. However, children can be very insightful. Rabbi Harold Schulweiss tells of this poignant exchange with his teenage son. One evening, Schulweiss noticed his son studying at his desk. He walked into the room and put his arm around him. The boy shrugged him off. After recovering from the shock, Schulweiss asked his son why. "Because, Dad," his son replied, "the only time you put your arm around me is when I am studying, doing something you approve of, never when I am watching TV." For many of us, we may not even give our kids the necessary time to ever put an arm on their shoulder (see **Way #13 — Your Leisure Time**). Ultimately, the best inheritance we can give to our children is a little time each day.

We are all human and fallible, though we rarely admit any weakness to our children, as realized by the parent who said to her teenage daughter: "I told you so. You would not have made such a foolish (stupid) mistake if you had used good judgment." The daughter responded: "Well, how do I get good judgment?" The mother then reflected a bit and said: "By making mistakes." In *Sefer Hassidim*,[1] we read: "Parents must not so frustrate a child that he cannot restrain himself from rebelling against them."

And so our children's characters are molded. Good ceases to mean gentle, kind and compassionate. It gets translated into the ability to bring home the signs of "success:" high grades and test scores in the best schools. And if our kids do well, we often find ourselves forgiving all sorts of aberrant behavior. Being products of the Sixties, we are part of that permissive era. In truth, in too many cases, our manner of discipline follows an undisciplined manner. We need to lead by example: "When you lead your sons and daughters in the good way, let your words be tender and caressing, in terms of discipline that wins the heart's assent" (*Alim L'Terufa*, Elijah Gaon).[2] In fact, children seldom misquote their parents. They

---

1. A collection of wisdom parables and sayings, compiled by Judah HeHasid, c. 1150-1217.
2. Elijah Gaon (1720-1797) was a Lithuanian talmudist from Vilna, referred to as the Gaon of Vilna.

usually repeat word for word what we should not have said, and copy what we should not have done. "Little children do not lie until they are taught to do so" (*Letters of Saadia Gaon*).[1]

The simple rule should be: just as we are commanded to honor our parents (see **Way #42 — Your Parents**), so too should we honor our children. If honoring your father and mother is one of the Ten Commandments, then we should come up with a parallel "Ten Suggestions," one of the first being: "Honor your children."

Our children are a reflection of what we leave behind (see Ethical Wills in **Way #35 — Your Aging**). Mutual respect is essential not only for building a solid relationship in our younger years, but also for solidifying that bond as our children grow older and we grow old. They provide us with our immortality: "Who rears his son in righteousness is like an immortal" (Rashi, *Commentary on Genesis* 18:19). If we "train our children in their youth, they won't train us in our old age" (Judah Lazerov).[2]

Judaism provides some basic truisms for raising children: 1) "Love equally all your children. Sometimes the favored disappoint and the neglected make you happy" (Berekia HaNakdan, *Mishlei Shualim*);[3] 2) "Reprimand not a child immediately on the offense. Wait until the irritation has been replaced by serenity" (Moses Hasid, *Iggeret HaMusar*);[4] 3) "It is easier to grow a legion of olive trees in Galilee than to rear one child in the household of Israel" (Eleazar Ben Simeon, *Genesis Rabba* 20:6);[5] 4) "A child's babbling out-of-doors comes from either his father or his mother" (*Talmud Sukkah* 56b); and 5) "Be faithful shepherds to your flock...and be in

---

1. Saadia Ben Joseph (882-942) was a scholar who wrote one the earliest works of Jewish medieval philosophy. He was appointed Gaon, the head of an academy, of Sura.
2. Judah Leib Lazerov (1868-1939) was a Yiddish preacher in New York.
3. A Provencal Hebrew fabulist of 12th or 13th century.
4. Moses Hasid (17th century) was a Prague moralist.
5. Eleazar Ben Simeon was a 2nd century commentator.

your conduct a light to their paths" (Elijah Ben Raphael, *Tzavah* 18c).[1]

Children are a blessing. It is no accident that the first commandment in the Bible is to procreate. "Truly children are a gift from the Lord, a blessing of the fruit of the womb...Happy the one who has a quiver filled with these arrows" (*Psalm* 127:3-5). **The forty-eighth way to be Jewish is to treat our children with love and respect, and, by example. Children may soon forget our presents, but they will always remember our presence. If we are essentially good people, then in all likelihood so too will our children be.** "May it be God's will that all the plants that grow from you be like you" (*Talmud Ta'anit* 5b).

---

1. Elijah Ben Raphael de Veali Saba (1738-1792) was an Italian kabbalist, poet and rabbi of Alessandria.

YOUR SINATRA[1]

or:

"I Did it my Way"[2]

A dmittedly, it may seem a bit strange to place Frank Sinatra as the penultimate **Way** in this book. But what non-fictional account on virtually any subject, written primarily for the Fifties and Sixties generation, could possibly exclude Frankie? So many of Sinatra's songs relate to the Jewish life cycle that it would have been quite easy to use his music instead of Simon & Garfunkel's as one of the underlying elements in this primer.

Many of Sinatra's songs speak to us, as they provide a retrospective on one's life, like: *It was a Very Good Year, Love and Marriage, Young at Heart, That's Life and All the Way.* But Sinatra's *My Way*

---

1. See **Way #5 — Your Singers**.
2. From the Frank Sinatra anthem *My Way*, written by Paul Anka, Claude Francois Ravaux and Gilles Thibault, to be found on numerous Sinatra albums.

became his theme song, and the sentiments expressed in it became the watchword for many of us — the wisdom being that we must stick to our guns and be certain to always do things "our way." Without exaggerating the existential meaning of the words of the song, it does begin ominously enough, as the person in the song looks back on his or her life and takes pride that throughout all the ups and downs, he or she can feel proud, indeed complete, that he or she did things "his or her way."

And now, the end is near
And so I face the final curtain.
My friend, I'll say it clear,
I'll state my case, of which I'm certain.
I've lived a life that's full,
I've traveled each and every highway,
And more, much more than this, I did it my way.

Yes, there were times, I'm sure you knew,
When I bit off more than I could chew,
But through it all,
When there was doubt,
I ate it up and spit it out,
I faced it all and I stood tall
And did it my way.

Regrets I've had a few,
But then again, too few to mention.
I did what I had to do,
And saw it through without exemption.
I planned each chartered course,
Each careful step along the byway,
But more, much more than this, I did it my way.

I've loved, I've laughed and cried,
I've had my fill, my share of losing,
And now, as tears subside, I find it all so amusing.
To think I did all that,
And may I say, not in a shy way.
"Oh no, oh, no, not me,
I did it my way."

For what is a man, what has he got?
If not himself, then he has not,
To say the things he truly feels,
And not the words of one who kneels,
The record shows, I took the blows
And did it my way.... Yes, it was my way.

While the themes in this song are most touching, upon even a surface examination, they really depict something very different from what Judaism is all about. The same thing can be said for the

Beatle's song *Let it Be,* a sort of mantra that we made our own when growing up, whose laissez-faire (almost fatalistic) approach to life deprives, as well as absolves one of taking responsibility for his or her actions (see **Way #18 — Your Social Activism**). The Jewish answer to *My Way* should be **"No Way, Jose!"** (I apologize for the Jose part.) While Sinatra may have been a supporter of Israel — having proven this with his substantial contribution to Israeli institutions, particularly the Hebrew University, which hosts the Frank Sinatra Student Center — this song is problematic for someone wanting to fashion a Jewish approach to life.

The famous biblical saying, "love your neighbor (friend) as yourself," has been interpreted in Jewish terms as loving your neighbor as much as you love yourself (see **Way #41 — Your Friends**). The notion that we have to feel good about ourselves is deeply ingrained in Judaism. But to do things exclusively "my way" essentially means to dwell only on our "self," against which we are forewarned, individually and collectively: "It is not only individuals, a people too cannot live only for itself" (I. L. Peretz).

While one should be able to look back on his or her life with satisfaction, the notion that if I had to do it all over again, I would do things exactly the same way, leaves no possibility for repentance or atonement, let alone self-examination. What does it mean to take such unabashed pride in always "doing it my way?" Let's listen to the words of Maimonides: "The ignorant man believes the world exists only for him...Therefore, if anything happens that gets in **his way**, he at once concludes that the whole universe is evil" (*Guide to the Perplexed* 3:12).

We cannot always get "our way." And "our way" is not always the "best way," as my father-in-law frequently reminds me: "You're entitled to your own wrong opinion!" To see things through without exemption, and to eat something up and then spit it out (I never liked that lyric) when doubts cloud your thoughts, defies all sense of humility, whereby one believes the earth revolves around him or her. But we must keep in mind: "The humble shall inherit the earth" (*Psalm* 37:11).

Humility, selflessness, introspection, self-criticism, reflection lead to what is known in Judaism as *derech eretz*[1] — common decency and consideration, or the "right way." There are two minor tractates that are appended to the *Babylonian Talmud, Derech Eretz Rabba* and *Derech Eretz Zuta*, which form a collection of ethical teachings containing rules of conduct that urge gentleness and patience, all the while emphasizing the importance of fulfilling one's moral and social duties. One of the most famous sayings in Judaism is: "Where there is no *Torah*, there is no *Derech Eretz*, and where there is no *Derech Eretz*, there is no *Torah...*" (*Sayings of the Fathers* 3:17).

The forty-ninth way to be Jewish is to be able to say that I tried to do things the "right way," not my way or his way or her way, but rather a Jewish way (which hopefully will become "my way"): with care, sensitivity, thoroughness, respect, dignity, reflection and wisdom. Sinatra asks: "For what is a man, what has he got? If not himself..." Hillel the Sage supplies the Jewish answer: "If I am not for myself, who will be? But if I am only for myself, what type of person am I..." (*Sayings of the Fathers* 1:14).

---

1. Literally translated means "the way of the earth."

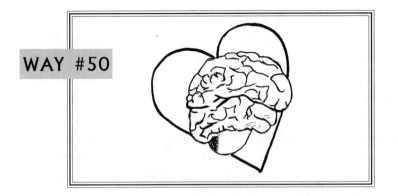

YOUR INSTINCTS

or:

Homeward Bound[1]

A young Israeli, upon finishing her army service, went on a trip to the United States. Needing some fast cash, she entered a bank and, in her halting English, asked to exchange several one hundred dollar traveler checks. When the teller inquired, "What denomination?" she instinctively replied, "Jewish!"

How does one measure instincts? Cain kills Abel. He immediately hides. Why? There is no concept of death in the Bible at that point, let alone of killing. He instinctively knew that to kill is simply wrong.[2] But God catches Cain red-handed, asking him

---

1. Song from the Simon & Garfunkel Album *Parsley, Sage, Rosemary and Thyme.*
2. Recognizing that a human being does not instinctively know it is wrong to kill someone, God felt compelled to inscribe this notion in the Ten Commandments: "You shall not murder" (*Exodus* 20:13).

where his brother is. To which Cain utters his famous response: "Am I my brother's keeper" (*Genesis* 4:9)? Well, for Jews, we are our brothers and sisters' keepers (see **Way #18 — Your Social Activism**). "All Israel is responsible for one another" (*Talmud Shavuot* 39a).[1]

I am not suggesting that when a plane crashes, we should automatically look through the list of deaths to seek out the Jewish names; and thus prove our instinctively Jewish sensitivities. Such parochialism is antithetical to the universal message of Judaism, as outlined in **Way #18 — Your Social Activism**. What is instinctive is to feel immediately the pain of all the relatives and friends who may have lost someone in that plane crash or any other tragedy,[2] because we are commanded: "The stranger who sojourns with you will be unto you as the home-born among you, and you will love himself as yourself..." (*Leviticus* 19:34).

In the Introduction to this book, it was stated that most of us "are truly uninformed when it comes to the basic elements of Jewish life. This lack of knowledge has not been shaped by any intellectual rejection of Judaism on our part; rather it has been colored by an indifference, which is born out of ignorance." For many of us, given our Jewish illiteracy and thus, incompetence, it is relatively simple to be Jewishly wise: all we need to do is to think of something to say about Judaism, which in all likelihood will be embarrassingly foolish, and then say the opposite! Sadly, our instincts have directed us away from taking our Judaism seriously, wherein we would have had to invest the necessary time and effort required to be Jewishly intelligent. Too often, our Jewish instinctive reaction is one of an unchecked acculturation at the expense of a

---

1. The traditional interpretation of this verse is that, just as the guarantor of a loan is responsible for the borrower's debt, so too are all Jews liable — and may be punished — for the sins of an individual Jew.
2. I am also not suggesting here that we instinctively root for a Mark Spitz, the 1972 Jewish Olympian champion swimmer (see **Way #20 — Your Heroes** and **Way #19 — Your Sports**).

personal commitment; of a runaway universalism at the expense of a particular identity; of an uneducated rejection at the expense of a learned acceptance.

Instinct is a natural or innate impulse to respond. It is motivated by some undefined inner force. It may imply natural intuitive power, although not necessarily to do that which is right. So, what of Jewish instinct? Simply put, this author has posited, that if one adopts as part of his or her daily routine the previous forty-nine **Ways** in this guidebook, then chances are his or her Jewish instincts will, by now, be relatively fine-tuned. Indeed, the purpose behind this primer is to have the reader let Judaism impact on all aspects of his or her life, so that Jewish life becomes a twenty-four-hour-a-day proposition. Should this happen, then reacting to people and events — whoever and whatever they are — with a Jewish heart and mind will become a natural and instinctive part of one's very being.

Tonight I'll sing my songs again,
I'll play the game and pretend.
But all my words come back to me in shades of mediocrity,
Like emptiness in harmony I need someone to comfort me.

Homeward Bound,
I wish I was,
Homeward Bound.
Home where my thought's escaping,
Home where my music's playing,
Home where my love is waiting
Silently for me.

Since the subtitle of this book is: *Simon & Garfunkel, Jesus loves you less than you will know*, it is interesting to note that Simon & Garfunkel's *Homeward Bound*, while not instinctively Jewish, stresses something very Jewishly instinctive — the deep-rooted need of an individual to be part of a home, a community, a family.

This ideal sustained the Jewish People for two thousand years. For Jews, Judaism provides a home, a community and a family. It is the totality of our being. It entices us with its music, with words and melodies we must learn, so that we can compose a Jewish song of our own, which we will instinctively sing: "...to our children; and when we are sitting in our house and walking on our way, when we lie down at night and when we rise in the morning. Then will our Jewish thoughts not escape our eyes and our hands, or when we enter our home" (*Deuteronomy* 6:7-9). Indeed, Judaism awaits our return. It is the "love of our Jewish life." These fifty **Ways** to be Jewish are an invitation to return home to Jewish life.

If we let Judaism envelop our lives — our names, our neighborhood, our trips abroad, our language, our singers, our home, our vote, our clothes, our cars, our culture, our flicks, our synagogue, our leisure time, our book shelf, our God, our animals, our money, our social activism, our sports, our heroes, our Israel quotient, our moral Mitzvot, our ritual Mitzvot, our miracles, our Internet, our profession, our holidays, our Shabbat, our Jewish education, our gay and lesbian friends, our personality, our environment, our food, our sex life, our aging, our Holocaust awareness, our body, our prayers, our marriage, our spirituality, our friends, our parents, our dreams, our life cycle events, our relatives, our death, our peace, our kids and our Sinatra — then instinctively we will have reached the fiftieth way to be Jewish.

Thank you Simon & Garfunkel:

> Life, I love you.
> All is "Jew-vy!"

A FINAL WORD

I hope that you, the reader, have found *Fifty Ways to be Jewish* not only informative and helpful, but also compelling enough to motivate you to develop an interest in Judaism that is fuller than might presently be the case. I hope that this guidebook has helped you in some "small way" to find "your way" to a Jewish life that can be replete with meaning and excitement.

In the widely known song that appears in the Passover *Haggaddah*, "Dayeinu," which means, "that would have been enough," at first glance each verse seems to stand on its own merit. For example:

> Had God brought us out of Egypt and not divided the sea for us,
> Dayeinu!
> Had God divided the sea and not permitted us to cross on dry land,
> Dayeinu!
> Had God given us the Sabbath and not brought us to Mount Sinai,
> Dayeinu!
> Had God brought us to Mount Sinai and not given us the *Torah*,
> Dayeinu!

The song continues for many stanzas. Yet while the simple interpretation of this song indicates that just one of these acts would be sufficient to sustain our Judaism, a deeper understanding clearly suggests that each event or "way" is dependent on the other. In order to become a "more complete Jew," we must integrate the many facets of Judaism into our life. What is critically important here is that we must continually strive throughout our life to reach higher and higher.

In *Talmud*, there is a general concept called: "To go up to holiness." It is based on the story of Jacob's ladder (*Genesis* 28:12-13). We are essentially commanded to make every effort to improve our Jewish self, and thereby our human self, by ascending toward the heavens in order to cultivate the Divine within us. We accomplish this by taking one step at a time. Just as a child builds his or her vocabulary by learning new words one by one, storing them up so that sentences flow, in order that ideas and thoughts can be articulated and communicated, and then eventually put into practice, so too must we adopt "one Jewish way after another Jewish way," in order to achieve a fuller Jewish life.

Lastly, my ultimate hope is that after reading this book, you will pursue Judaism in a "Big Way," that the *Torah*, our "way of life," will guide you, as it is written:

> The *Torah* is a tree of life to those who cling to it,
> And whoever holds on to it is happy.
> Its **Ways** are **Ways** of pleasantness,
> And all its paths are peace.
>
> (*Proverbs* 3:17-18)